Historical Atlas of the World

6th Edition

ISBN: 0-528-01447-1

Table of Contents

Introduction

Information about the past is compiled, stored, and made accessible in a variety of ways. One of these ways is historical maps. Historical maps provide a chronology of important events and show the impact these events had on the places where they occurred. Historical maps support and extend information from primary historical resources such as letters, treaties, and census data. Historical maps are summaries of past events presented in graphic form.

The maps in the Rand McNally *Historical Atlas of the World* portray the rich panoply of the world's history from preliterate times to the present. They show how cultures and civilizations were linked and how they interacted. These maps make it clear that history is not static. Rather, it is about change and movement across time. The maps in this atlas show change by presenting the dynamics of expansion, cooperation, and conflict.

Benefits of Using the Rand McNally *Historical Atlas of the World*

Events gain fuller meaning.
Knowing where events took place gives them fuller meaning and often explains causes and effects. For example, the map showing Russia's expansion in Europe clearly illustrates a major territorial goal of the czars was to access warm-water ports that would connect their realm to the world's seas and oceans.

Connections among events are clarified.
Through the visual power of historical maps, the links between and among events become clearer. The maps showing diffusion of languages and religions are good illustrations of this, as is the map of Native Americans that details the rise and fall of indigenous peoples of North and South America.

Similarities and differences become apparent.
The maps in this historical atlas provide the opportunity to compare and contrast places over time. The maps of Africa in the 10th and 15th centuries present time capsules of human migrations. They also act as an inventory of the continent's resources in two specific time frames.

The influence of sense of place is conveyed.
Maps in this atlas can convey a people's sense of place at a particular time in history. The map of Europe's Age of Discovery is a good illustration. The cartographer has deliberately centered the continent so the map's projection reflects the extent and ambition of Europe's exploration at the end of the Renaissance.

Trends emerge.
Another benefit of using this historical atlas is that trends emerge. Maps of the westward expansion of the United States show how the nation was settled, what technologies were used, who was displaced, and in what sequence. In another example, the map of the Mogul Empire in India under Aurangzeb reveals how a dynasty can become powerfully established in little more than a century.

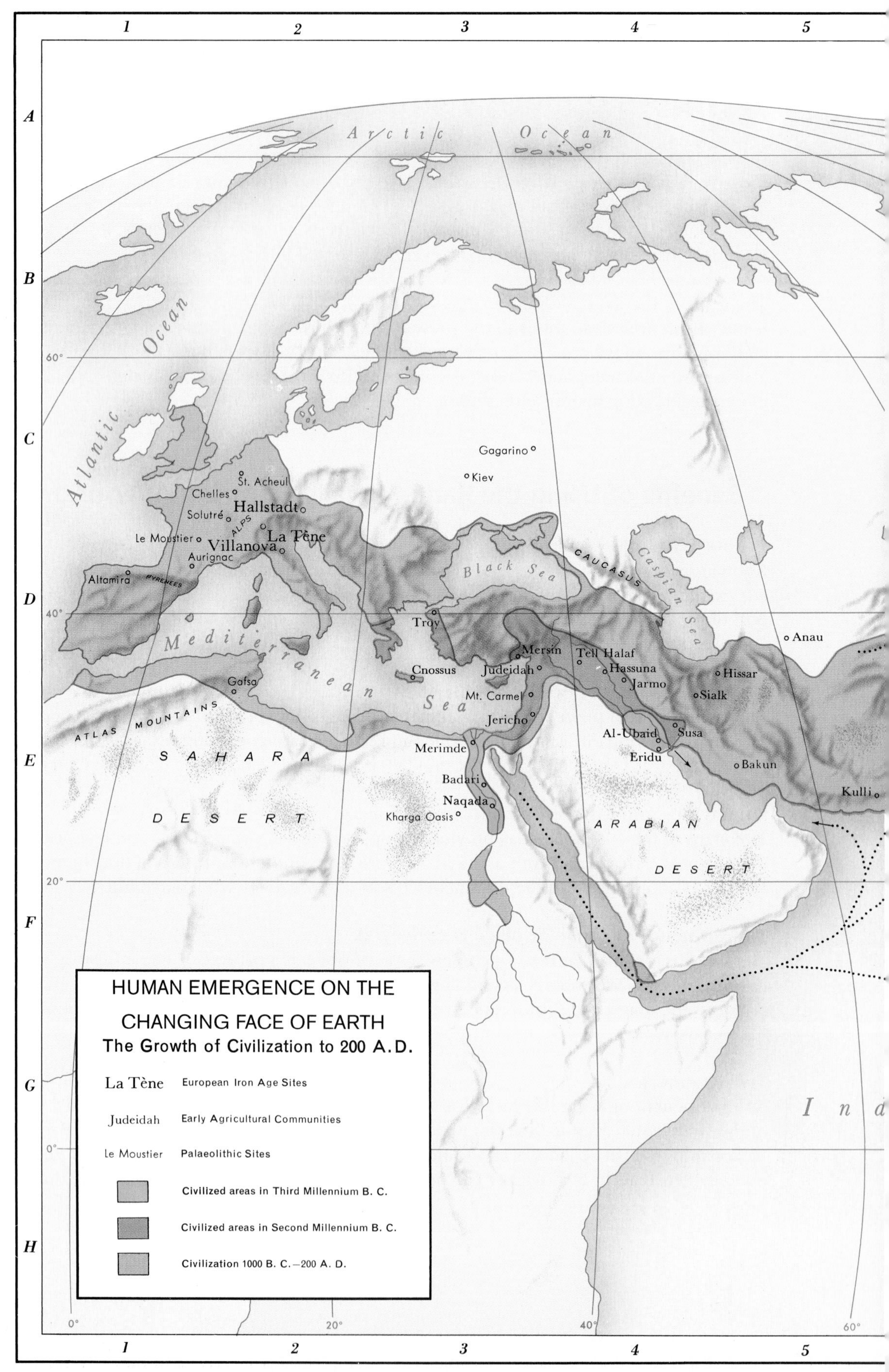
HUMAN EMERGENCE ON THE
CHANGING FACE OF EARTH
The Growth of Civilization to 200 A.D.
La Tène European Iron Age Sites
Judeidah Early Agricultural Communities
Le Moustier Palaeolithic Sites
Civilized areas in Third Millennium B. C.
Civilized areas in Second Millennium B. C.
Civilization 1000 B. C.—200 A. D.
Arctic Ocean
Atlantic Ocean
Mediterranean Sea
Black Sea
Caspian Sea
CAUCASUS
ALPS
PYRENEES
ATLAS MOUNTAINS
SAHARA DESERT
ARABIAN DESERT
Ind
Gagarino
Kiev
St. Acheul
Chelles
Solutré
Hallstadt
La Tène
Le Moustier
Villanova
Aurignac
Altamira
Troy
Cnossus
Mersin
Judeidah
Mt. Carmel
Jericho
Tell Halaf
Hassuna
Jarmo
Hissar
Sialk
Anau
Al-Ubaid
Susa
Eridu
Bakun
Kulli
Gafsa
Merimde
Badari
Naqada
Kharga Oasis
60°
40°
20°
0°
1 2 3 4 5
A B C D E F G H

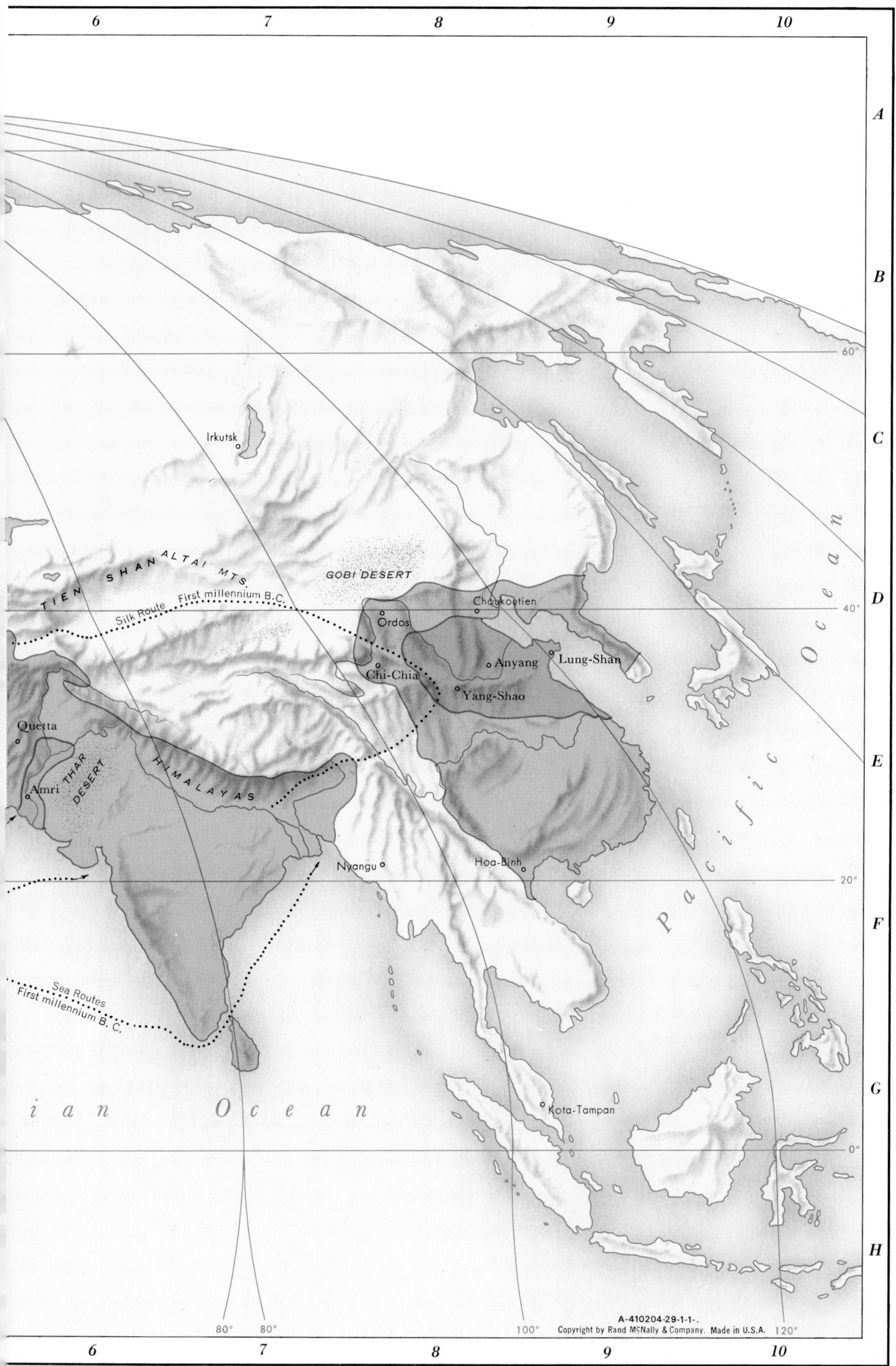

6
7
8
9
10
A
B
C
D
E
F
G
H
60°
40°
20°
0°
Irkutsk
TIEN SHAN
ALTAI MTS.
GOBI DESERT
Silk Route
First millennium B.C.
Choukoutien
Ordos
Anyang
Lung-Shan
Chi-Chia
Yang-Shao
Quetta
THAR DESERT
Amri
HIMALAYAS
Nyangu
Hoa-Binh
Pacific Ocean
Sea Routes
First millennium B.C.
ian Ocean
Kota-Tampan
80°
80°
100°
120°
A-410204-29-1-1-.
Copyright by Rand McNally & Company. Made in U.S.A.

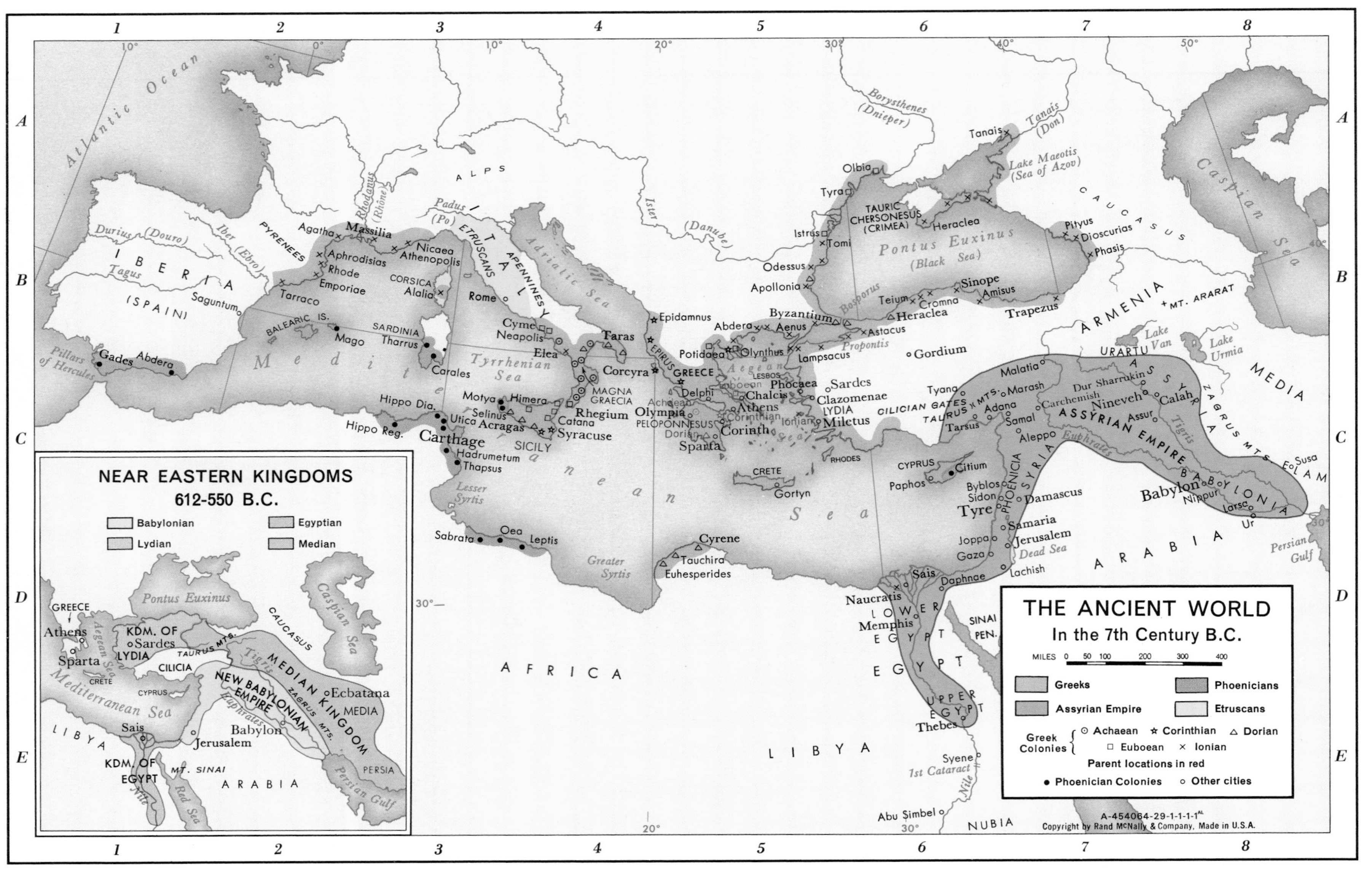
THE ANCIENT WORLD
In the 7th Century B.C.
MILES 0 50 100 200 300 400
Greeks
Phoenicians
Assyrian Empire
Etruscans
Greek Colonies
Achaean
Corinthian
Dorian
Euboean
Ionian
Parent locations in red
Phoenician Colonies
Other cities
A-454064-29-1-1-1
Copyright by Rand McNally & Company, Made in U.S.A.
NEAR EASTERN KINGDOMS
612-550 B.C.
Babylonian
Egyptian
Lydian
Median
GREECE
Athens
Sparta
Aegean Sea
CRETE
Mediterranean Sea
KDM. OF LYDIA
Sardes
TAURUS MTS.
CILICIA
CYPRUS
Pontus Euxinus
CAUCASUS
Caspian Sea
MEDIAN KINGDOM
Ecbatana
MEDIA
NEW BABYLONIAN EMPIRE
ZAGRUS MTS.
Tigris
Euphrates
Babylon
Jerusalem
Sais
KDM. OF EGYPT
Nile
MT. SINAI
Red Sea
ARABIA
PERSIA
Persian Gulf
LIBYA
Atlantic Ocean
Pillars of Hercules
Gades
Abdera
IBERIA
(SPAIN)
Durius (Douro)
Tagus
Iber (Ebro)
Saguntum
PYRENEES
Tarraco
Emporiae
Rhode
Aphrodisias
Agatha
Massilia
Rhodanus (Rhône)
Nicaea
Athenopolis
CORSICA
Alalia
BALEARIC IS.
Mago
SARDINIA
Tharrus
Carales
Mediterranean Sea
ALPS
Padus (Po)
ETRUSCANS
ITALY
APENNINES
Rome
Cyme
Neapolis
Elea
Tyrrhenian Sea
Hippo Dia.
Hippo Reg.
Utica
Carthage
Hadrumetum
Thapsus
Motya
Himera
Selinus
Acragas
SICILY
Catana
Syracuse
Rhegium
MAGNA GRAECIA
Taras
Corcyra
Adriatic Sea
Lesser Syrtis
Sabrata
Oea
Leptis
Greater Syrtis
AFRICA
Ister
(Danube)
Epidamnus
EPIRUS
GREECE
Delphi
Achaean
Olympia
PELOPONNESUS
Dorian
Sparta
Corinth
Athens
Chalcis
Euboean
Potidaea
Olynthus
Abdera
Aenus
Byzantium
LESBOS
Aegean
Phocaea
Sardes
Clazomenae
LYDIA
Ionian
Miletus
RHODES
CRETE
Gortyn
Cyrene
Tauchira
Euhesperides
LIBYA
Borysthenes (Dnieper)
Olbia
Tyra
Istrus
Tomi
Odessus
Apollonia
TAURIC CHERSONESUS (CRIMEA)
Heraclea
Pontus Euxinus (Black Sea)
Bosporus
Propontis
Lampsacus
Astacus
Teium
Heraclea
Cromna
Sinope
Amisus
Trapezus
Gordium
Tanais
Tanais (Don)
Lake Maeotis (Sea of Azov)
CAUCASUS
Pityus
Dioscurias
Phasis
Caspian Sea
ARMENIA
MT. ARARAT
URARTU
Lake Van
Lake Urmia
MEDIA
CILICIAN GATES
TAURUS MTS.
Tyana
Tarsus
Adana
Marash
Malatia
Samal
Carchemish
Aleppo
Dur Sharrukin
Nineveh
Calah
Assur
ASSYRIAN EMPIRE
ASSYRIA
ZAGRUS MTS.
Tigris
Euphrates
ELAM
Susa
BABYLONIA
Babylon
Nippur
Larsa
Ur
Persian Gulf
ARABIA
CYPRUS
Citium
Paphos
PHOENICIA
SYRIA
Byblos
Sidon
Tyre
Damascus
Samaria
Jerusalem
Dead Sea
Joppa
Gaza
Lachish
Sais
Daphnae
Naucratis
LOWER EGYPT
Memphis
EGYPT
SINAI PEN.
UPPER EGYPT
Thebes
Syene
1st Cataract
Nile
Abu Simbel
NUBIA

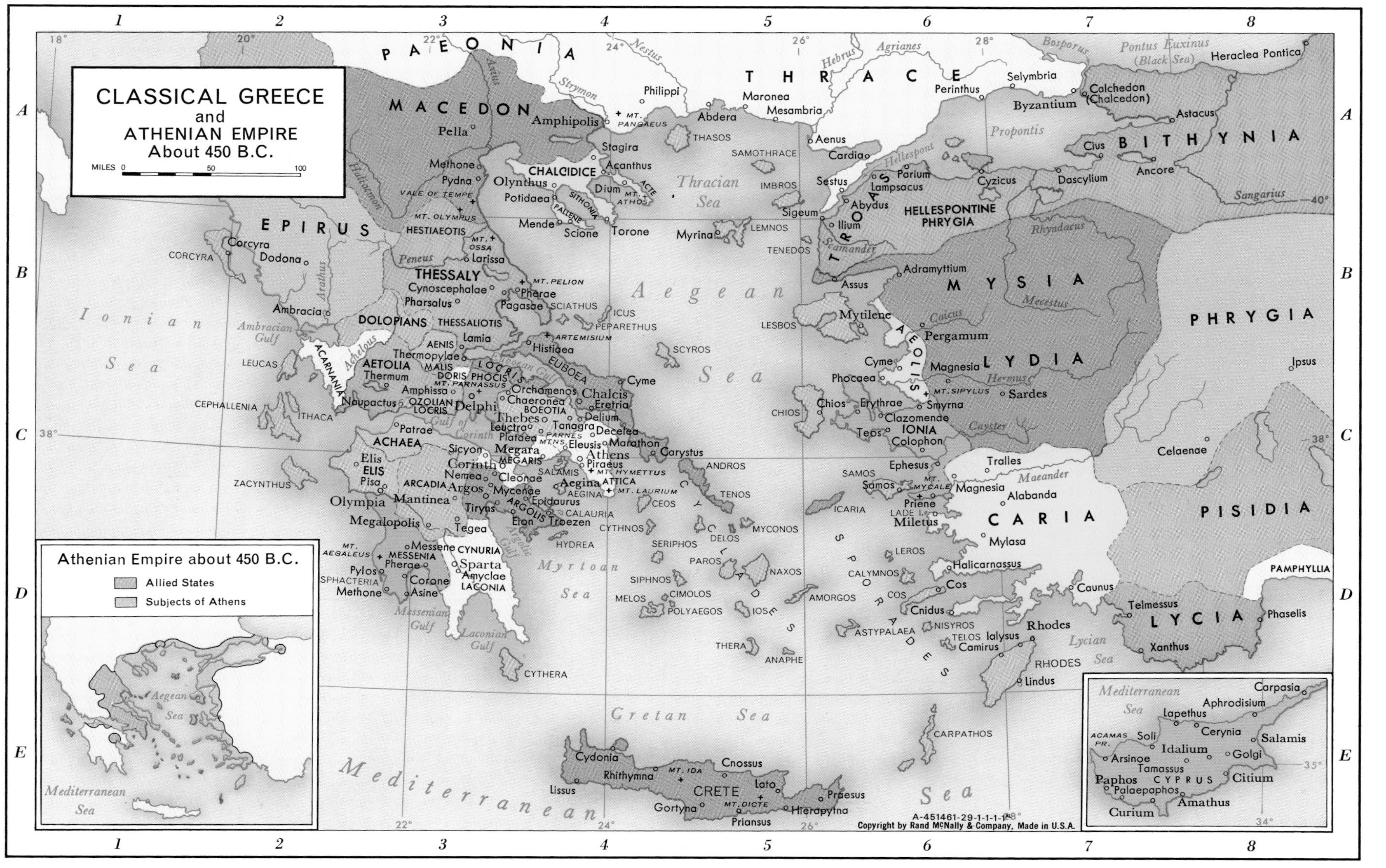
CLASSICAL GREECE
and
ATHENIAN EMPIRE
About 450 B.C.
MILES 0 50 100
Athenian Empire about 450 B.C.
Allied States
Subjects of Athens
A-451461-29-1-1-1
Copyright by Rand McNally & Company, Made in U.S.A.

ANCIENT PERSIA 549 B.C. – 651 A.D.

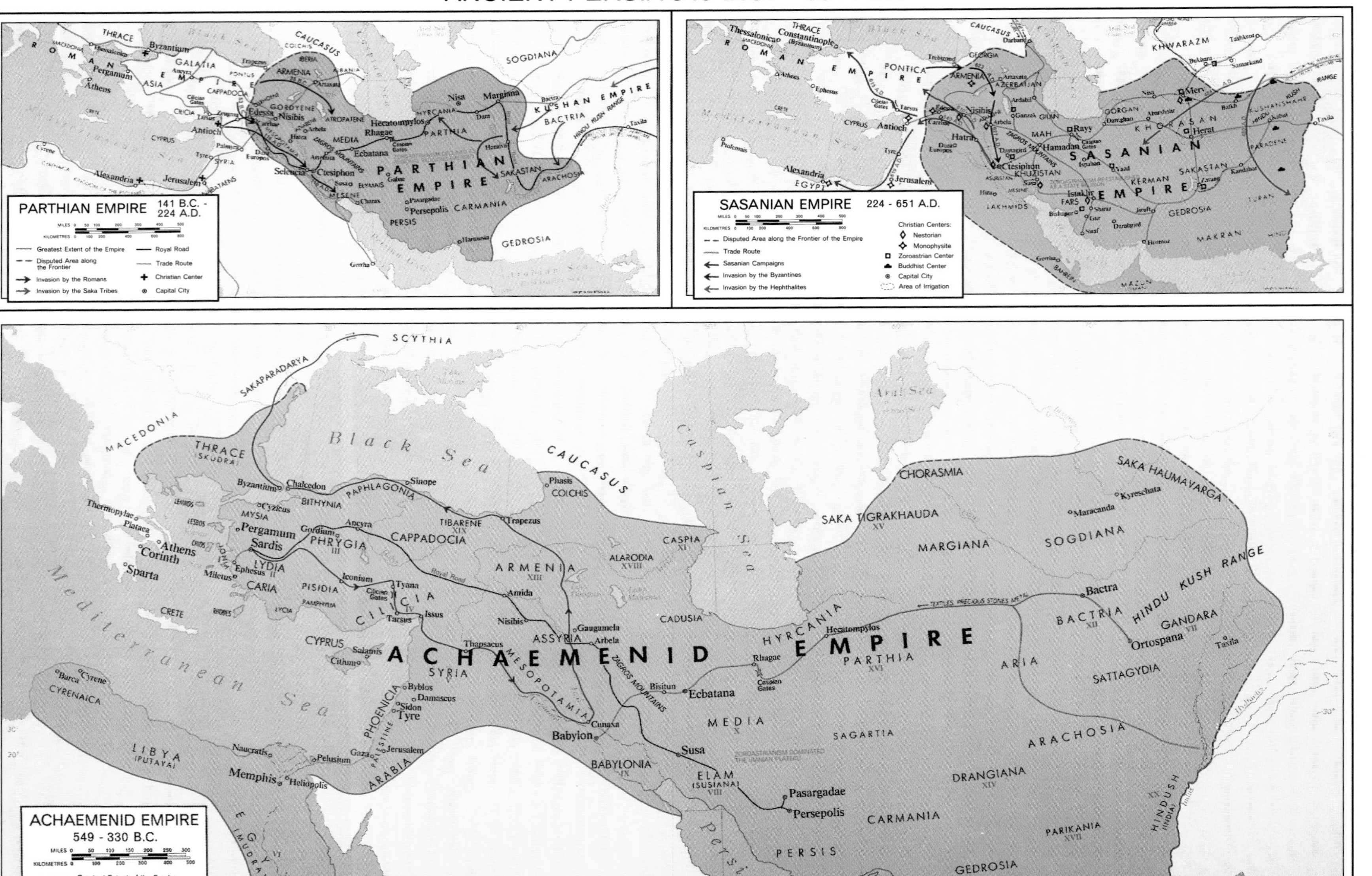

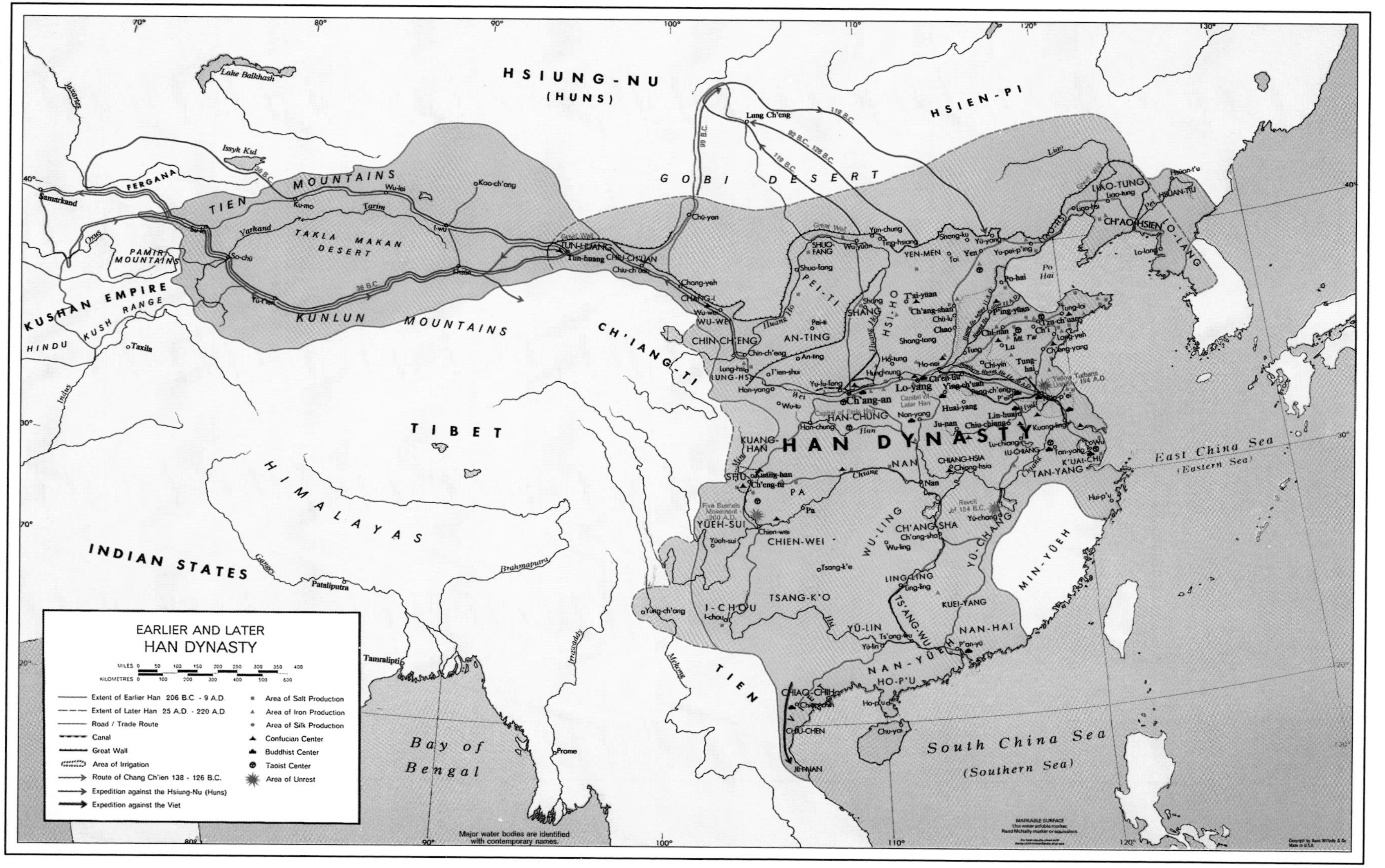
EARLIER AND LATER
HAN DYNASTY
MILES 0 50 100 150 200 250 300 350 400
KILOMETRES 0 100 200 300 400 500 600
Extent of Earlier Han 206 B.C. - 9 A.D.
Extent of Later Han 25 A.D. - 220 A.D.
Road / Trade Route
Canal
Great Wall
Area of Irrigation
Route of Chang Ch'ien 138 - 126 B.C.
Expedition against the Hsiung-Nu (Huns)
Expedition against the Viet
Area of Salt Production
Area of Iron Production
Area of Silk Production
Confucian Center
Buddhist Center
Taoist Center
Area of Unrest
HSIUNG-NU
(HUNS)
HSIEN-PI
GOBI DESERT
TIEN MOUNTAINS
TAKLA MAKAN DESERT
KUNLUN MOUNTAINS
PAMIR MOUNTAINS
KUSHAN EMPIRE
HINDU KUSH RANGE
FERGANA
CH'IANG-TI
TIBET
HIMALAYAS
INDIAN STATES
HAN DYNASTY
TIEN
MIN-YÜEH
NAN-YÜEH
East China Sea
(Eastern Sea)
South China Sea
(Southern Sea)
Bay of Bengal
Lake Balkhash
Issyk Kul
Samarkand
Taxila
Pataliputra
Tamralipti
Prome
Tun-huang
Ch'ang-an
Lo-yang
Lung Ch'eng
Yellow Turbans 184 A.D.
Revolt of 154 B.C.
Five Bushels Movement 200 A.D.
Major water bodies are identified with contemporary names.

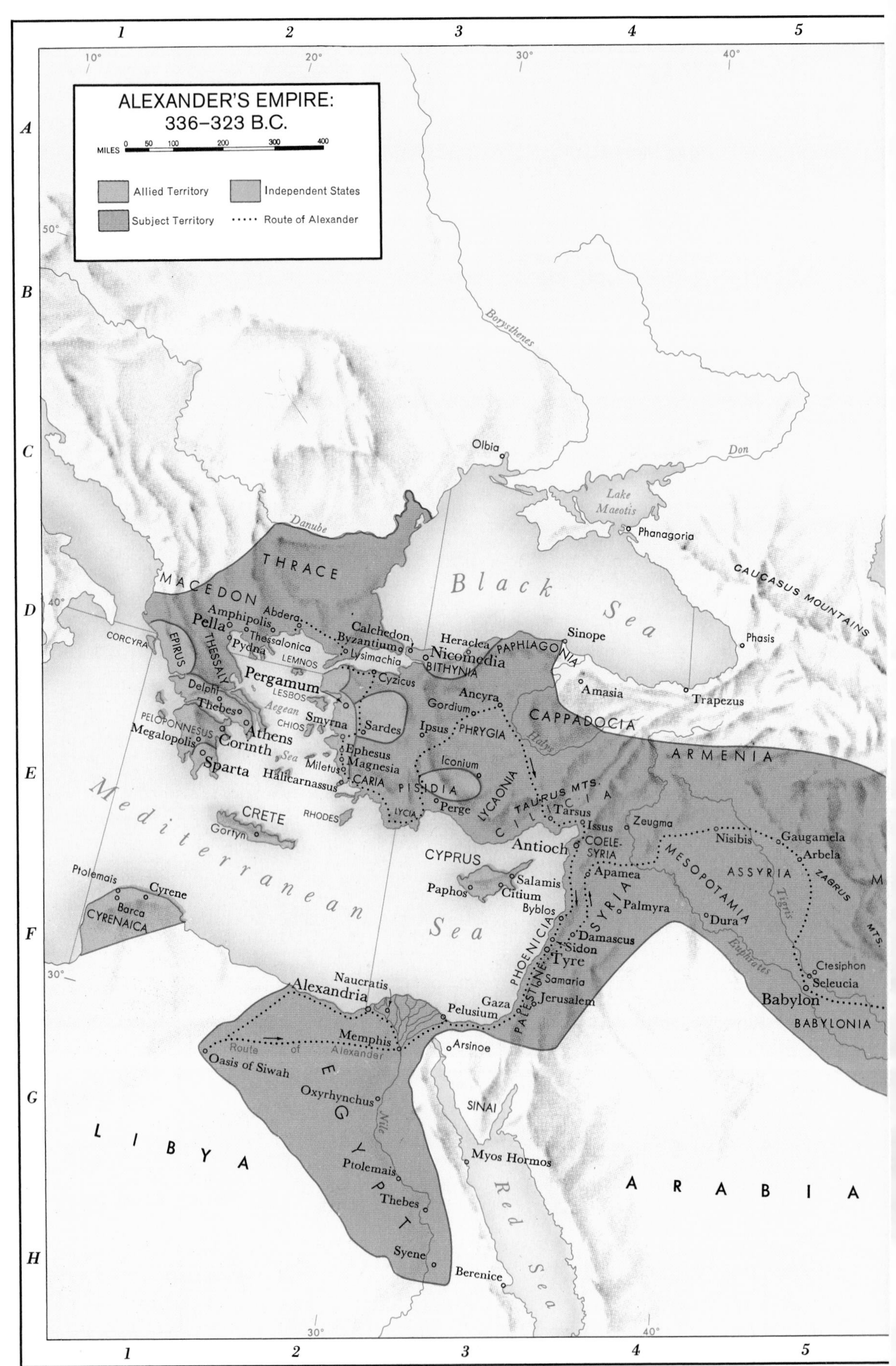
ALEXANDER'S EMPIRE: 336–323 B.C.
MILES 0 50 100 200 300 400
Allied Territory
Independent States
Subject Territory
Route of Alexander
1
2
3
4
5
A
B
C
D
E
F
G
H
10°
20°
30°
40°
50°
40°
30°
Borysthenes
Olbia
Don
Lake Maeotis
Phanagoria
Danube
THRACE
MACEDON
Black Sea
CAUCASUS MOUNTAINS
Phasis
Sinope
Amasia
Trapezus
Abdera
Amphipolis
Pella
Thessalonica
Pydna
CORCYRA
EPIRUS
THESSALY
LEMNOS
Calchedon
Byzantium
Lysimachia
Heraclea
Nicomedia
BITHYNIA
PAPHLAGONIA
Cyzicus
Pergamum
LESBOS
Delphi
Thebes
Aegean
CHIOS
Smyrna
Sardes
Ancyra
Gordium
Ipsus
PHRYGIA
CAPPADOCIA
Halys
ARMENIA
PELOPONNESUS
Megalopolis
Athens
Corinth
Sea
Ephesus
Magnesia
Miletus
Sparta
Halicarnassus
CARIA
Iconium
PISIDIA
LYCAONIA
TAURUS MTS.
CILICIA
Tarsus
Issus
Zeugma
Perge
LYCIA
RHODES
CRETE
Gortyn
Mediterranean Sea
Antioch
COELE-SYRIA
Nisibis
Gaugamela
Arbela
CYPRUS
Salamis
Paphos
Citium
Apamea
MESOPOTAMIA
ASSYRIA
ZAGRUS
Tigris
Byblos
Palmyra
Dura
SYRIA
Damascus
Sidon
Tyre
PHOENICIA
Samaria
Jerusalem
PALESTINE
Euphrates
Ctesiphon
Seleucia
Babylon
BABYLONIA
Ptolemais
Cyrene
Barca
CYRENAICA
Naucratis
Alexandria
Gaza
Pelusium
Memphis
Route of Alexander
Arsinoe
Oasis of Siwah
EGYPT
Oxyrhynchus
SINAI
Nile
LIBYA
Myos Hormos
Ptolemais
Red Sea
ARABIA
Thebes
Syene
Berenice

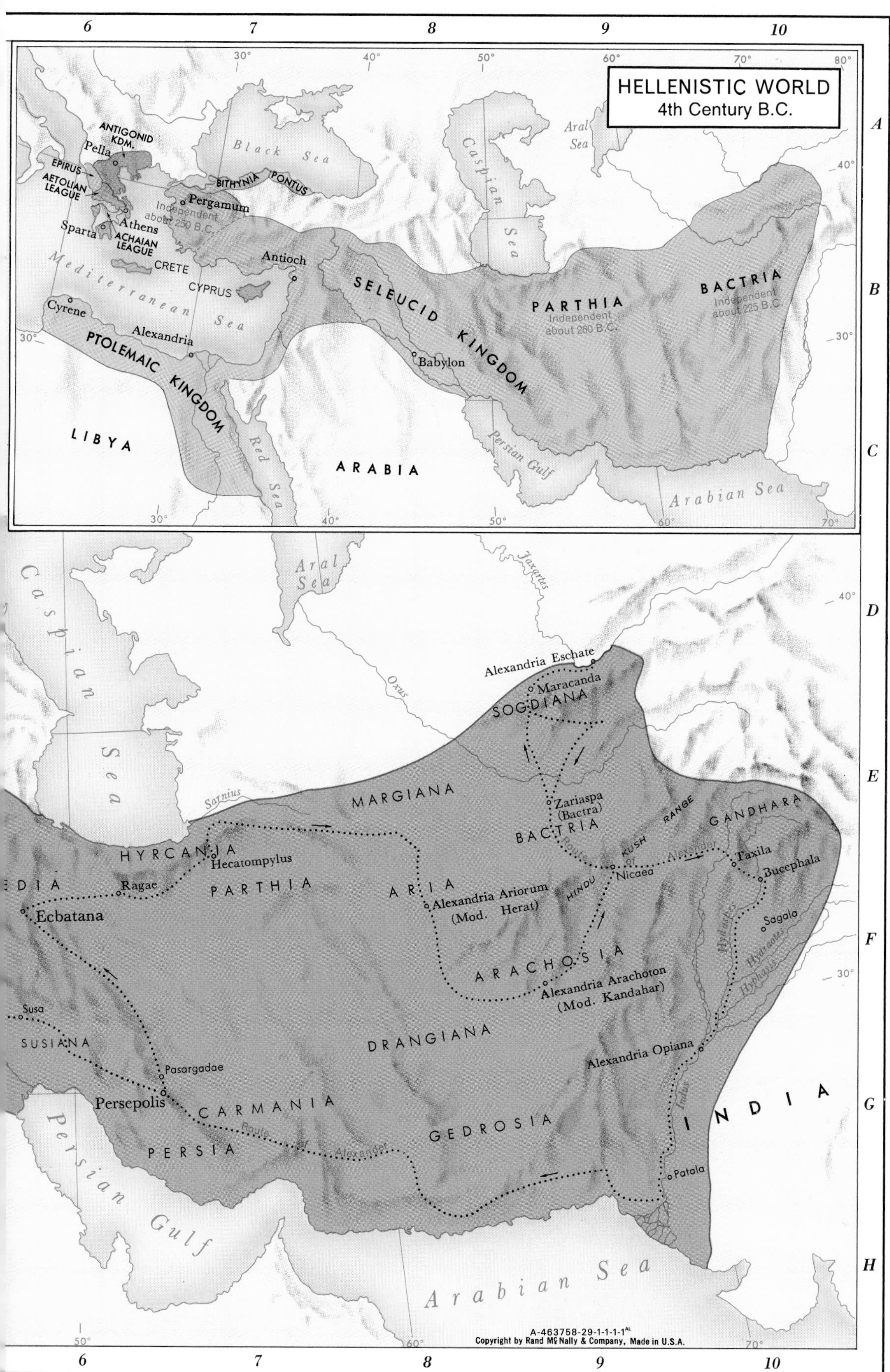
HELLENISTIC WORLD
4th Century B.C.
ANTIGONID KDM.
Pella
EPIRUS
AETOLIAN LEAGUE
Athens
Sparta
ACHAIAN LEAGUE
CRETE
CYPRUS
Black Sea
BITHYNIA
PONTUS
Pergamum
Independent about 250 B.C.
Antioch
Mediterranean Sea
Cyrene
Alexandria
PTOLEMAIC KINGDOM
LIBYA
Red Sea
ARABIA
SELEUCID KINGDOM
Babylon
Persian Gulf
Caspian Sea
Aral Sea
PARTHIA
Independent about 260 B.C.
BACTRIA
Independent about 225 B.C.
Arabian Sea
Aral Sea
Jaxartes
Oxus
Caspian Sea
Alexandria Eschate
Maracanda
SOGDIANA
Sarnius
MARGIANA
Zariaspa (Bactra)
BACTRIA
HINDU KUSH RANGE
GANDHARA
Route of Alexander
Taxila
Bucephala
Nicaea
HYRCANIA
Hecatompylus
MEDIA
Ragae
PARTHIA
ARIA
Alexandria Ariorum (Mod. Herat)
Ecbatana
Hydaspes
Sagala
Hydraotes
Hyphasis
ARACHOSIA
Alexandria Arachoton (Mod. Kandahar)
Susa
SUSIANA
DRANGIANA
Alexandria Opiana
Pasargadae
Persepolis
CARMANIA
Route of Alexander
GEDROSIA
Indus
INDIA
PERSIA
Patala
Persian Gulf
Arabian Sea
A-463758-29-1-1-1-1

INDIA 250 B.C. AND 400 A.D.

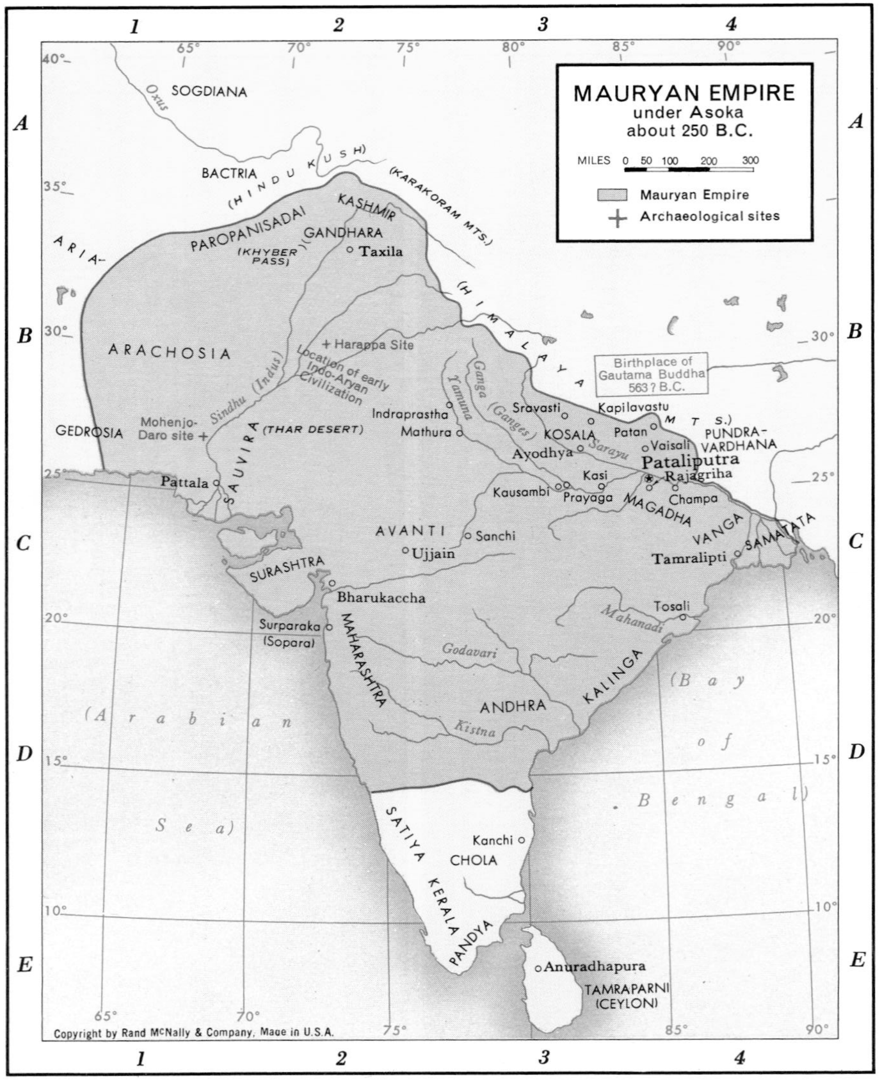

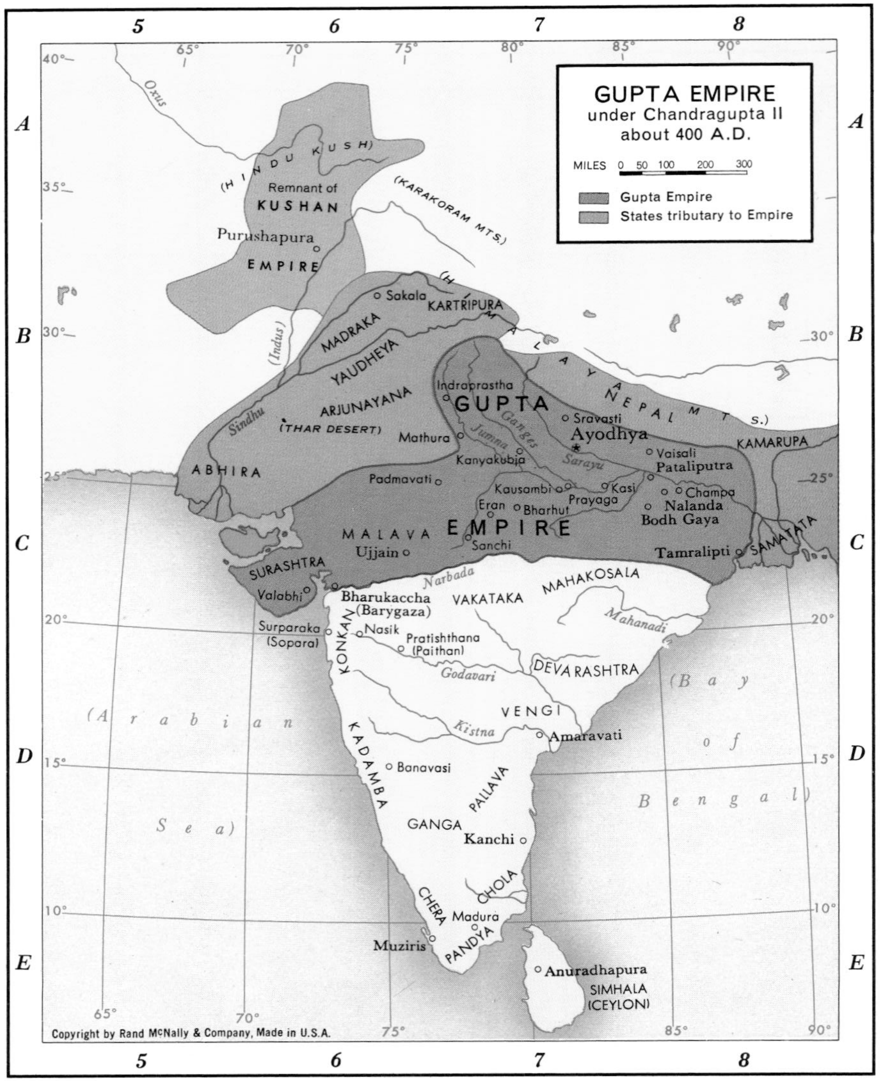

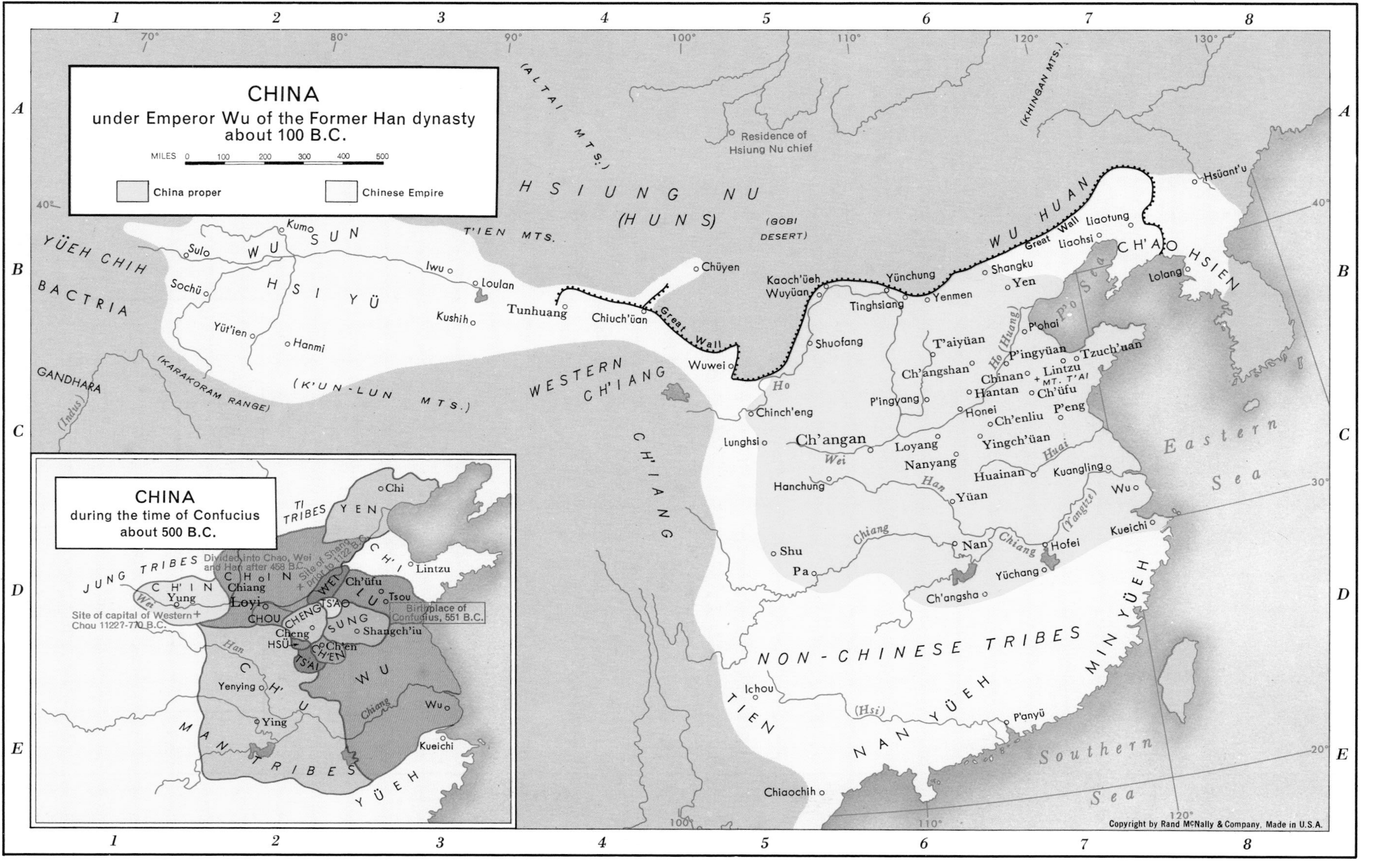
CHINA
under Emperor Wu of the Former Han dynasty
about 100 B.C.
MILES 0 100 200 300 400 500
China proper
Chinese Empire
HSIUNG NU
(HUNS)
(GOBI DESERT)
(ALTAI MTS.)
(KHINGAN MTS.)
Residence of Hsiung Nu chief
T'IEN MTS.
WU SUN
HSI YÜ
YÜEH CHIH
BACTRIA
GANDHARA
(Indus)
(KARAKORAM RANGE)
(K'UN-LUN MTS.)
WESTERN CH'IANG
CH'IANG
WU HUAN
CH'AO HSIEN
NON-CHINESE TRIBES
TIEN
NAN YÜEH
MIN YÜEH
Great Wall
Kumo
Sulo
Sochü
Yüt'ien
Hanmi
Iwu
Loulan
Kushih
Tunhuang
Chiuch'üan
Chüyen
Wuwei
Kaoch'üeh
Wuyüan
Shuofang
Tinghsiang
Yünchung
Yenmen
Shangku
Yen
Liaohsi
Liaotung
Lolang
Hsüant'u
P'ohai
Po Sea
T'aiyüan
Ch'angshan
P'ingyüan
Tzuch'uan
Chinan
Lintzu
MT. T'AI
Hantan
Ch'üfu
P'ingyang
Honei
Ch'enliu
P'eng
Ho
Ho (Huang)
Chinch'eng
Lunghsi
Ch'angan
Wei
Loyang
Yingch'üan
Nanyang
Huai
Huainan
Kuangling
Hanchung
Han
Yüan
Wu
Kueichi
(Yangtze)
Shu
Pa
Chiang
Nan
Hofei
Yüchang
Ch'angsha
Ichou
(Hsi)
P'anyü
Chiaochih
Eastern Sea
Southern Sea
CHINA
during the time of Confucius
about 500 B.C.
TI TRIBES
YEN
Chi
CH'I
Lintzu
JUNG TRIBES
CH'IN
Yung
Wei
Site of capital of Western Chou 1122?-770 B.C.
CHIN
Chiang
Divided into Chao, Wei and Han after 458 B.C.
Site of Shang prior to 1122 B.C.
WEI
LU
Ch'üfu
Tsou
Birthplace of Confucius, 551 B.C.
Loyi
CHOU
CHENG
Cheng
TSAO
SUNG
Shangch'iu
HSÜ
Ch'en
CH'EN
TS'AI
WU
Han
CH'U
Yenying
Ying
Chiang
Wu
Kueichi
MAN TRIBES
YÜEH
Copyright by Rand McNally & Company, Made in U.S.A.

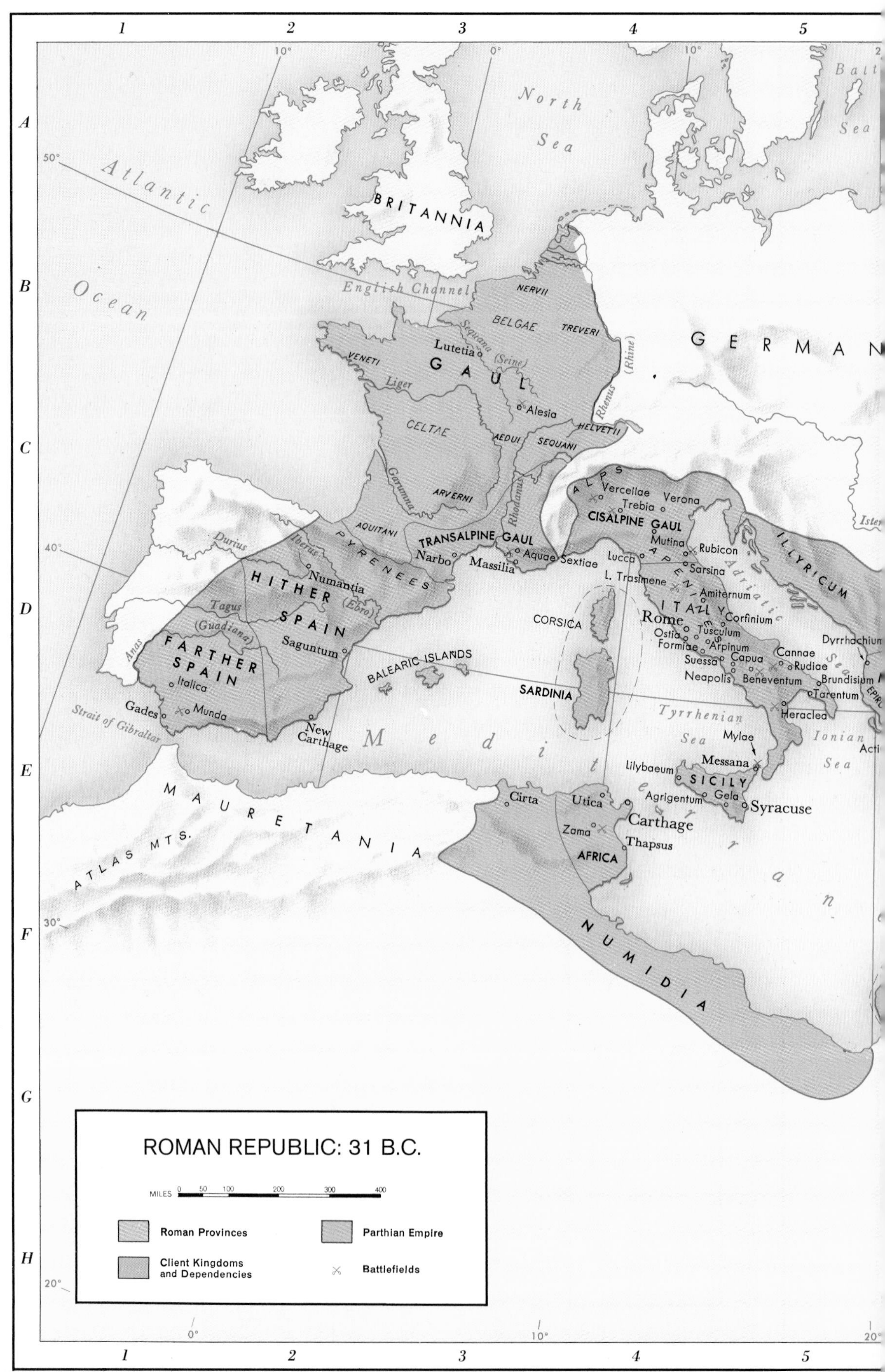
ROMAN REPUBLIC: 31 B.C.
MILES 0 50 100 200 300 400
Roman Provinces
Parthian Empire
Client Kingdoms and Dependencies
Battlefields
BRITANNIA
GAUL
HITHER SPAIN
FARTHER SPAIN
TRANSALPINE GAUL
CISALPINE GAUL
ITALY
ILLYRICUM
SICILY
SARDINIA
CORSICA
AFRICA
NUMIDIA
MAURETANIA
GERMAN
North Sea
Baltic Sea
Atlantic Ocean
English Channel
Mediterranean
Tyrrhenian Sea
Ionian Sea
Adriatic Sea
Lutetia
Alesia
Narbo
Massilia
Aquae Sextiae
Numantia
Saguntum
Italica
Gades
Munda
New Carthage
Vercellae
Trebia
Verona
Mutina
Rubicon
Lucca
Sarsina
L. Trasimene
Amiternum
Corfinium
Rome
Ostia
Tusculum
Formiae
Arpinum
Suessa
Capua
Neapolis
Beneventum
Cannae
Rudiae
Brundisium
Tarentum
Heraclea
Dyrrhachium
Mylae
Messana
Lilybaeum
Agrigentum
Gela
Syracuse
Cirta
Utica
Zama
Carthage
Thapsus
NERVII
BELGAE
TREVERI
VENETI
CELTAE
AEDUI
SEQUANI
HELVETII
ARVERNI
AQUITANI
PYRENEES
ALPS
APENNINES
ATLAS MTS.
BALEARIC ISLANDS
Strait of Gibraltar
Sequana (Seine)
Liger
Garumna
Rhodanus
Rhenus (Rhine)
Durius
Iberus (Ebro)
Tagus
Anas (Guadiana)

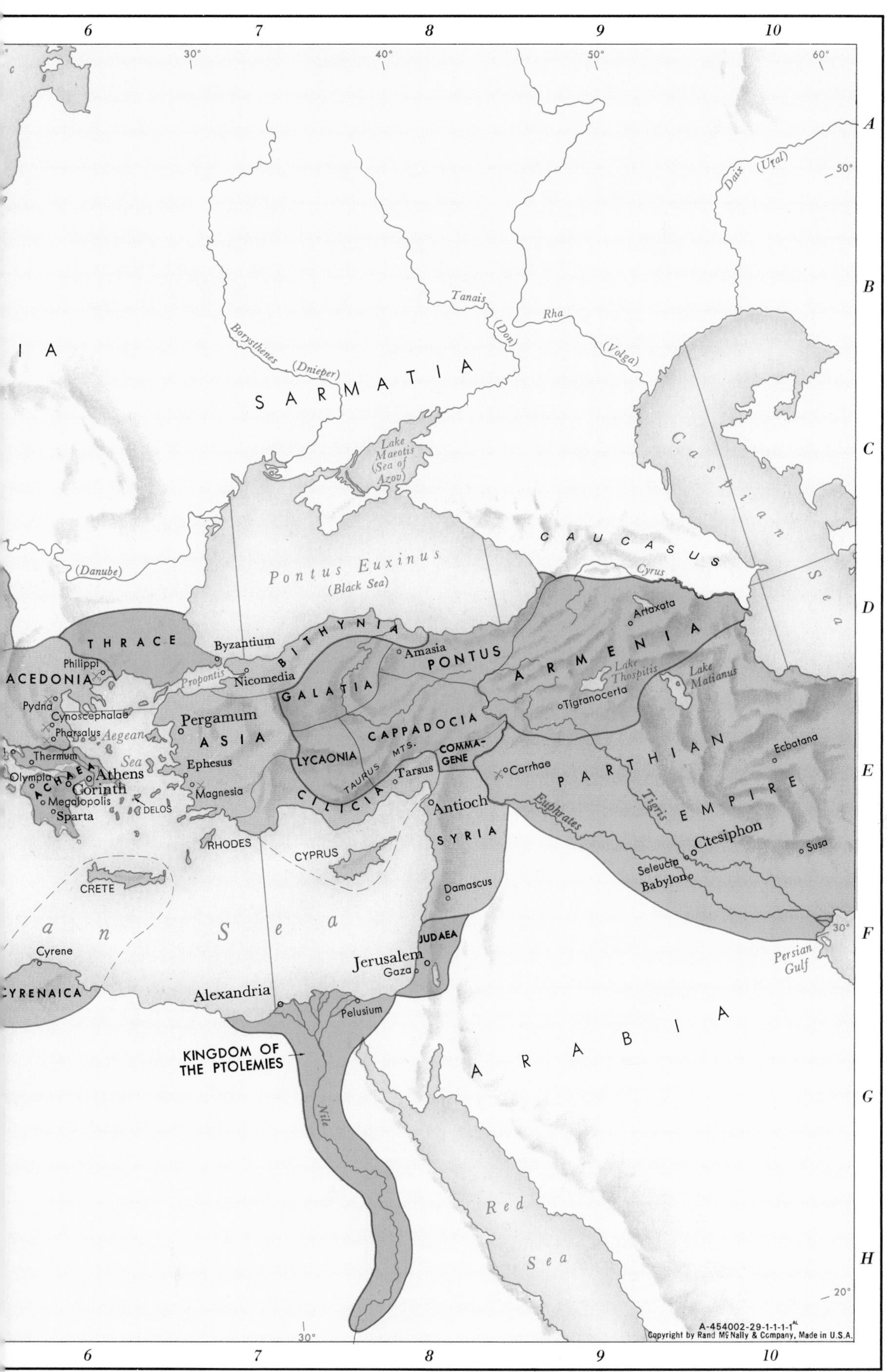

SARMATIA
Borysthenes (Dnieper)
Tanais (Don)
Rha (Volga)
Daix (Ural)
Lake Maeotis (Sea of Azov)
(Danube)
Pontus Euxinus (Black Sea)
CAUCASUS
Cyrus
Caspian Sea
THRACE
Byzantium
Philippi
MACEDONIA
Propontis
Nicomedia
BITHYNIA
Amasia
PONTUS
GALATIA
ARMENIA
Artaxata
Lake Thospitis
Lake Matianus
Tigranocerta
Pydna
Cynoscephalae
Pharsalus
Aegean Sea
Thermum
Pergamum
ASIA
CAPPADOCIA
Ephesus
LYCAONIA
TAURUS MTS.
COMMAGENE
Olympia
ACHAEA
Athens
Corinth
Megalopolis
Sparta
DELOS
Magnesia
CILICIA
Tarsus
Antioch
Carrhae
PARTHIAN EMPIRE
Ecbatana
Euphrates
Tigris
RHODES
CYPRUS
SYRIA
Ctesiphon
Susa
Seleucia
Babylon
CRETE
Damascus
Sea
JUDAEA
Cyrene
Jerusalem
Gaza
Persian Gulf
CYRENAICA
Alexandria
Pelusium
KINGDOM OF THE PTOLEMIES
ARABIA
Nile
Red Sea
A-454002-29-1-1-1-1
Copyright by Rand McNally & Company, Made in U.S.A.

Roman City Names and Modern Equivalents

ROMAN NAME	MODERN NAME
Ancyra	Ankara
Aquincum	Budapest
Arelate	Arles
Augusta Treverorum	Trier, Treves
Augusta Vindelicorum	Augsburg
Augustodunum	Autun
Bononia	Bologna
Burdigala	Bordeaux
Caesar Augusta	Saragossa
Camulodunum	Colchester
Carales	Cagliari
Colonia Agrippina	Cologne
Deva	Chester
Eburacum	York
Emerita Augusta	Merida
Gades	Cadiz
Hispalis	Seville
Lindum	Lincoln

ROMAN NAME	MODERN NAME
Londinium	London
Lugdunum	Lyon
Lugdunum Batavorum	Leiden
Lutetia	Paris
Malaca	Malaga
Massilia	Marseille
Mazaca Caesarea	Kayseri
Mediolanum	Milan
Moguntiacum	Mainz
Nemausus	Nimes
Olisipo	Lisbon
Patavium	Padua
Salmantica	Salamanca
Thessalonica	Salonika
Toletum	Toledo
Tolosa	Toulouse
Valentia	Valencia
Vindobona	Vienna

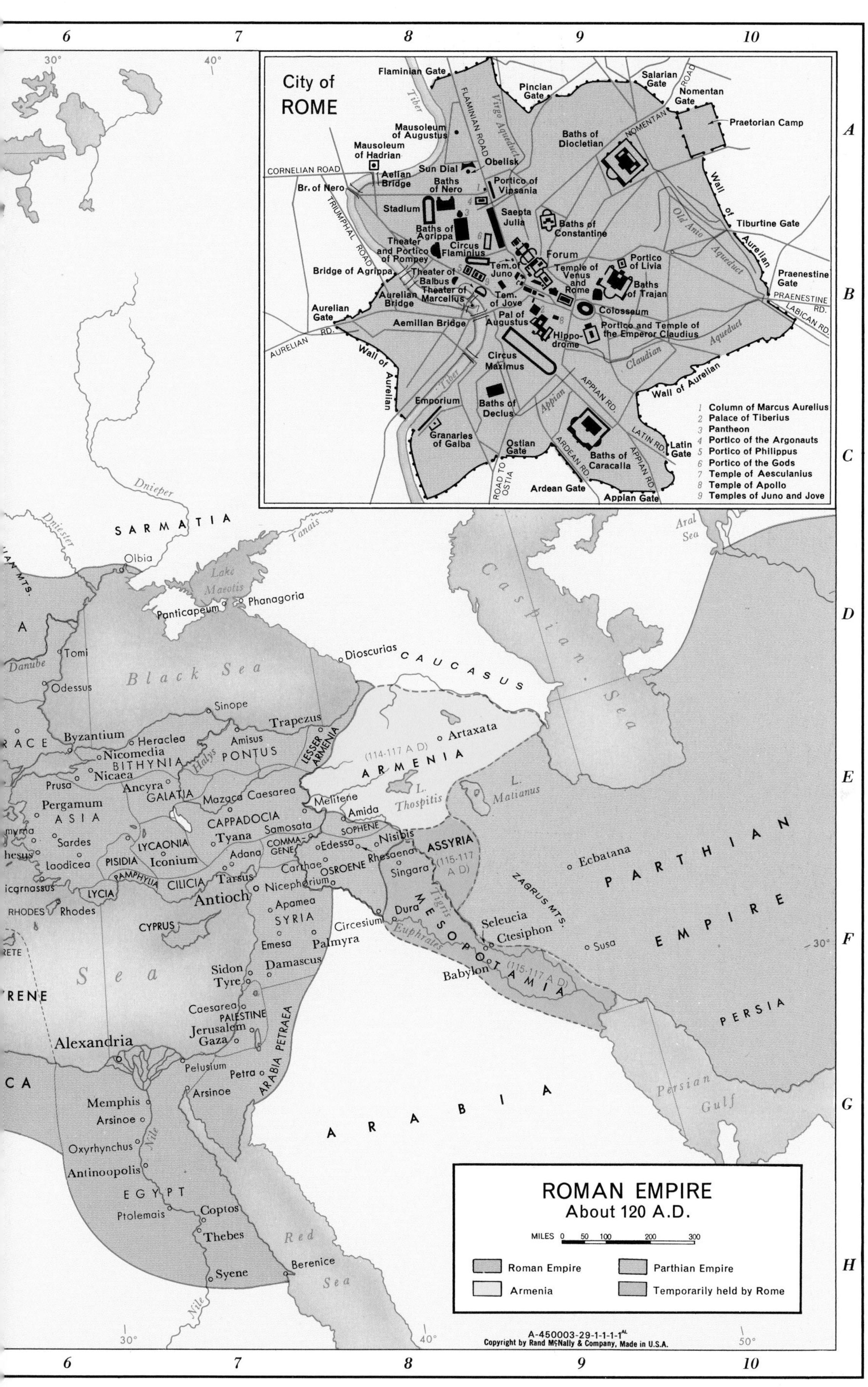
City of ROME
Flaminian Gate
Pincian Gate
Salarian Gate
Nomentan Gate
Praetorian Camp
Mausoleum of Augustus
Mausoleum of Hadrian
Baths of Diocletian
Cornelian Road
Aelian Bridge
Sun Dial
Obelisk
Br. of Nero
Baths of Nero
Portico of Vipsania
Stadium
Saepta Julia
Baths of Constantine
Baths of Agrippa
Circus Flaminius
Theater and Portico of Pompey
Forum
Portico of Livia
Bridge of Agrippa
Theater of Balbus
Tem. of Juno
Temple of Venus and Rome
Baths of Trajan
Praenestine Gate
Aurelian Bridge
Theater of Marcellus
Tem. of Jove
Colosseum
Aurelian Gate
Aemilian Bridge
Pal of Augustus
Portico and Temple of the Emperor Claudius
Hippodrome
Circus Maximus
Wall of Aurelian
Tiburtine Gate
Emporium
Baths of Decius
Granaries of Galba
Ostian Gate
Baths of Caracalla
Latin Gate
Ardean Gate
Appian Gate
1 Column of Marcus Aurelius
2 Palace of Tiberius
3 Pantheon
4 Portico of the Argonauts
5 Portico of Philippus
6 Portico of the Gods
7 Temple of Aesculanius
8 Temple of Apollo
9 Temples of Juno and Jove
SARMATIA
Olbia
Lake Maeotis
Panticapeum
Phanagoria
Dioscurias
CAUCASUS
Caspian Sea
Aral Sea
Black Sea
Tomi
Odessus
Sinope
Trapezus
Byzantium
Heraclea
Nicomedia
BITHYNIA
Nicaea
Amisus
PONTUS
LESSER ARMENIA
Artaxata
ARMENIA (114-117 A.D.)
L. Thospitis
L. Matianus
Prusa
Pergamum
ASIA
Ancyra
GALATIA
Mazaca Caesarea
CAPPADOCIA
Melitene
Amida
Tyana
Samosata
Sardes
LYCAONIA
Iconium
COMMAGENE
Edessa
Nisibis
ASSYRIA (115-117 A.D.)
Laodicea
PISIDIA
Adana
Carrhae
OSROENE
Rhesaena
Singara
Ecbatana
PARTHIAN EMPIRE
ZAGRUS MTS.
PAMPHYLIA
CILICIA
Tarsus
LYCIA
Nicephorium
Antioch
Apamea
Rhodes
CYPRUS
SYRIA
Dura
MESOPOTAMIA
Seleucia
Ctesiphon
Circesium
Emesa
Palmyra
Susa
Sidon
Tyre
Damascus
Babylon
(115-117 A.D.)
PERSIA
Caesarea
PALESTINE
Jerusalem
Gaza
ARABIA PETRAEA
Alexandria
Pelusium
Petra
Arsinoe
Persian Gulf
Memphis
ARABIA
Oxyrhynchus
Antinoopolis
EGYPT
Ptolemais
Coptos
Thebes
Red Sea
Berenice
Syene
Nile
Euphrates
Tigris
Danube
Dnieper
Dniester
Tanais
Halys
ROMAN EMPIRE
About 120 A.D.
MILES 0 50 100 200 300
Roman Empire
Parthian Empire
Armenia
Temporarily held by Rome
A-450003-29-1-1-1
Copyright by Rand McNally & Company, Made in U.S.A.

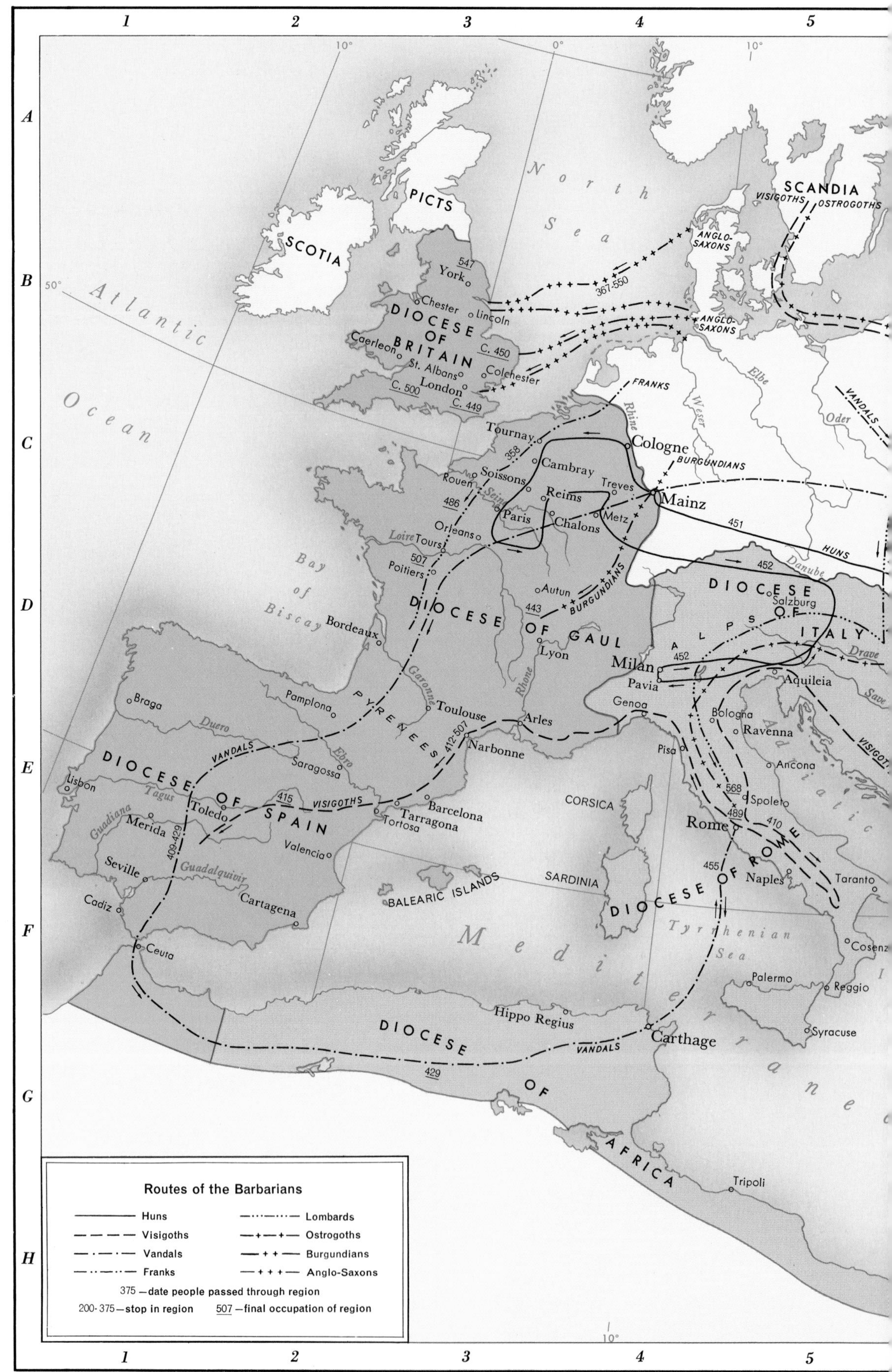

Routes of the Barbarians
Huns
Visigoths
Vandals
Franks
Lombards
Ostrogoths
Burgundians
Anglo-Saxons
375 —date people passed through region
200-375—stop in region
507—final occupation of region
SCANDIA
PICTS
SCOTIA
DIOCESE OF BRITAIN
DIOCESE OF GAUL
DIOCESE OF SPAIN
DIOCESE OF ITALY
DIOCESE OF ROME
DIOCESE OF AFRICA
Atlantic Ocean
North Sea
Bay of Biscay
Mediterranean
Tyrrhenian Sea
York
Chester
Lincoln
Caerleon
St. Albans
Colchester
London
Tournay
Cologne
Cambray
Soissons
Rouen
Reims
Treves
Mainz
Paris
Chalons
Metz
Orleans
Tours
Poitiers
Autun
Bordeaux
Lyon
Milan
Pavia
Salzburg
Aquileia
Genoa
Bologna
Ravenna
Toulouse
Arles
Narbonne
Pamplona
Saragossa
Braga
Lisbon
Toledo
Merida
Barcelona
Tarragona
Tortosa
Valencia
Seville
Cadiz
Cartagena
Ceuta
CORSICA
SARDINIA
BALEARIC ISLANDS
Pisa
Ancona
Spoleto
Rome
Naples
Taranto
Cosenza
Palermo
Reggio
Syracuse
Hippo Regius
Carthage
Tripoli
PYRENEES
ALPS

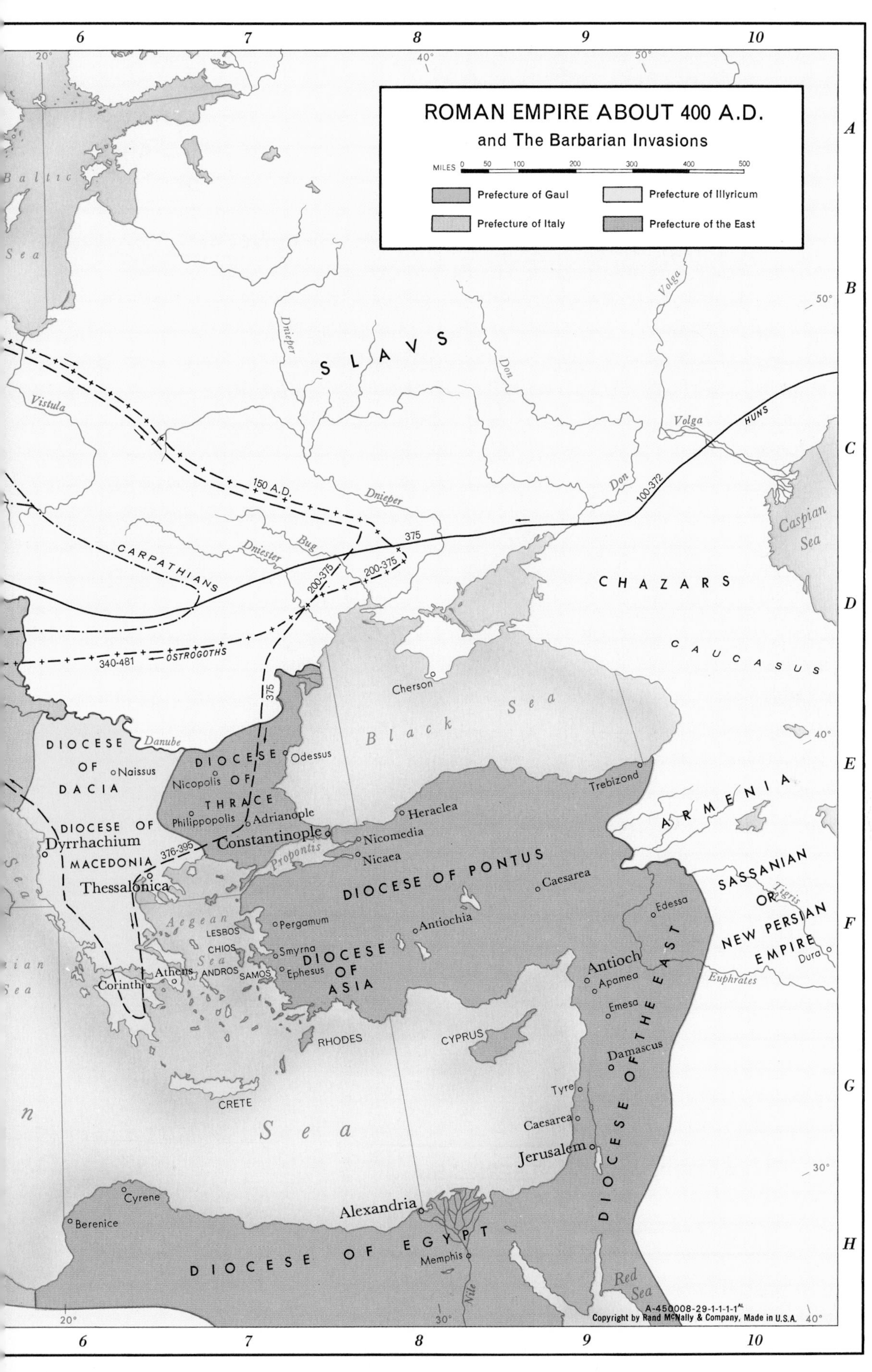

ROMAN EMPIRE ABOUT 400 A.D.
and The Barbarian Invasions
MILES 0 50 100 200 300 400 500
Prefecture of Gaul
Prefecture of Illyricum
Prefecture of Italy
Prefecture of the East
SLAVS
HUNS
CHAZARS
CAUCASUS
CARPATHIANS
OSTROGOTHS
150 A.D.
100-372
375
200-375
340-481
376-395
Baltic Sea
Vistula
Dnieper
Don
Volga
Bug
Dniester
Danube
Caspian Sea
Black Sea
Cherson
Odessus
Trebizond
ARMENIA
SASSANIAN OR NEW PERSIAN EMPIRE
Tigris
Euphrates
Dura
Edessa
DIOCESE OF DACIA
Naissus
DIOCESE OF THRACE
Nicopolis
Philippopolis
Adrianople
Constantinople
Propontis
Heraclea
Nicomedia
Nicaea
DIOCESE OF MACEDONIA
Dyrrhachium
Thessalonica
DIOCESE OF PONTUS
Caesarea
Aegean Sea
LESBOS
CHIOS
ANDROS
SAMOS
Pergamum
Smyrna
Ephesus
DIOCESE OF ASIA
Antiochia
Athens
Corinth
RHODES
CYPRUS
CRETE
DIOCESE OF THE EAST
Antioch
Apamea
Emesa
Damascus
Tyre
Caesarea
Jerusalem
Sea
Cyrene
Berenice
Alexandria
DIOCESE OF EGYPT
Memphis
Nile
Red Sea
A-450008-29-1-1-1-1
Copyright by Rand McNally & Company, Made in U.S.A.

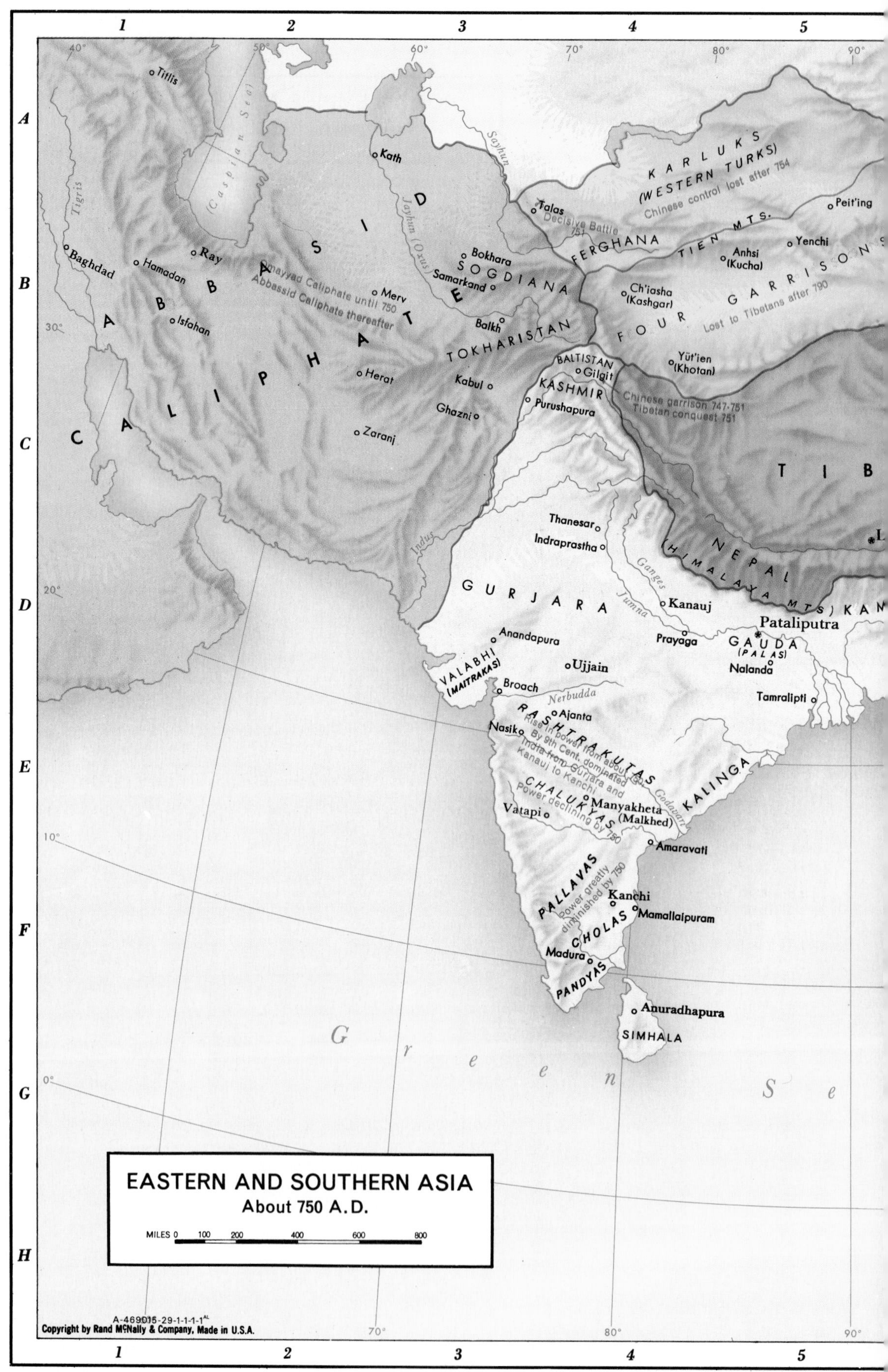
EASTERN AND SOUTHERN ASIA
About 750 A.D.
MILES 0 100 200 400 600 800
ABBASID CALIPHATE
Omayyad Caliphate until 750
Abbassid Caliphate thereafter
Tiflis
Baghdad
Hamadan
Ray
Isfahan
Merv
Herat
Zaranj
Kath
Bokhara
Samarkand
SOGDIANA
Balkh
TOKHARISTAN
Kabul
Ghazni
Talas
Decisive Battle 751
FERGHANA
KARLUKS (WESTERN TURKS)
Chinese control lost after 754
TIEN MTS.
Peit'ing
Yenchi
Anhsi (Kucha)
Ch'iasha (Kashgar)
FOUR GARRISONS
Lost to Tibetans after 790
Yüt'ien (Khotan)
BALTISTAN
Gilgit
KASHMIR
Purushapura
Chinese garrison 747-751
Tibetan conquest 751
TIB
NEPAL
HIMALAYA MTS.
Thanesar
Indraprastha
GURJARA
Kanauj
Prayaga
Pataliputra
GAUDA (PALAS)
Nalanda
Tamralipti
Anandapura
VALABHI (MAITRAKAS)
Ujjain
Broach
Nerbudda
Ajanta
Nasik
RASHTRAKUTAS
Rise in power from about 750
By 9th Cent. dominated India from Gurjara and Kanauj to Kanchi
CHALUKYAS
Power declining by 750
Manyakheta (Malkhed)
Vatapi
KALINGA
Godavari
Amaravati
PALLAVAS
Power greatly diminished by 750
Kanchi
Mamallaipuram
CHOLAS
Madura
PANDYAS
Anuradhapura
SIMHALA
Green Se
Tigris
(Caspian Sea)
Jayhun (Oxus)
Sayhun
Indus
Ganges
Jumna
A-469015-29-1-1-1
Copyright by Rand McNally & Company, Made in U.S.A.

6
7
8
9
10
A
B
C
D
E
F
G
H
Uighur Capital
Orkhon
UIGHURS (EASTERN TURKS)
(GOBI DESERT)
KHITANS
Capital
P'O HAI
Liaotung
SILLA
Hanchow
Capital
Capital from 794
Heian
Nara
Capital from 710-784
JAPAN
Great Wall
Huang
Tunhuang
LUNG YU
T'UYÜHUNS
Shan
KUANNEI
HO TUNG
T'aiyüan
HOPEI
Weichow
Yün
HO NAN
Loyang
TUCHI
Plen
Sung
Grand Canal
Yangchow
Eastern Sea
CHINGCHI
Ch'angan
SHANNAN HSI
SHANNAN TUNG
HUAINAN
Soochow
Yüeh
Hsüan
Hangchow
Chiangling
Yangtze
CHINA
Ch'engtu
CHIENNAN
CH'IENCHUNG
CHIANGNAN HSI
CHIANGNAN TUNG
Ch'üanchow
hasa
Brahmaputra
Tali
NAN CHAO (T'AI)
LINGNAN
(Hsi)
Kwangchow
Southern Sea
Halin
PYU
ANNAM
Chiaochow
(HAINAN)
UPPER (LAND) CHENLA
Srikshetra
MONS
Thaton
CHAMPA
Amaravati
Mekong
LOWER (MARITIME) CHENLA
KAUTHARA
Virapura
PANDURANGA
DVARAVATI
TAMBRALINGA
LANGKASUKA
KEDAH
(SUMATRA)
(BORNEO)
Malayu
BANKA
SRIVIJAYA
Srivijaya
(JAVA)
SAILENDRAS
Borobodur Built 772?
MATARAM
TARUMA
100°
110°
120°
130°
140°
30°
20°
10°
0°
The Srivijayan Empire, perhaps under a Sailendran ruler, probably included more of Sumatra and Java and even portions of the Malay peninsula and Borneo by the end of the 8th Century

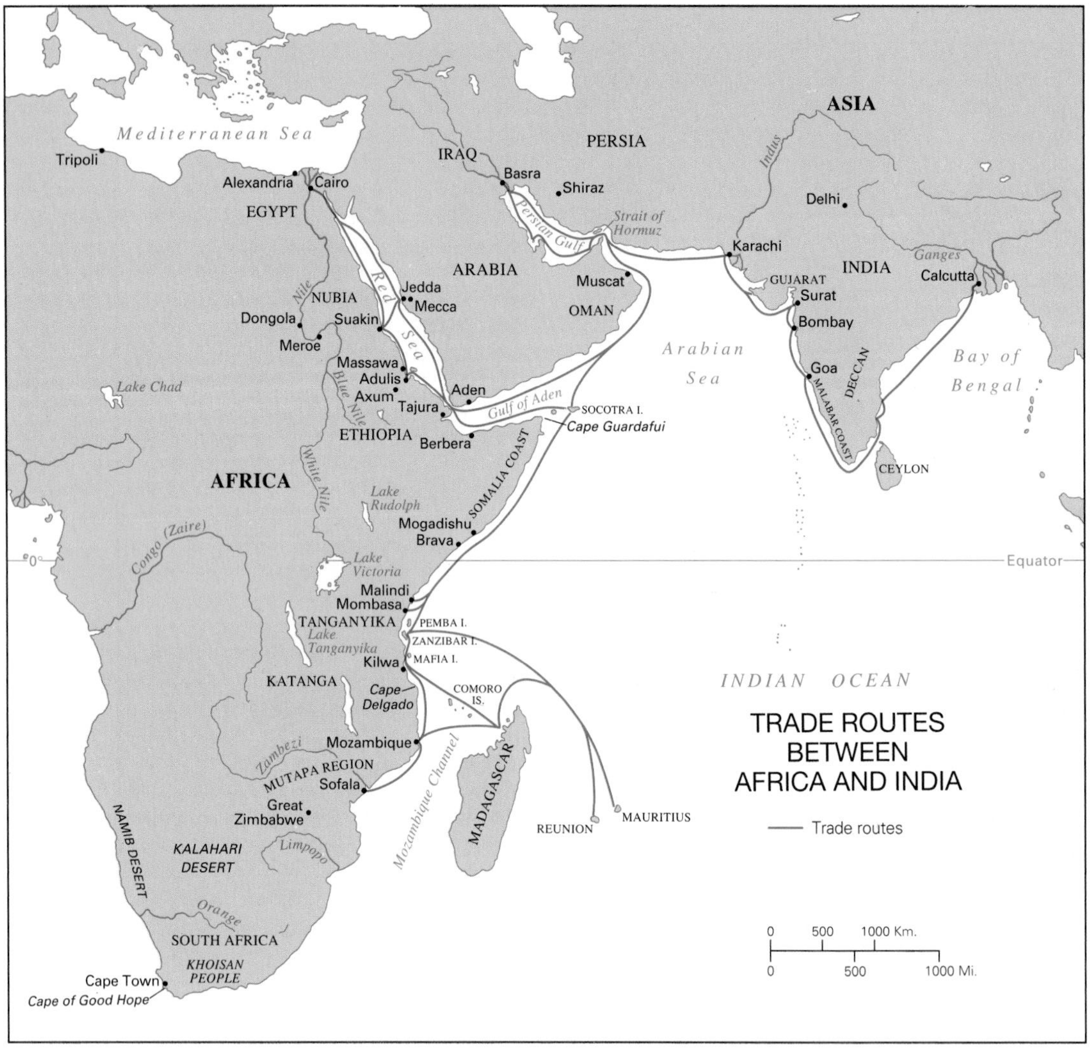

TRADE ROUTES
BETWEEN
AFRICA AND INDIA
Trade routes
Mediterranean Sea
Tripoli
Alexandria
Cairo
EGYPT
IRAQ
Basra
PERSIA
Shiraz
ASIA
Indus
Delhi
Persian Gulf
Strait of Hormuz
Karachi
GUJARAT
Surat
Bombay
INDIA
Ganges
Calcutta
Bay of Bengal
Goa
DECCAN
MALABAR COAST
CEYLON
Arabian Sea
ARABIA
Muscat
OMAN
Jedda
Mecca
Red Sea
NUBIA
Nile
Dongola
Suakin
Meroe
Massawa
Adulis
Axum
Aden
Tajura
Gulf of Aden
SOCOTRA I.
Cape Guardafui
Lake Chad
Blue Nile
ETHIOPIA
Berbera
AFRICA
White Nile
Lake Rudolph
SOMALIA COAST
Mogadishu
Brava
Congo (Zaire)
0
Equator
Lake Victoria
Malindi
Mombasa
TANGANYIKA
Lake Tanganyika
PEMBA I.
ZANZIBAR I.
MAFIA I.
Kilwa
KATANGA
Cape Delgado
COMORO IS.
INDIAN OCEAN
Mozambique
Zambezi
MUTAPA REGION
Sofala
MADAGASCAR
Mozambique Channel
Great Zimbabwe
REUNION
MAURITIUS
NAMIB DESERT
KALAHARI DESERT
Limpopo
Orange
SOUTH AFRICA
KHOISAN PEOPLE
Cape Town
Cape of Good Hope
0 500 1000 Km.
0 500 1000 Mi.

THE KINGDOM
OF MALI
Kingdom of Ghana, 11th century
Kingdom of Mali, 1337
Trans-Saharan trade routes
SPAIN
ATLANTIC OCEAN
Mediterranean Sea
Tunis
Tripoli
Fez
Marrakech
ATLAS MTS.
Sijilmassa
Canary Is.
Ghadames
To Egypt
Ghat
Taghaza
SAHARA
Wadane
Awlil
Awdaghost
Walata
Timbuktu
Gao
Senegal
KANGABA
Jenne
Segou
Niani
Niger
Lake Chad
HAUSALAND
Kano
Volta
Benue
GOLD COAST
Gulf of Guinea
0 300 600 Km.
0 300 600 Mi.

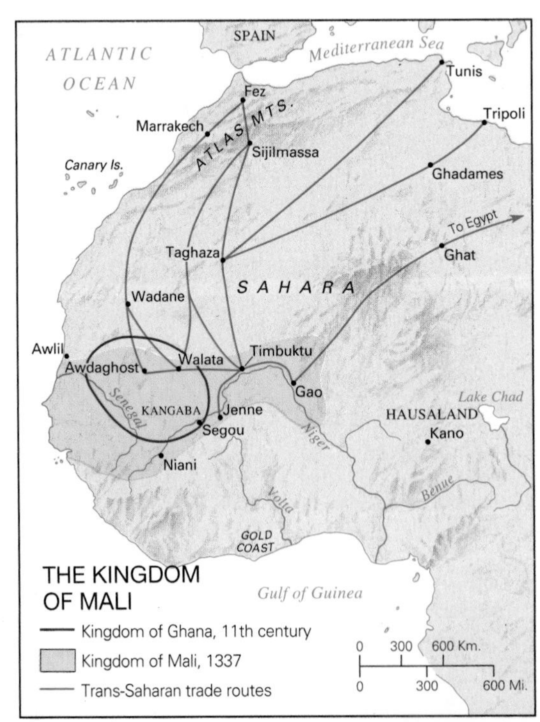

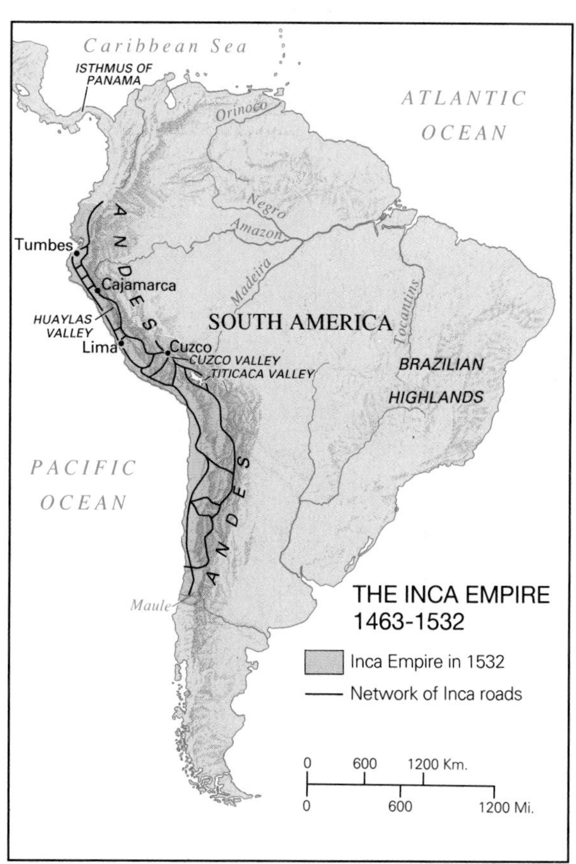
Caribbean Sea
ISTHMUS OF PANAMA
Orinoco
ATLANTIC OCEAN
Negro
Amazon
Madeira
Tocantins
Tumbes
Cajamarca
HUAYLAS VALLEY
Lima
Cuzco
CUZCO VALLEY
TITICACA VALLEY
SOUTH AMERICA
BRAZILIAN HIGHLANDS
ANDES
PACIFIC OCEAN
Maule
THE INCA EMPIRE 1463-1532
Inca Empire in 1532
Network of Inca roads
0 600 1200 Km.
0 600 1200 Mi.

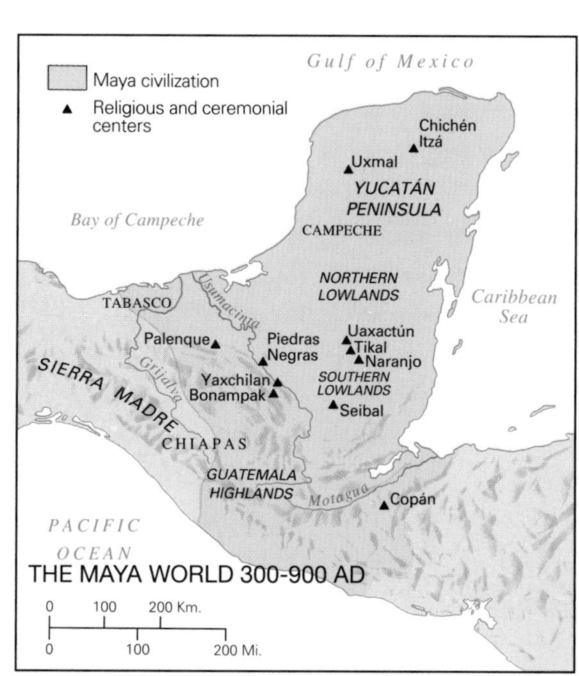
Gulf of Mexico
Maya civilization
Religious and ceremonial centers
Chichén Itzá
Uxmal
YUCATÁN PENINSULA
Bay of Campeche
CAMPECHE
TABASCO
Usumacinta
NORTHERN LOWLANDS
Caribbean Sea
Palenque
Piedras Negras
Uaxactún
Tikal
Naranjo
SIERRA MADRE
Grijalva
Yaxchilan
Bonampak
SOUTHERN LOWLANDS
Seibal
CHIAPAS
GUATEMALA HIGHLANDS
Motagua
Copán
PACIFIC OCEAN
THE MAYA WORLD 300-900 AD
0 100 200 Km.
0 100 200 Mi.

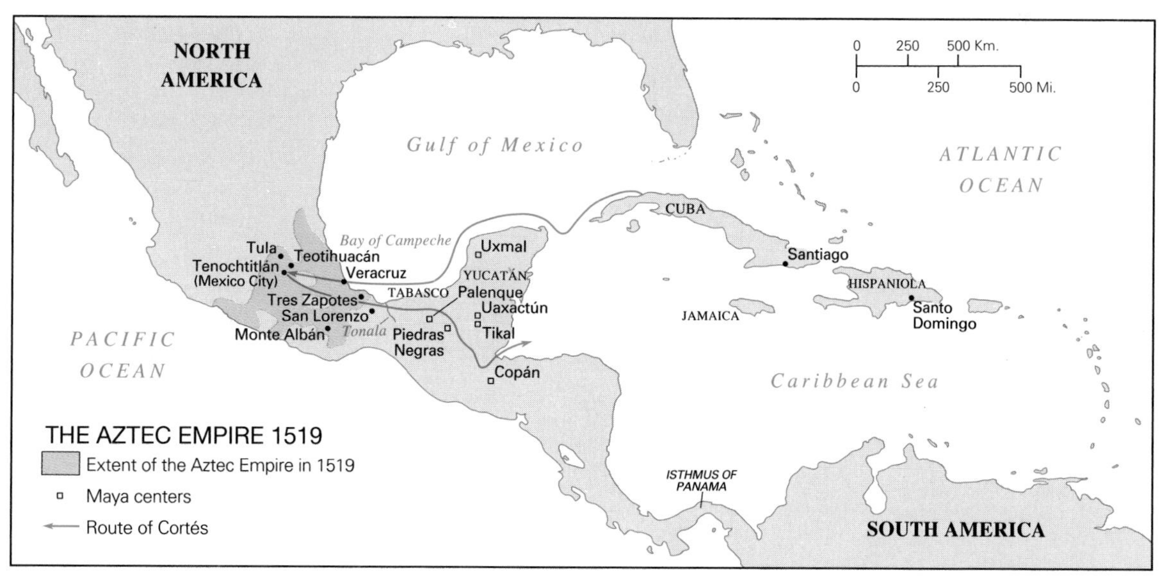
NORTH AMERICA
0 250 500 Km.
0 250 500 Mi.
Gulf of Mexico
ATLANTIC OCEAN
CUBA
Bay of Campeche
Uxmal
Tula
Teotihuacán
Tenochtitlán (Mexico City)
Veracruz
YUCATÁN
Santiago
TABASCO
Palenque
HISPANIOLA
Tres Zapotes
San Lorenzo
Uaxactún
Santo Domingo
JAMAICA
PACIFIC OCEAN
Monte Albán
Tonala
Piedras Negras
Tikal
Copán
Caribbean Sea
THE AZTEC EMPIRE 1519
Extent of the Aztec Empire in 1519
Maya centers
Route of Cortés
ISTHMUS OF PANAMA
SOUTH AMERICA

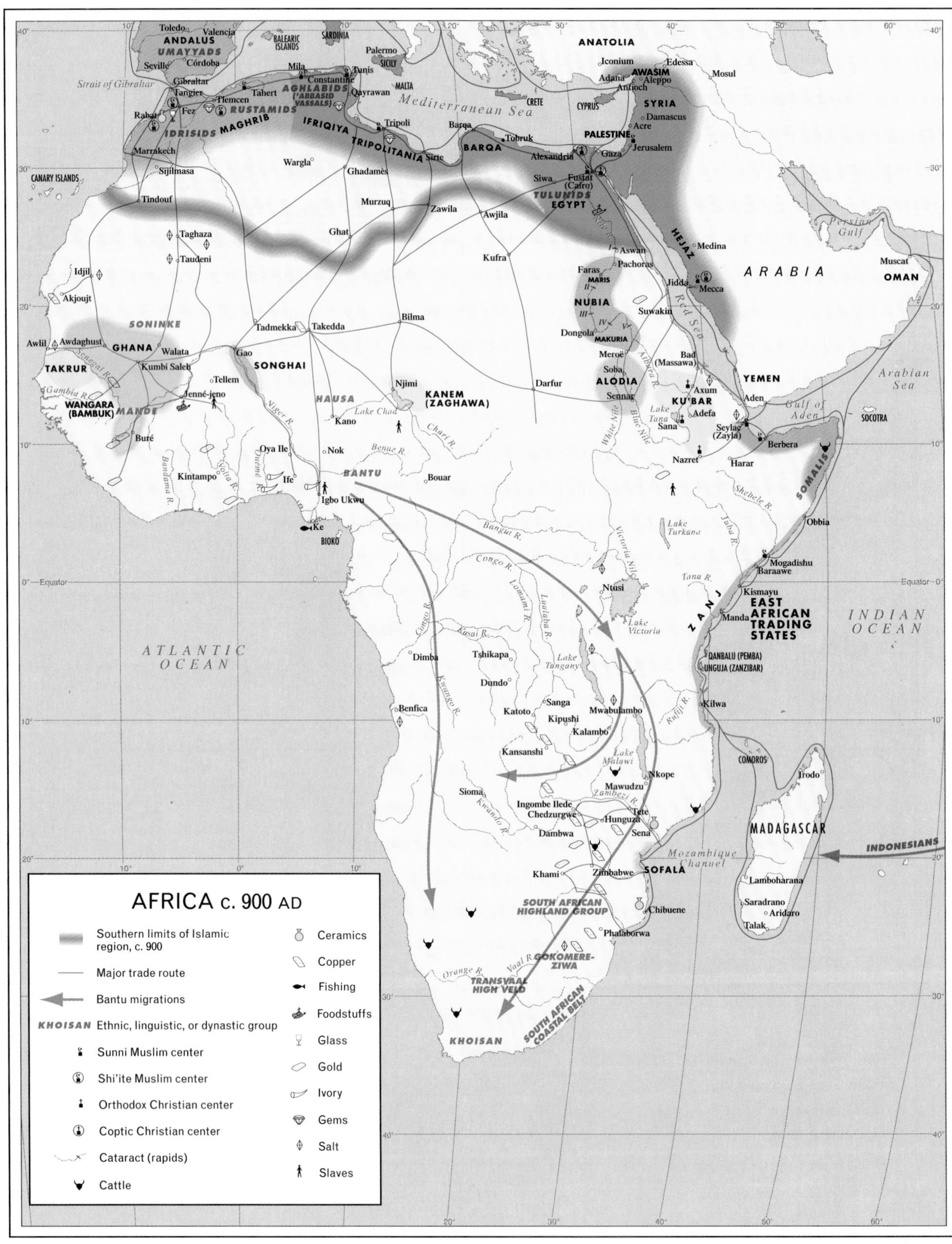

AFRICA c. 900 AD
Southern limits of Islamic region, c. 900
Major trade route
Bantu migrations
KHOISAN Ethnic, linguistic, or dynastic group
Sunni Muslim center
Shi'ite Muslim center
Orthodox Christian center
Coptic Christian center
Cataract (rapids)
Cattle
Ceramics
Copper
Fishing
Foodstuffs
Glass
Gold
Ivory
Gems
Salt
Slaves
ANDALUS
UMAYYADS
Toledo
Valencia
Seville
Córdoba
BALEARIC ISLANDS
SARDINIA
Palermo
SICILY
MALTA
CRETE
CYPRUS
ANATOLIA
Iconium
Adana
Antioch
Edessa
AWASIM
Aleppo
Mosul
SYRIA
Damascus
Acre
PALESTINE
Jerusalem
Gaza
Strait of Gibraltar
Gibraltar
Tangier
Tlemcen
Tahert
Mila
Constantine
Tunis
Qayrawan
AGHLABIDS
('ABBASID VASSALS)
RUSTAMIDS
Rabat
Fez
IDRISIDS
MAGHRIB
IFRIQIYA
TRIPOLITANIA
Tripoli
Mediterranean Sea
Barqa
BARQA
Tobruk
Alexandria
Marrakech
Sijilmasa
CANARY ISLANDS
Wargla
Ghadames
Sirte
Siwa
Fustat (Cairo)
TULUNIDS
EGYPT
Tindouf
Murzuq
Zawila
Awjila
Ghat
Taghaza
Taudeni
Kufra
Aswan
Pachoras
HEJAZ
Medina
Mecca
Jidda
ARABIA
Muscat
OMAN
Persian Gulf
Idjil
Akjoujt
Faras
MARIS
NUBIA
Suwakin
Red Sea
SONINKE
Tadmekka
Takedda
Bilma
Dongola
MAKURIA
Meroë
Soba
ALODIA
Sennar
Awlil
Awdaghust
GHANA
Walata
Kumbi Saleh
TAKRUR
Senegal R.
Gao
SONGHAI
Bad (Massawa)
Axum
Adefa
YEMEN
Aden
Gulf of Aden
Arabian Sea
SOCOTRA
Tellem
Jenné-jeno
Gambia R.
WANGARA (BAMBUK)
MANDE
HAUSA
Njimi
KANEM (ZAGHAWA)
Lake Chad
Kano
Darfur
Atbara R.
KU'BAR
Lake Tana
Sana
Seylac (Zayla)
Berbera
Buré
Niger R.
Oya Ile
Nok
Benue R.
Chari R.
White Nile
Blue Nile
Nazret
Harar
SOMALIS
Kintampo
Bandama R.
Volta R.
Oueme R.
Ife
BANTU
Igbo Ukwu
Bouar
Shebele R.
Ke
BIOKO
Bangui R.
Lake Turkana
Juba R.
Obbia
Congo R.
Lomami R.
Lualaba R.
Victoria Nile
Mogadishu
Baraawe
Ntusi
Tana R.
Kismayu
Equator
EAST AFRICAN TRADING STATES
Manda
ZANJ
Lake Victoria
INDIAN OCEAN
ATLANTIC OCEAN
Kasai R.
Dimba
Tshikapa
Lake Tanganyika
QANBALU (PEMBA)
UNGUJA (ZANZIBAR)
Dundo
Sanga
Katoto
Kipushi
Mwabulambo
Kilwa
Rufiji R.
Benfica
Kwango R.
Kalambo
Kansanshi
Lake Malawi
COMOROS
Irodo
Nkope
Mawudzu
Zambezi R.
Sioma
Kwando R.
Ingombe Ilede
Chedzurgwe
Hunguza
Tete
Sena
Dambwa
MADAGASCAR
INDONESIANS
Mozambique Channel
Khami
Zimbabwe
SOFALA
Lamboharana
Saradrano
Aridaro
Talak
SOUTH AFRICAN HIGHLAND GROUP
Chibuene
Phalaborwa
GOKOMERE-ZIWA
Orange R.
Vaal R.
TRANSVAAL HIGH VELD
SOUTH AFRICAN COASTAL BELT
KHOISAN

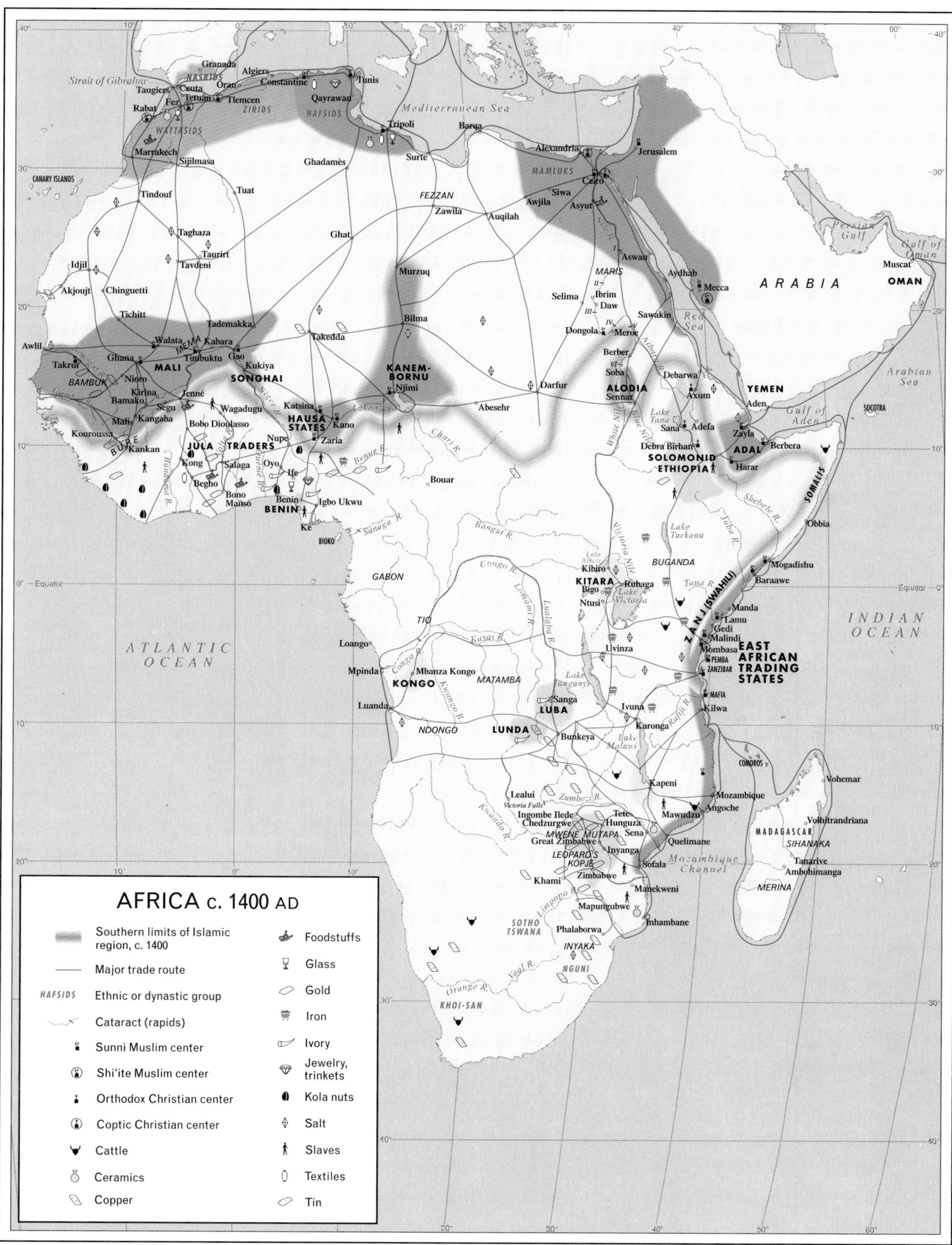
AFRICA c. 1400 AD
Southern limits of Islamic region, c. 1400
Major trade route
HAFSIDS Ethnic or dynastic group
Cataract (rapids)
Sunni Muslim center
Shi'ite Muslim center
Orthodox Christian center
Coptic Christian center
Cattle
Ceramics
Copper
Foodstuffs
Glass
Gold
Iron
Ivory
Jewelry, trinkets
Kola nuts
Salt
Slaves
Textiles
Tin
Strait of Gibraltar
Granada
NASRIDS
Algiers
Constantine
Tunis
Taugiers
Ceuta
Tetuan
Oran
Tlemcen
Rabat
Fez
ZIRIDS
Qayrawan
HAFSIDS
WATTASIDS
Marrakech
Sijilmasa
Mediterranean Sea
Tripoli
Barqa
Alexandria
Jerusalem
MAMLUKS
Cairo
Siwa
Awjila
Asyut
Ghadamès
Surte
CANARY ISLANDS
Tindouf
Tuat
FEZZAN
Zawila
Auqilah
Taghaza
Ghat
Taurirt
Tavdeni
Idjil
Akjoujt
Chinguetti
Murzuq
Aswan
MARIS
Aydhab
Mecca
ARABIA
Persian Gulf
Gulf of Oman
Muscat
OMAN
Selima
Ibrim
Daw
Tichitt
Bilma
Tademakka
Sawakin
Red Sea
Dongola
Meroe
Awlil
Walata
MEMA
Kabara
Takedda
Berber
Takrur
Ghana
MALI
Timbuktu
Gao
Kukiya
SONGHAI
KANEM-BORNU
Soba
BAMBUK
Nioro
Njimi
Darfur
ALODIA
Sennar
Debarwa
Axum
YEMEN
Arabian Sea
Kirina
Bamako
Jenné
Segu
Wagadugu
Katsina
HAUSA STATES
Kano
Lake Chad
Abesehr
Lake Tana
Aden
Gulf of Aden
SOCOTRA
Mali
Kangaba
Bobo Dioulasso
Sana
Adefa
Zayla
Kouroussa
BURE
Nupe
Zaria
Debra Birhan
ADAL
Berbera
Kankan
JULA TRADERS
Chari R.
SOLOMONID ETHIOPIA
Harar
Kong
Salaga
Oyo
Ife
Benue R.
Begho
Bono Manso
Benin
BENIN
Igbo Ukwu
Bouar
SOMALIS
Shebele R.
Ke
BIOKO
Sanaga R.
Bangui R.
Lake Turkana
Obbia
Juba R.
GABON
Congo R.
Lake Albert
Kibiro
BUGANDA
Mogadishu
Equator
KITARA
Bigo
Rubaga
Lake Victoria
Ntusi
Tana R.
Baraawe
TIO
Lomami R.
Lualaba R.
ZANJ (SWAHILI)
Manda
Lamu
Gedi
INDIAN OCEAN
ATLANTIC OCEAN
Loango
Kasai R.
Uvinza
Malindi
Mombasa
PEMBA
ZANZIBAR
EAST AFRICAN TRADING STATES
Mpinda
Mbanza Kongo
KONGO
MATAMBA
Kwango R.
Lake Tanganyika
Sanga
LUBA
MAFIA
Luanda
Kilwa
Ivuna
Karonga
Rufiji R.
NDONGO
LUNDA
Bunkeya
Lake Malawi
COMOROS
Kapeni
Vohemar
Lealui
Victoria Falls
Zambezi R.
Mozambique
Angoche
Mawudzu
Ingombe Ilede
Chedzurgwe
Tete
Hunguza
MWENE MUTAPA
Sena
Great Zimbabwe
Quelimane
MADAGASCAR
Volhitrandriana
SIHANAKA
LEOPARD'S KOPJE
Inyanga
Sofala
Mozambique Channel
Tanarive
Ambohimanga
Khami
Zimbabwe
Limpopo R.
Manekweni
MERINA
Mapungubwe
Inhambane
SOTHO TSWANA
Phalaborwa
INYAKA
NGUNI
Vaal R.
Orange R.
KHOI-SAN
Kwando R.

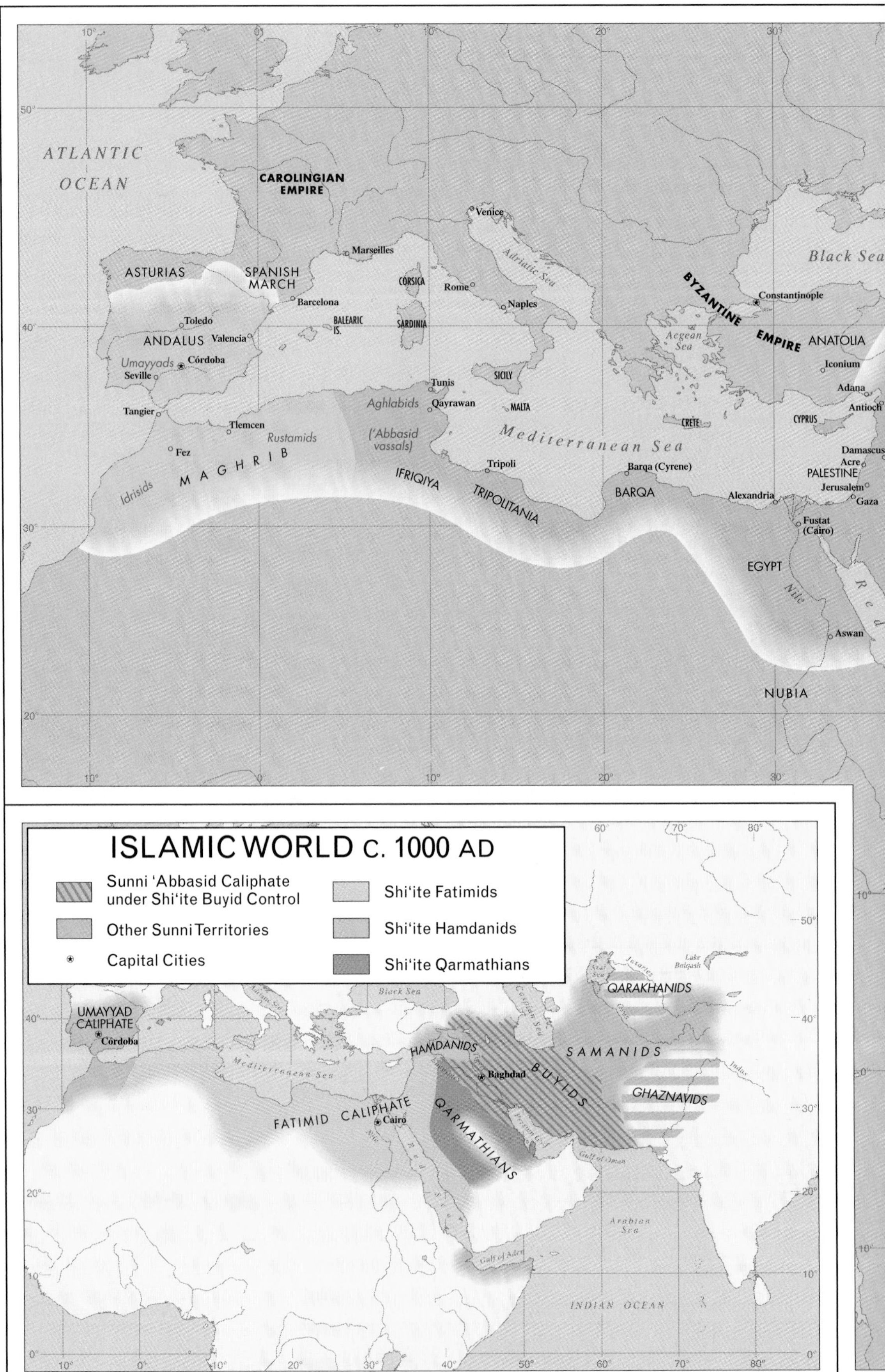

ATLANTIC OCEAN
CAROLINGIAN EMPIRE
Venice
Marseilles
Adriatic Sea
Black Sea
ASTURIAS
SPANISH MARCH
CORSICA
Rome
BYZANTINE EMPIRE
Constantinople
Barcelona
Naples
Toledo
BALEARIC IS.
SARDINIA
Aegean Sea
ANDALUS
Valencia
ANATOLIA
Umayyads
Córdoba
Seville
Iconium
Tunis
SICILY
Adana
Aghlabids
Qayrawan
MALTA
Antioch
Tangier
CRETE
CYPRUS
Tlemcen
Rustamids
('Abbasid vassals)
Mediterranean Sea
Damascus
Fez
Acre
MAGHRIB
Tripoli
Barqa (Cyrene)
PALESTINE
Idrisids
IFRIQIYA
TRIPOLITANIA
BARQA
Alexandria
Jerusalem
Gaza
Fustat (Cairo)
EGYPT
Nile
Aswan
NUBIA
ISLAMIC WORLD C. 1000 AD
Sunni 'Abbasid Caliphate under Shi'ite Buyid Control
Shi'ite Fatimids
Other Sunni Territories
Shi'ite Hamdanids
Capital Cities
Shi'ite Qarmathians
Black Sea
QARAKHANIDS
UMAYYAD CALIPHATE
Córdoba
HAMDANIDS
SAMANIDS
Baghdad
BUYIDS
GHAZNAVIDS
Mediterranean Sea
FATIMID CALIPHATE
Cairo
QARMATHIANS
Arabian Sea
INDIAN OCEAN

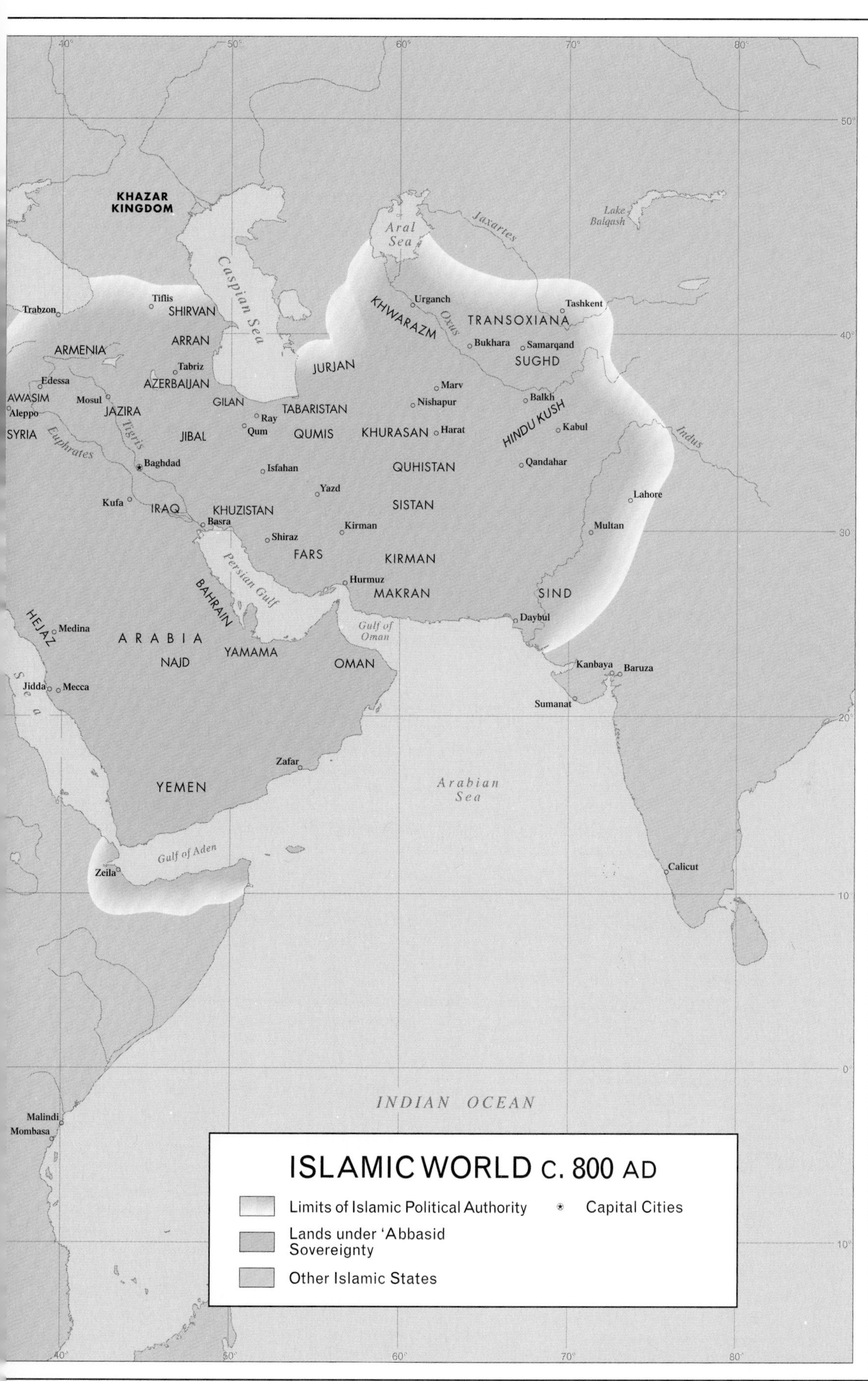
ISLAMIC WORLD c. 800 AD
Limits of Islamic Political Authority
Capital Cities
Lands under ʻAbbasid Sovereignty
Other Islamic States
KHAZAR KINGDOM
Caspian Sea
Aral Sea
Jaxartes
Lake Balqash
Oxus
Indus
Trabzon
Tiflis
SHIRVAN
ARRAN
ARMENIA
Tabriz
AZERBAIJAN
Edessa
AWASIM
Aleppo
SYRIA
Mosul
JAZIRA
Tigris
Euphrates
GILAN
Ray
Qum
JIBAL
Baghdad
Kufa
IRAQ
KHUZISTAN
Basra
Isfahan
Shiraz
FARS
TABARISTAN
QUMIS
JURJAN
KHWARAZM
Urganch
TRANSOXIANA
Tashkent
Bukhara
Samarqand
SUGHD
Marv
Nishapur
KHURASAN
Harat
Balkh
HINDU KUSH
Kabul
Qandahar
QUHISTAN
Yazd
SISTAN
Kirman
KIRMAN
Hurmuz
MAKRAN
SIND
Daybul
Lahore
Multan
Persian Gulf
BAHRAIN
Gulf of Oman
HEJAZ
Medina
ARABIA
NAJD
YAMAMA
OMAN
Jidda
Mecca
Sea
Zafar
YEMEN
Gulf of Aden
Zeila
Arabian Sea
Kanbaya
Baruza
Sumanat
Calicut
INDIAN OCEAN
Malindi
Mombasa

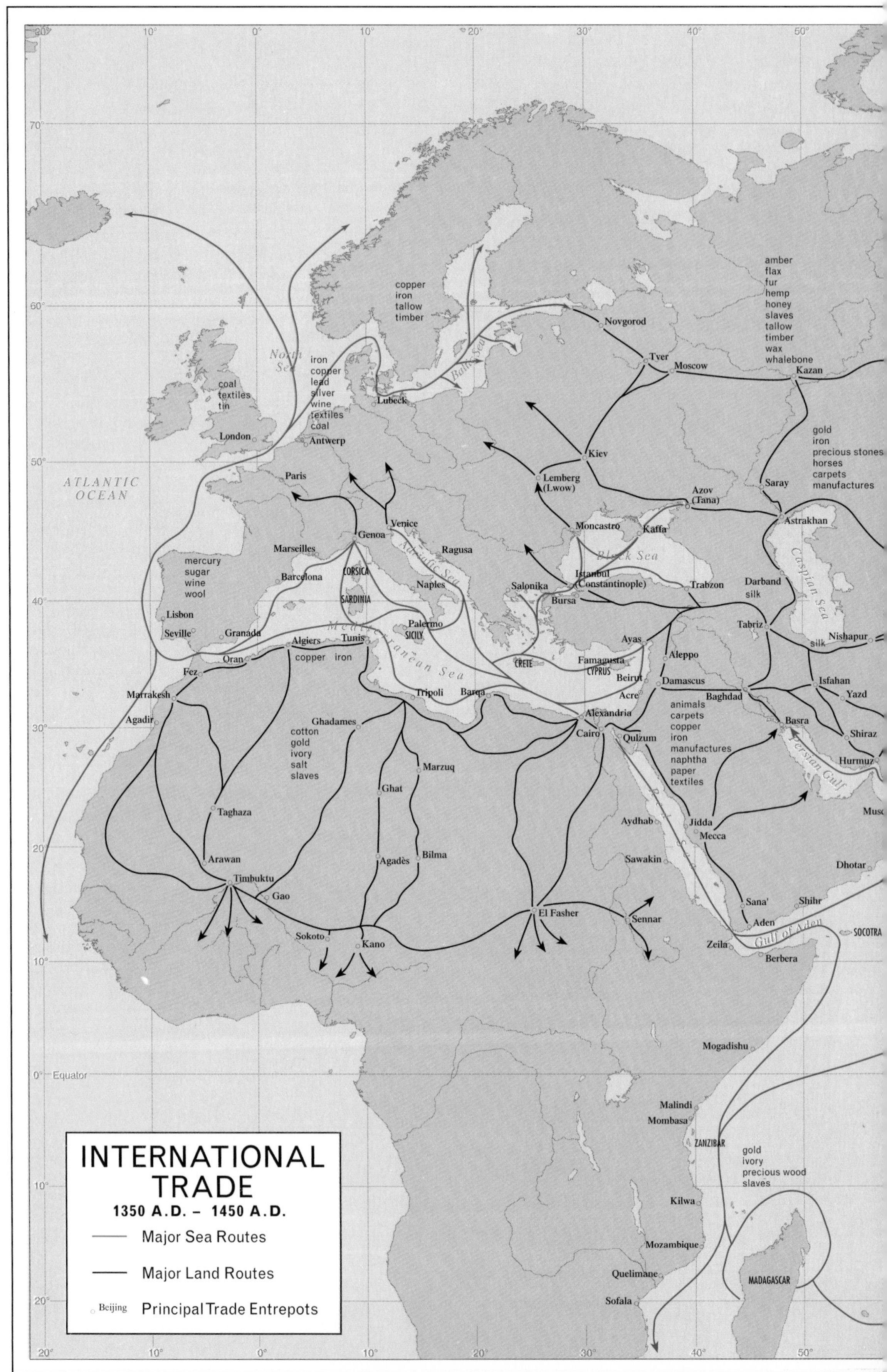

INTERNATIONAL TRADE
1350 A.D. – 1450 A.D.
Major Sea Routes
Major Land Routes
Beijing Principal Trade Entrepots
ATLANTIC OCEAN
North Sea
Baltic Sea
Adriatic Sea
Black Sea
Caspian Sea
Mediterranean Sea
Persian Gulf
Gulf of Aden
Equator
copper iron tallow timber
iron copper lead silver wine textiles coal
coal textiles tin
mercury sugar wine wool
copper iron
cotton gold ivory salt slaves
amber flax fur hemp honey slaves tallow timber wax whalebone
gold iron precious stones horses carpets manufactures
silk
animals carpets copper iron manufactures naphtha paper textiles
gold ivory precious wood slaves
London
Lubeck
Antwerp
Paris
Novgorod
Tver
Moscow
Kazan
Kiev
Lemberg (Lwow)
Saray
Azov (Tana)
Astrakhan
Venice
Genoa
Marseilles
Barcelona
CORSICA
SARDINIA
Ragusa
Naples
Moncastro
Kaffa
Istanbul (Constantinople)
Trabzon
Darband
Salonika
Bursa
Lisbon
Seville
Granada
Palermo
SICILY
Tabriz
Nishapur
Algiers
Tunis
Oran
Fez
CRETE
Ayas
Aleppo
Famagusta
CYPRUS
Beirut
Damascus
Isfahan
Yazd
Marrakesh
Tripoli
Barqa
Acre
Baghdad
Agadir
Ghadames
Alexandria
Cairo
Qulzum
Basra
Shiraz
Hurmuz
Marzuq
Ghat
Taghaza
Aydhab
Jidda
Mecca
Arawan
Agadès
Bilma
Sawakin
Dhotar
Timbuktu
Gao
Sana'
Shihr
El Fasher
Sennar
Aden
SOCOTRA
Sokoto
Kano
Zeila
Berbera
Mogadishu
Malindi
Mombasa
ZANZIBAR
Kilwa
Mozambique
Quelimane
MADAGASCAR
Sofala

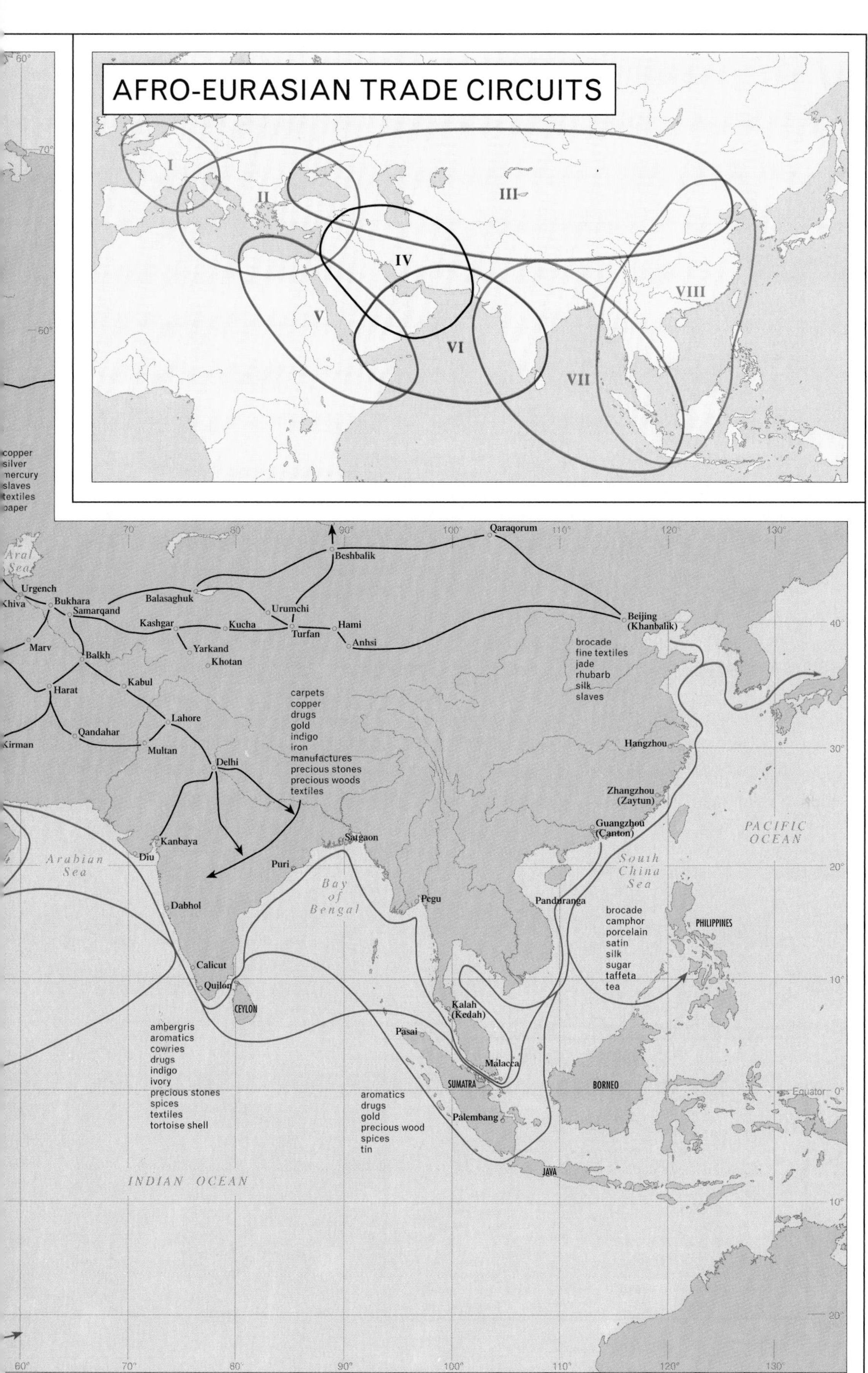

AFRO-EURASIAN TRADE CIRCUITS
I
II
III
IV
V
VI
VII
VIII
copper
silver
mercury
slaves
textiles
paper
Aral Sea
Urgench
Khiva
Bukhara
Samarqand
Balasaghuk
Beshbalik
Qaraqorum
Urumchi
Kashgar
Kucha
Turfan
Hami
Anhsi
Yarkand
Khotan
Beijing (Khanbalik)
Marv
Balkh
Harat
Kabul
Lahore
Qandahar
Kirman
Multan
Delhi
brocade
fine textiles
jade
rhubarb
silk
slaves
carpets
copper
drugs
gold
indigo
iron
manufactures
precious stones
precious woods
textiles
Hangzhou
Zhangzhou (Zaytun)
Guangzhou (Canton)
PACIFIC OCEAN
Kanbaya
Diu
Arabian Sea
Satgaon
Puri
Bay of Bengal
South China Sea
Dabhol
Pegu
Pandurangа
brocade
camphor
porcelain
satin
silk
sugar
taffeta
tea
PHILIPPINES
Calicut
Quilon
CEYLON
Kalah (Kedah)
ambergris
aromatics
cowries
drugs
indigo
ivory
precious stones
spices
textiles
tortoise shell
Pasai
Malacca
SUMATRA
BORNEO
Equator
aromatics
drugs
gold
precious wood
spices
tin
Palembang
JAVA
INDIAN OCEAN

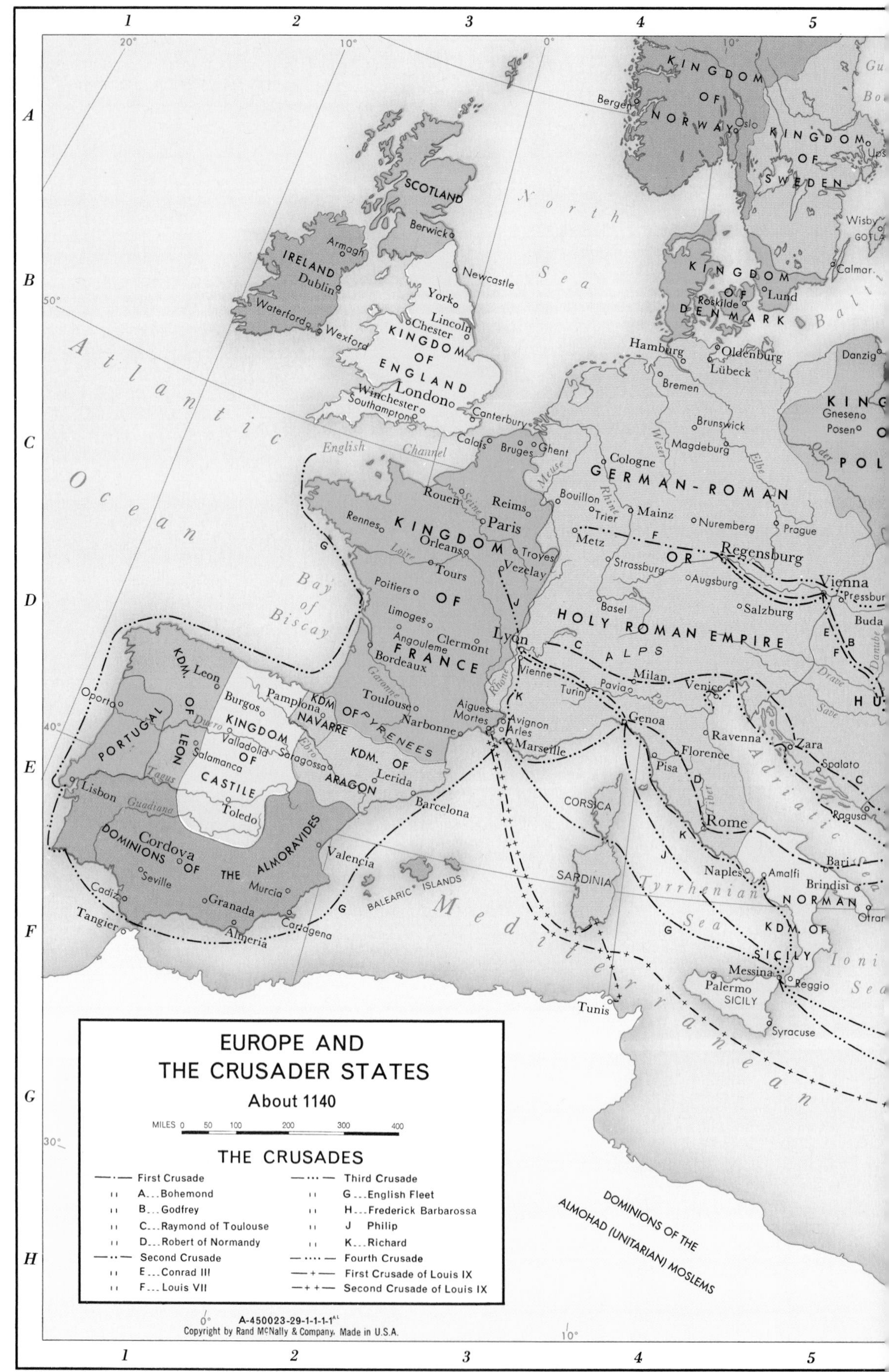

EUROPE AND
THE CRUSADER STATES
About 1140
MILES 0 50 100 200 300 400
THE CRUSADES
First Crusade
A...Bohemond
B...Godfrey
C...Raymond of Toulouse
D...Robert of Normandy
Second Crusade
E...Conrad III
F...Louis VII
Third Crusade
G...English Fleet
H...Frederick Barbarossa
J Philip
K...Richard
Fourth Crusade
First Crusade of Louis IX
Second Crusade of Louis IX
KINGDOM OF NORWAY
KINGDOM OF SWEDEN
KINGDOM OF DENMARK
SCOTLAND
IRELAND
KINGDOM OF ENGLAND
KINGDOM OF FRANCE
GERMAN-ROMAN OR HOLY ROMAN EMPIRE
KDM. OF LEON
PORTUGAL
KINGDOM OF CASTILE
KDM OF NAVARRE
KDM. OF ARAGON
PYRENEES
DOMINIONS OF THE ALMORAVIDES
NORMAN KDM. OF SICILY
DOMINIONS OF THE ALMOHAD (UNITARIAN) MOSLEMS
North Sea
Atlantic Ocean
Bay of Biscay
English Channel
Mediterranean
Tyrrhenian Sea
Adriatic
Ionian Sea
ALPS
CORSICA
SARDINIA
SICILY
BALEARIC ISLANDS
Bergen
Oslo
Wisby
Calmar
Lund
Roskilde
Hamburg
Oldenburg
Lübeck
Danzig
Bremen
Brunswick
Magdeburg
Gneseno
Posen
Armagh
Dublin
Waterford
Wexford
Berwick
Newcastle
York
Lincoln
Chester
London
Winchester
Southampton
Canterbury
Calais
Bruges
Ghent
Cologne
Bouillon
Trier
Mainz
Nuremberg
Prague
Metz
Regensburg
Strassburg
Augsburg
Vienna
Pressburg
Salzburg
Basel
Buda
Rouen
Reims
Paris
Rennes
Orleans
Troyes
Vezelay
Tours
Poitiers
Limoges
Clermont
Angouleme
Bordeaux
Lyon
Vienne
Toulouse
Narbonne
Aigues-Mortes
Avignon
Arles
Marseille
Turin
Pavia
Milan
Venice
Genoa
Ravenna
Zara
Spalato
Florence
Pisa
Rome
Ragusa
Naples
Amalfi
Bari
Brindisi
Messina
Reggio
Palermo
Syracuse
Tunis
Leon
Oporto
Burgos
Pamplona
Valladolid
Saragossa
Salamanca
Lerida
Barcelona
Lisbon
Toledo
Cordova
Seville
Valencia
Murcia
Granada
Cadiz
Tangier
Almeria
Cartagena
Seine
Loire
Garonne
Rhone
Meuse
Rhine
Weser
Elbe
Oder
Danube
Drave
Save
Po
Tiber
Ebro
Duero
Tagus
Guadiana
A-450023-29-1-1-1-1

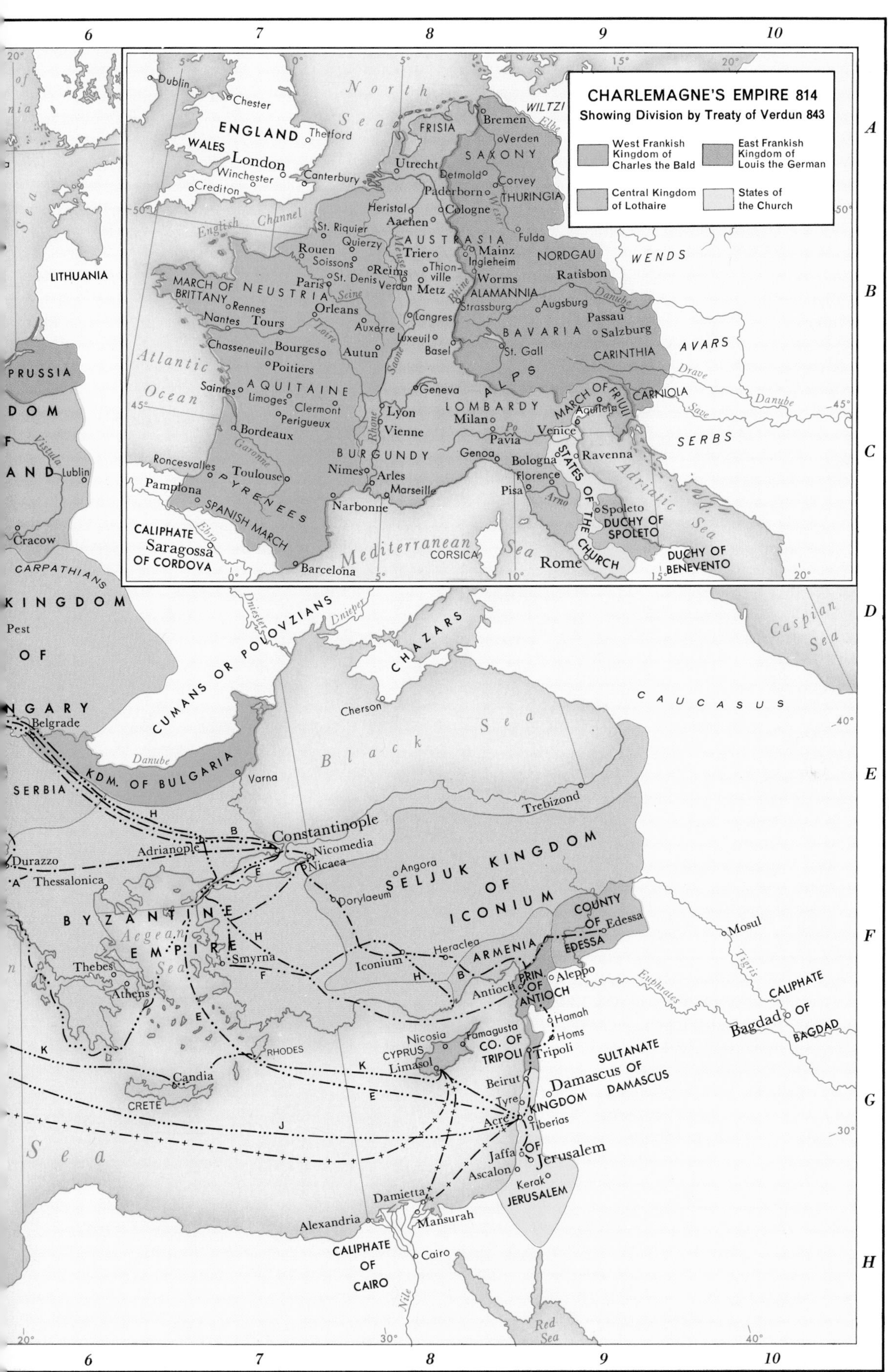
CHARLEMAGNE'S EMPIRE 814
Showing Division by Treaty of Verdun 843
West Frankish Kingdom of Charles the Bald
East Frankish Kingdom of Louis the German
Central Kingdom of Lothaire
States of the Church
ENGLAND
WALES
London
AUSTRASIA
NEUSTRIA
AQUITAINE
BURGUNDY
LOMBARDY
SAXONY
BAVARIA
ALAMANNIA
STATES OF THE CHURCH
DUCHY OF SPOLETO
DUCHY OF BENEVENTO
CALIPHATE OF CORDOVA
SPANISH MARCH
KDM. OF BULGARIA
BYZANTINE EMPIRE
SELJUK KINGDOM OF ICONIUM
COUNTY OF EDESSA
PRIN. OF ANTIOCH
CO. OF TRIPOLI
KINGDOM OF JERUSALEM
SULTANATE OF DAMASCUS
CALIPHATE OF BAGDAD
CALIPHATE OF CAIRO
CUMANS OR POLOVZIANS
CHAZARS
Constantinople
Jerusalem
Black Sea
Mediterranean Sea
Caspian Sea

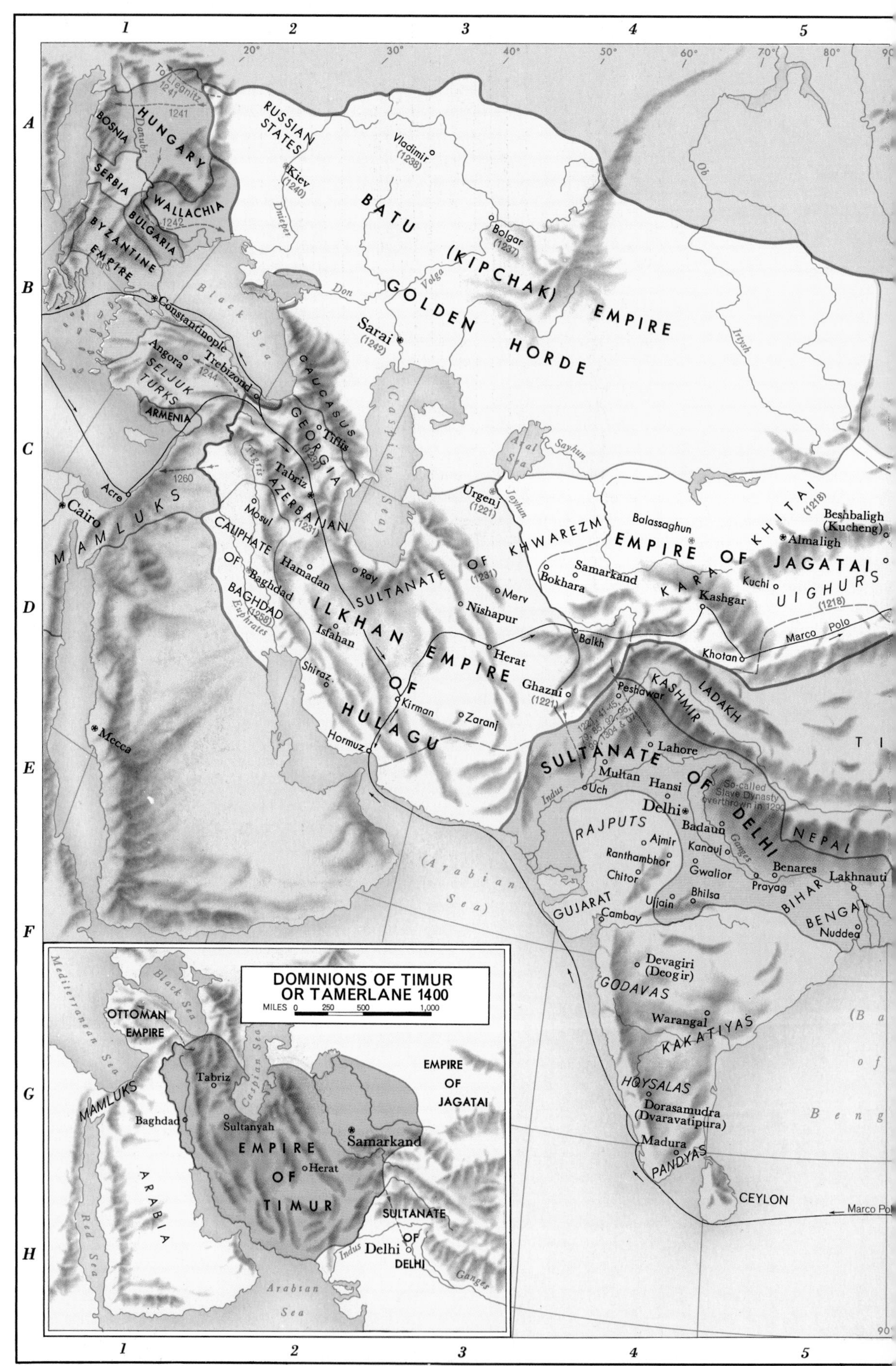

A
B
C
D
E
F
G
H
1
2
3
4
5
HUNGARY
BOSNIA
SERBIA
WALLACHIA
BULGARIA
BYZANTINE EMPIRE
RUSSIAN STATES
Kiev (1240)
Vladimir (1238)
Bolgar (1237)
BATU (KIPCHAK) EMPIRE
GOLDEN HORDE
Sarai (1242)
Black Sea
Constantinople
Angora
Trebizond
SELJUK TURKS
ARMENIA
CAUCASUS
GEORGIA
Tiflis
Caspian Sea
Aral Sea
Acre
Cairo
MAMLUKS
Tabriz
AZERBAIJAN
Mosul
CALIPHATE OF BAGHDAD
Baghdad (1258)
Hamadan
Ray
Isfahan
Shiraz
ILKHAN EMPIRE OF HULAGU
Kirman
Hormuz
Zaranj
Urgenj (1221)
SULTANATE OF KHWAREZM
Merv
Nishapur
Herat
Bokhara
Samarkand
Balkh
Ghazni (1221)
Balassaghun
EMPIRE OF KARA KHITAI
EMPIRE OF JAGATAI
Almaligh
Beshbaligh (Kucheng)
Kuchi
UIGHURS
Kashgar
Khotan
Marco Polo
Peshawar
KASHMIR
LADAKH
Lahore
SULTANATE OF DELHI
Multan
Uch
Hansi
Delhi
So-called Slave Dynasty overthrown in 1290
NEPAL
RAJPUTS
Badaun
Ajmir
Kanauj
Ranthambhor
Gwalior
Chitor
Benares
Prayag
Lakhnauti
BIHAR
BENGAL
Nuddea
Ujjain
Bhilsa
GUJARAT
Cambay
Arabian Sea
Mecca
Devagiri (Deogir)
GODAVAS
Warangal
KAKATIYAS
HOYSALAS
Dorasamudra (Dvaravatipura)
Madura
PANDYAS
CEYLON
Bay of Bengal
Danube
Dnieper
Don
Volga
Ob
Irtysh
Sayhun
Jayhun
Tigris
Euphrates
Indus
Ganges
DOMINIONS OF TIMUR OR TAMERLANE 1400
MILES 0 250 500 1,000
Mediterranean Sea
Black Sea
OTTOMAN EMPIRE
MAMLUKS
Tabriz
Caspian Sea
Baghdad
Sultanyah
EMPIRE OF TIMUR
Herat
Samarkand
EMPIRE OF JAGATAI
ARABIA
Red Sea
SULTANATE OF DELHI
Delhi
Indus
Ganges
Arabian Sea

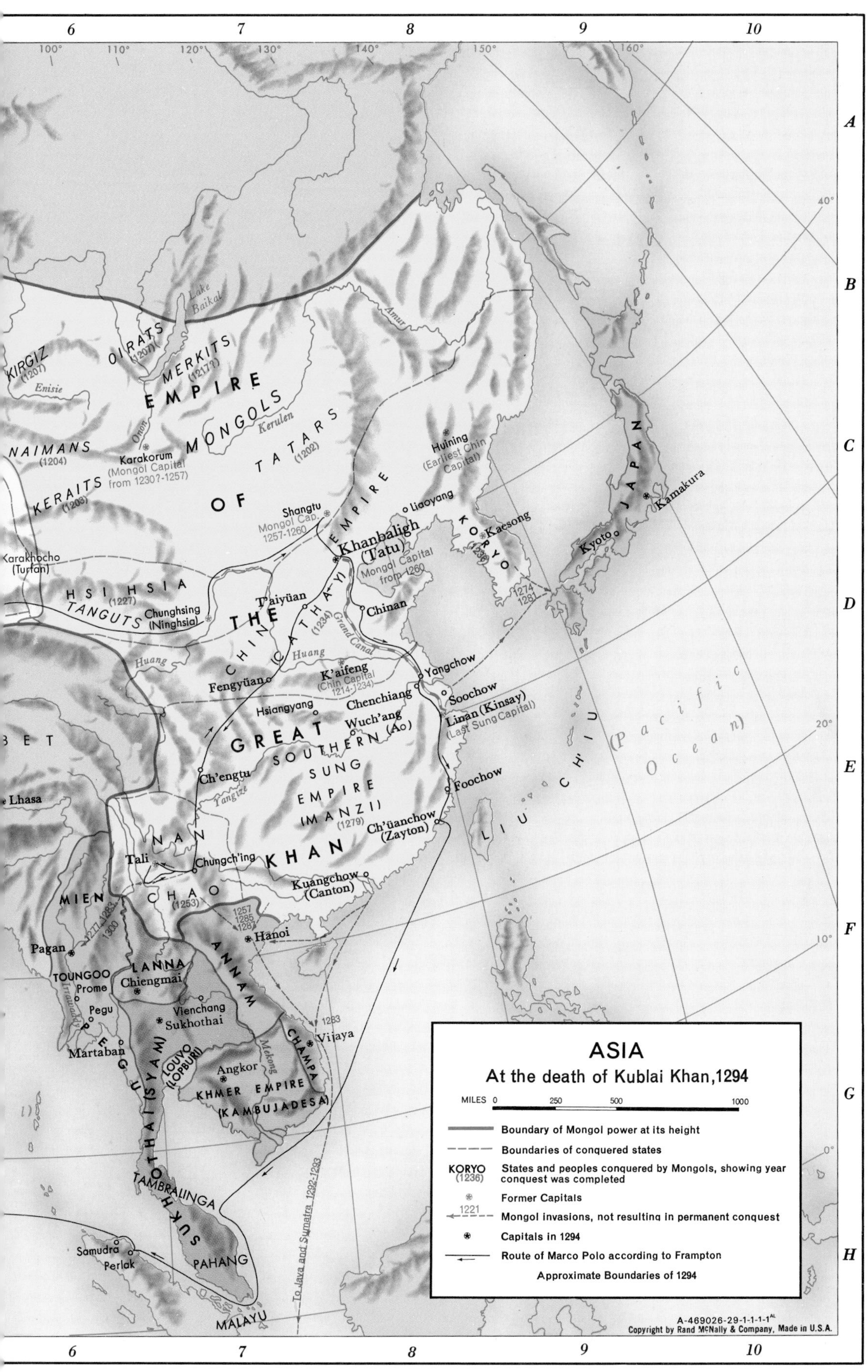
ASIA
At the death of Kublai Khan, 1294
MILES 0 250 500 1000
Boundary of Mongol power at its height
Boundaries of conquered states
KORYO (1236) States and peoples conquered by Mongols, showing year conquest was completed
Former Capitals
1221 Mongol invasions, not resulting in permanent conquest
Capitals in 1294
Route of Marco Polo according to Frampton
Approximate Boundaries of 1294
EMPIRE OF THE GREAT KHAN
MONGOLS
TATARS (1202)
OIRATS (1207)
MERKITS (1217?)
KIRGIZ (1207)
NAIMANS (1204)
KERAITS (1203)
Karakorum (Mongol Capital from 1230?-1257)
Shangtu Mongol Cap. 1257-1260
Khanbaligh (Tatu) Mongol Capital from 1260
HSI HSIA (1227) TANGUTS
Chunghsing (Ninghsia)
Karakhocho (Turfan)
CHIN (1234)
CATHAY
T'aiyüan
Chinan
Huining (Earliest Chin Capital)
Liaoyang
KORYO (1236)
Kaesong
1274 1281
JAPAN
Kyoto
Kamakura
K'aifeng (Chin Capital 1214-1234)
Fengyüan
Hsiangyang
Yangchow
Chenchiang
Soochow
Wuch'ang (Ao)
Linan (Kinsay) (Last Sung Capital)
SOUTHERN SUNG EMPIRE (MANZI) (1279)
Ch'engtu
Foochow
Ch'üanchow (Zayton)
Kuangchow (Canton)
Chungch'ing
NAN CHAO (1253)
Tali
Lhasa
LIU CH'IU
Pacific Ocean
MIEN
1277, 1283, 1300
Pagan
TOUNGOO
Prome
Pegu
PEGU
Martaban
LANNA
Chiengmai
Vienchang
Sukhothai
ANNAM
1257 1285 1287
Hanoi
CHAMPA
1283
Vijaya
LOUVO (LOPBURI)
Angkor
KHMER EMPIRE (KAMBUJADESA)
SUKHOTHAI (SYAM)
TAMBRALINGA
PAHANG
MALAYU
Samudra
Perlak
To Java and Sumatra 1292-1293
Lake Baikal
Amur
Kerulen
Onon
Enisie
Huang
Grand Canal
Yangtze
Mekong
Irrawaddy
A-469026-29-1-1-1
Copyright by Rand McNally & Company, Made in U.S.A.

EUROPE
About 1360
MILES 0 50 100 200 300
Boundary of Holy Roman Empire
Boundary of France
FAEROES
NORWAY
SHETLAND ISLANDS
ORKNEY ISLANDS
HEBRIDES
Bergen
Oslo
Upsala
SCOTLAND
Aberdeen
Bannockburn
Edinburgh
Falkirk
Berwick
Armagh
IRELAND
Dublin
Carlisle
North Sea
DENMARK
Calmar
Copenhagen
York
Lincoln
Chester
Wexford
Cork
WALES
ENGLAND
Norwich
Thames
London
Atlantic Ocean
Lubeck
Stralsund
POMERANIA
Hamburg
Bremen
HOLLAND
Magdeburg
BRANDENBURG
Gnesen
Posen
Bruges
Calais
BRABANT
Ghent
English Channel
Agincourt
Harfleur
Crecy
HAINAUT
Rhine
Cologne
HOLY
SILESIA
Elbe
Rouen
Seine
Caen
BRITTANY
Rennes
Paris
Bretigny
Reims
Compiegne
Vaucouleurs
LUXEMBURG
Trier
Frankfurt
Mainz
BOHEMIA
Prague
PALATINATE
FRANCE
Nantes
Loire
Orleans
Chinon
Troyes
LORRAINE
Domremy
Strassburg
ROMAN
Regensburg
MORAVIA
BAVARIA
Munich
Danube
Vienna
Poitiers
Dijon
Basel
Besancon
SWISS CONFED.
Constance
Salzburg
Bay of Biscay
Limoges
BURGUNDY
EMPIRE
AUSTRIA
Buda
Bordeaux
AQUITAINE
Garonne
Lyon
SAVOY
LANDS OF THE VISCONTI
Milan
Turin
Trieste
Drave
Santiago
Bayonne
Toulouse
Leon
Ebro
Pau
Rhone
DAUPHINY
Avignon
Po
Ferrara
Venice
REPUBLIC OF VENICE
Genoa
Bologna
BOSN
PORTUGAL
Duero
NAVARRE
Narbonne
PROVENCE
Marseille
Florence
Adriatic Sea
Salamanca
Saragossa
PAPAL STATES
Tagus
Toledo
CASTILE
Lisbon
Guadiana
ARAGON
Barcelona
CORSICA (To Genoa)
Rome
Ragusa
KINGDOM OF NAPLES
Seville
Cordova
Guadalquivir
Valencia
BALEARIC ISLANDS (To Aragon)
SARDINIA (To Aragon)
Naples
Taran
Cadiz
Granada
GRANADA
Gibraltar
Mediterranean
Palermo
Messina
Reggio
KINGDOM OF SICILY
MOSLEM STATES
Algiers
MARINIDS
Tunis
ZIANIDS
HAFSIDS
MALTA
A-450028-29-1-1-1-1

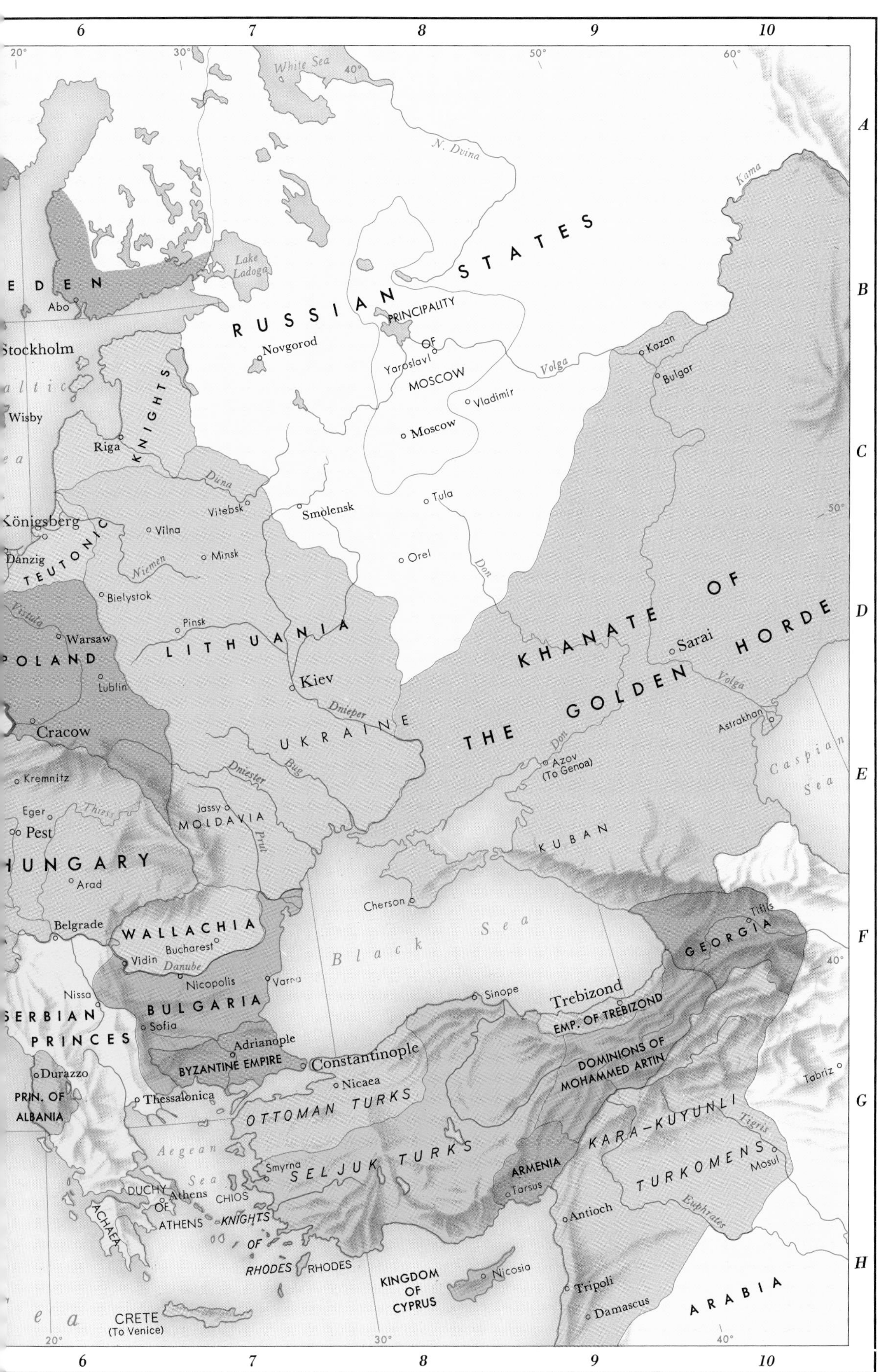

6
7
8
9
10
White Sea
N. Dvina
Kama
Lake Ladoga
EDEN
Abo
RUSSIAN STATES
PRINCIPALITY OF MOSCOW
Stockholm
Novgorod
Yaroslavl
Kazan
Bulgar
Volga
Wisby
KNIGHTS
Vladimir
Riga
Moscow
Düna
Vitebsk
Tula
Smolensk
Königsberg
Vilna
Minsk
Orel
Don
Danzig
TEUTONIC
Niemen
Bielystok
KHANATE OF THE GOLDEN HORDE
Vistula
Pinsk
Warsaw
LITHUANIA
Sarai
POLAND
Kiev
Lublin
Volga
Dnieper
Astrakhan
Cracow
UKRAINE
Bug
Dniester
Azov (To Genoa)
Caspian Sea
Kremnitz
Eger
Thiess
Jassy
MOLDAVIA
Prut
Pest
KUBAN
HUNGARY
Arad
Cherson
Tiflis
Belgrade
WALLACHIA
Black Sea
GEORGIA
Bucharest
Vidin
Danube
Nicopolis
Varna
Nissa
Sinope
Trebizond
SERBIAN PRINCES
BULGARIA
EMP. OF TREBIZOND
Sofia
Adrianople
Constantinople
DOMINIONS OF MOHAMMED ARTIN
BYZANTINE EMPIRE
Durazzo
Tabriz
Nicaea
PRIN. OF ALBANIA
Thessalonica
OTTOMAN TURKS
KARA-KUYUNLI
Tigris
Aegean Sea
SELJUK TURKS
ARMENIA
TURKOMENS
Mosul
Smyrna
Tarsus
DUCHY OF ATHENS
Athens
CHIOS
Euphrates
KNIGHTS OF RHODES
Antioch
ACHAEA
RHODES
KINGDOM OF CYPRUS
Nicosia
Tripoli
Damascus
ARABIA
CRETE (To Venice)
20°
30°
40°
50°
60°
A
B
C
D
E
F
G
H

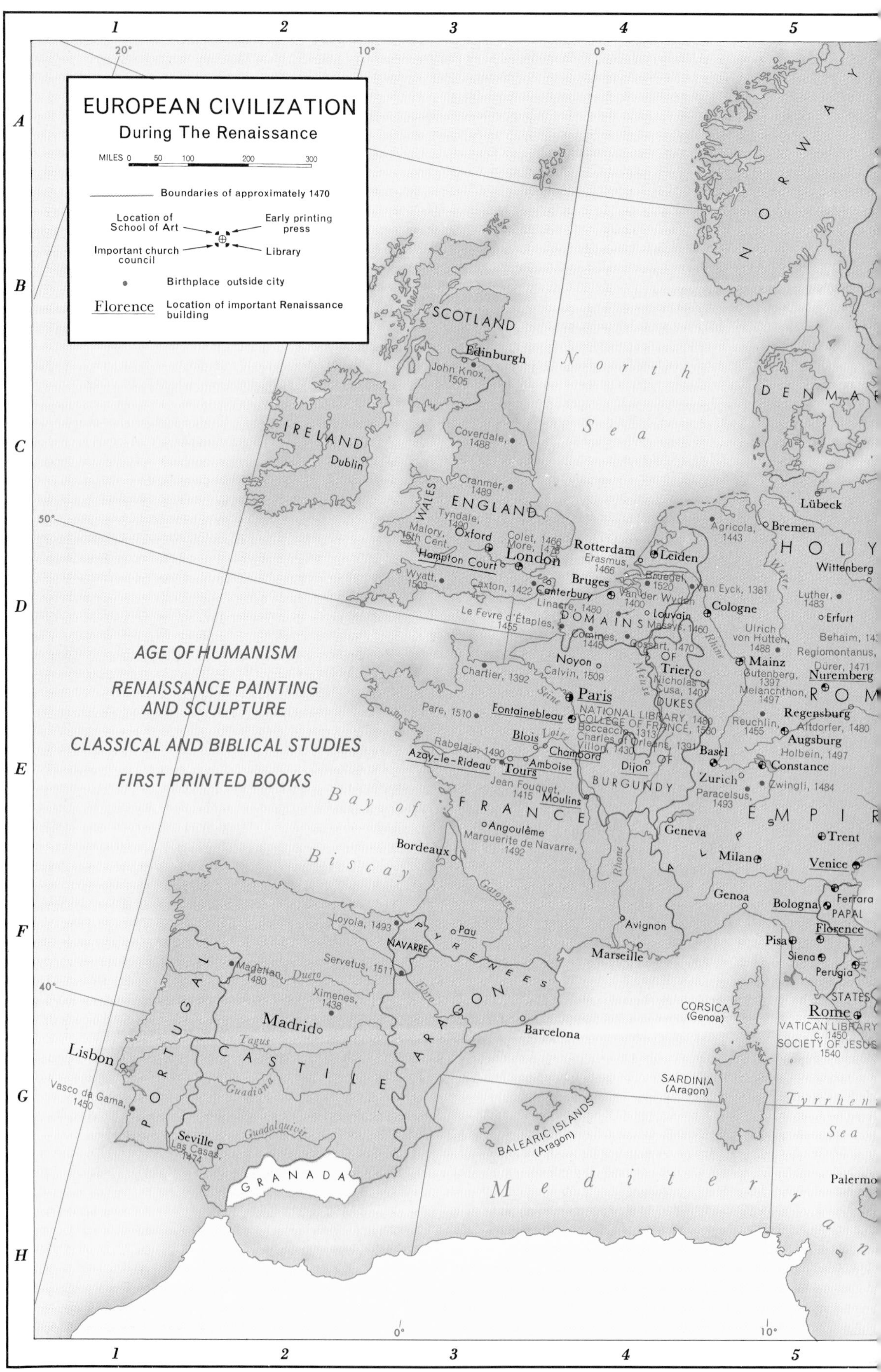

EUROPEAN CIVILIZATION
During The Renaissance
MILES 0 50 100 200 300
Boundaries of approximately 1470
Location of School of Art
Early printing press
Important church council
Library
Birthplace outside city
Florence Location of important Renaissance building
AGE OF HUMANISM
RENAISSANCE PAINTING AND SCULPTURE
CLASSICAL AND BIBLICAL STUDIES
FIRST PRINTED BOOKS
SCOTLAND
Edinburgh
John Knox, 1505
North Sea
IRELAND
Dublin
Coverdale, 1488
Cranmer, 1489
WALES
ENGLAND
Tyndale, 1490
Malory, 15th Cent.
Oxford
Colet, 1466
More, 1478
London
Hampton Court
Wyatt, 1503
Caxton, 1422
Canterbury
Linacre, 1480
Rotterdam
Erasmus, 1466
Leiden
Bruges
Bruegel, 1520
Van der Wyden, 1400
Louvain
Van Eyck, 1381
Cologne
Le Fevre d'Étaples, 1455
DOMAINS OF DUKES OF BURGUNDY
Massys, 1460
Comines, 1445
Gossart, 1470
Noyon
Calvin, 1509
Trier
Nicholas of Cusa, 1401
Chartier, 1392
Seine
Paris
NATIONAL LIBRARY, 1480
COLLEGE OF FRANCE, 1530
Pare, 1510
Fontainebleau
Boccaccio, 1313
Charles of Orleans, 1391
Villon, 1430
Blois
Loire
Chambord
Rabelais, 1490
Azay-le-Rideau
Tours
Amboise
Dijon
Jean Fouquet, 1415
Moulins
Bay of Biscay
FRANCE
Angoulême
Marguerite de Navarre, 1492
Bordeaux
Garonne
Rhone
Meuse
Rhine
Geneva
Avignon
Marseille
Loyola, 1493
NAVARRE
Pau
PYRENEES
Servetus, 1511
Ebro
Magellan, 1480
Duero
Ximenes, 1438
Madrid
ARAGON
Barcelona
PORTUGAL
CASTILE
Tagus
Lisbon
Vasco da Gama, 1450
Guadiana
Seville
Guadalquivir
Las Casas, 1474
GRANADA
BALEARIC ISLANDS (Aragon)
CORSICA (Genoa)
SARDINIA (Aragon)
Mediterranean
Tyrrhenian Sea
Palermo
NORWAY
DENMARK
Lübeck
Bremen
Agricola, 1443
HOLY ROMAN EMPIRE
Wittenberg
Weser
Luther, 1483
Erfurt
Ulrich von Hutten, 1488
Behaim, 1459
Regiomontanus
Mainz
Gutenberg, 1397
Dürer, 1471
Nuremberg
Melanchthon, 1497
Regensburg
Reuchlin, 1455
Altdorfer, 1480
Augsburg
Holbein, 1497
Basel
Constance
Zurich
Paracelsus, 1493
Zwingli, 1484
ALPS
Trent
Milan
Venice
Po
Genoa
Bologna
Ferrara
PAPAL STATES
Florence
Pisa
Siena
Perugia
Tiber
Rome
VATICAN LIBRARY c. 1450
SOCIETY OF JESUS 1540

THE ITALIAN RENAISSANCE
MILES 0 10 20 30 40 50 75 100
Boundaries after the Peace of Lodi, 1454
Birthplace outside city
SWITZERLAND
HAPSBURG LANDS
DUCHY OF MILAN
REPUBLIC OF VENICE
DUCHY OF SAVOY
MARQUISATE OF MONTFERRAT
REP. OF GENOA
DUCHY OF MODENA
DUCHY OF FERRARA
MANTUA
REP. OF LUCCA
REP. OF FLORENCE
REP. OF SIENA
STATES OF THE CHURCH
KINGDOM OF NAPLES (Aragon)
Titian, 1477
Giorgione 1478
Vicenza Mantegna, 1431
Venice ALDINE PRESS. c. 1490 J. Bellini, 1400 Alberti, 1404
Verona Fra. Giocondo, 1435 Paul Veronese, 1528
Milan
Pavia Cardan, 1501
Cremona
Piacenza
Mantua Pomponazzi, 1462
Parma Corregio, 1494
Ferrara Savonarola, 1452
Reggio Ariosto, 1474
Pico della Mirandola, 1462
Bologna
Genoa John Cabot, 1450 Columbus, 1451
Fra. Bartolomeo, 1472
Fra. Angelico, 1387
Lucca
Leonardo da Vinci, 1452
Pisa
Florence
Urbino Raphael, 1483
Michelangelo, 1475
PLATONIC ACADEMY, c. 1440
Brunelleschi, 1377
Donatello, c. 1386
Fra. Filippo Lippi, 1406
Ficino, 1433
Botticelli, 1447
Lorenzo Medici, the "Magnificent," 1449
Americus Vespucius, 1451
Machiavelli, 1469
Guicciardini, 1483
Andrea del Sarto, 1486
B. Cellini, 1500
Masaccio, 1402
Arezzo Petrarch, 1303 L. Bruni, 1370 P. Aretino, 1492
Siena Francesco Giorgio, 1439
Signorelli, 1441
Aeneas Sylvius, 1405
P. Vannuchi, 1446
ELBA
CORSICA
Tyrrhenian Sea
Adriatic Sea
Po
Arno
Tiber
Rome VATICAN LIBRARY, c. 1450 SISTINE CHAPEL, 1473 L. Valla, 1405 Lucrezia Borgia, 1480
Naples
SWEDEN
Baltic Sea
Königsberg
Danzig
Thorn Copernicus, 1473
POLAND
Oder
Vistula
Elbe
Prague
Vienna
Danube
Buda
Thiess
HUNGARY
Drave
Save
OTTOMAN EMPIRE
Black Sea
Constantinople
Salonika
Aegean Sea
Ionian Sea
NAPLES
SICILY (Aragon)
RHODES (Knights of Rhodes)
CYPRUS (Venice)
CRETE (Venice)
A-450030-29-1-2-1-1
Copyright by Rand McNally & Company, Made in U.S.A.

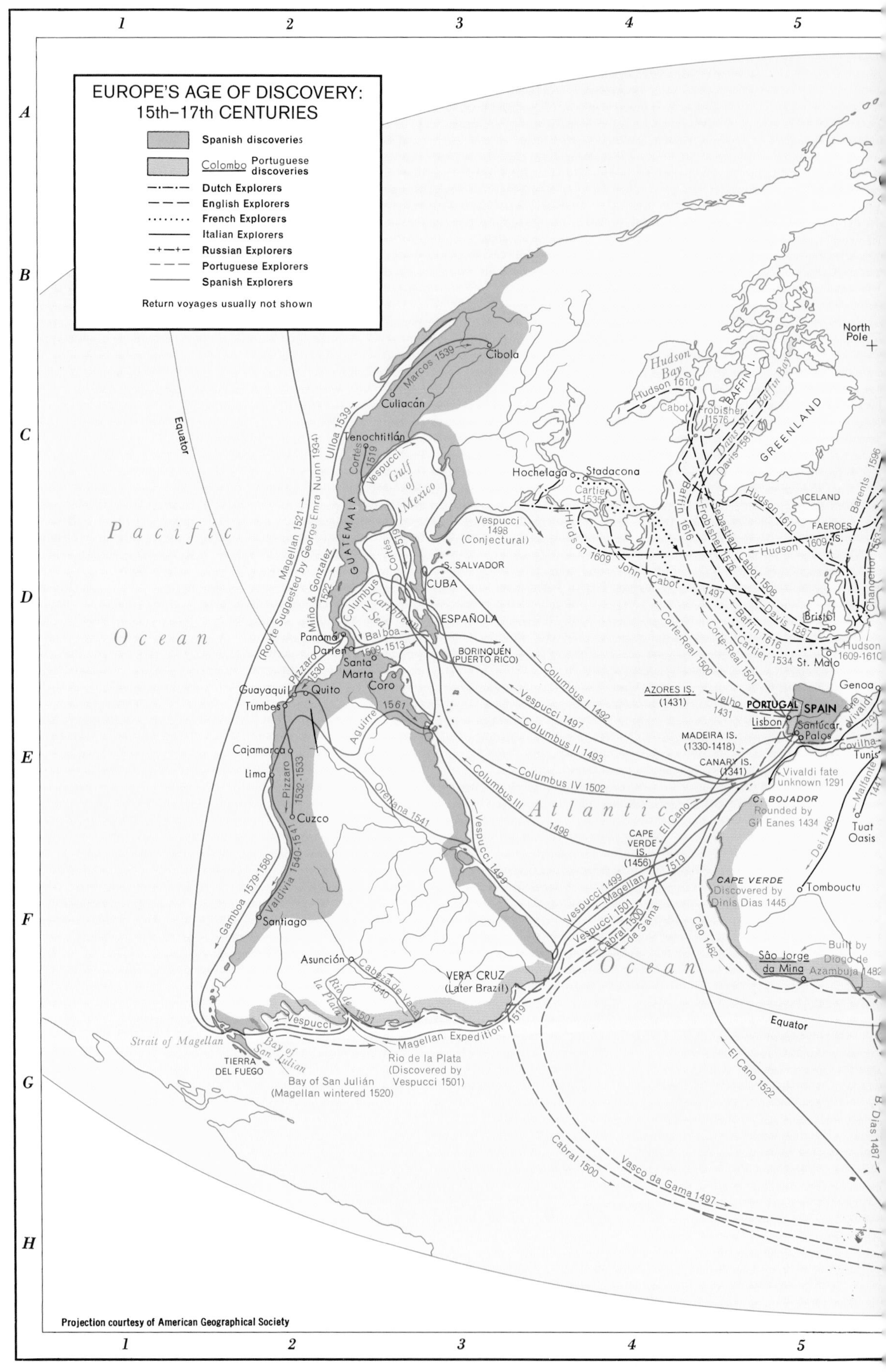

EUROPE'S AGE OF DISCOVERY: 15th–17th CENTURIES
Spanish discoveries
Colombo Portuguese discoveries
Dutch Explorers
English Explorers
French Explorers
Italian Explorers
Russian Explorers
Portuguese Explorers
Spanish Explorers
Return voyages usually not shown
Pacific Ocean
Atlantic Ocean
Equator
Cibola
Marcos 1539
Culiacán
Ulloa 1539
Tenochtitlán
Cortés 1519
Gulf of Mexico
Vespucci
GUATEMALA
Magellan 1521
(Route Suggested by George Emra Nunn 1934)
Miño & Gonzalez 1522
Caribbean Sea
Columbus IV
S. SALVADOR
CUBA
ESPAÑOLA
BORINQUÉN (PUERTO RICO)
Panamá
Darien
Balboa 1509-1513
Santa Marta
Coro
Guayaquil
Quito
Tumbes
Pizzaro 1530
Cajamarca
Lima
Pizzaro 1532-1533
Cuzco
Aguirre 1561
Orellana 1541
Valdivia 1540-1541
Gamboa 1579-1580
Santiago
Asunción
Cabeza de Vaca 1540
Rio de la Plata 1501
VERA CRUZ (Later Brazil)
Vespucci 1499
Strait of Magellan
TIERRA DEL FUEGO
Bay of San Julian
Bay of San Julián (Magellan wintered 1520)
Magellan Expedition 1519
Rio de la Plata (Discovered by Vespucci 1501)
Vespucci 1498 (Conjectural)
Hochelaga
Stadacona
Cartier 1535
Hudson Bay
Hudson 1610
Cabot
Frobisher 1576
BAFFIN I.
Baffin Bay
Davis Str.
Davis 1587
GREENLAND
North Pole
ICELAND
FAEROES IS.
Barents 1596
Hudson 1609
John Cabot 1497
Sebastian Cabot 1508
Frobisher 1576
Baffin 1616
Corte-Real 1500
Corte-Real 1501
Cartier 1534
Bristol
Chancellor 1553
Hudson 1609-1610
St. Malo
Genoa
Vivaldi
PORTUGAL
SPAIN
Lisbon
Santúcar
Palos
AZORES IS. (1431)
Velho 1431
MADEIRA IS. (1330-1418)
CANARY IS. (1341)
Vivaldi fate unknown 1291
Covilha
Tunis
Malfante 1447
C. BOJADOR Rounded by Gil Eanes 1434
Tuat Oasis
Dei 1469
CAPE VERDE IS. (1456)
CAPE VERDE Discovered by Dinis Dias 1445
Tombouctu
Columbus I 1492
Vespucci 1497
Columbus II 1493
Columbus IV 1502
Columbus III 1498
El Cano
Magellan 1519
Vespucci 1499
Vespucci 1501
Cabral 1500
da Gama
Cão 1482
São Jorge da Mina
Built by Diogo de Azambuja 1482
El Cano 1522
Cabral 1500
Vasco da Gama 1497
B. Dias 1487
Projection courtesy of American Geographical Society

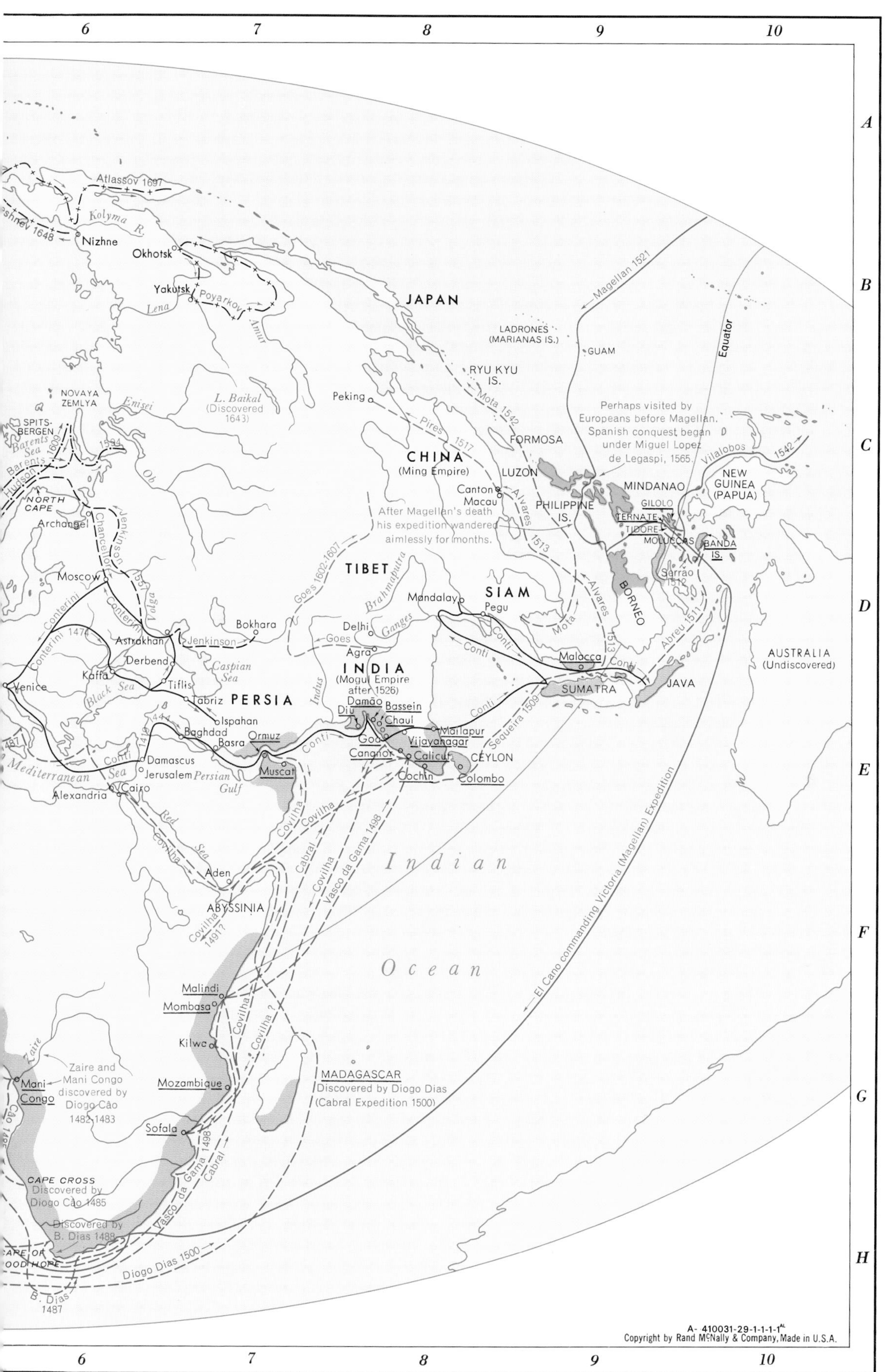

JAPAN
CHINA
(Ming Empire)
TIBET
SIAM
INDIA
(Mogul Empire after 1526)
PERSIA
ABYSSINIA
MADAGASCAR
Discovered by Diogo Dias
(Cabral Expedition 1500)
Indian
Ocean
AUSTRALIA
(Undiscovered)
NEW GUINEA
(PAPUA)
BORNEO
SUMATRA
JAVA
CEYLON
PHILIPPINE IS.
LUZON
MINDANAO
FORMOSA
RYU KYU IS.
LADRONES
(MARIANAS IS.)
GUAM
GILOLO
TERNATE
TIDORE
MOLUCCAS
BANDA IS.
Perhaps visited by Europeans before Magellan. Spanish conquest began under Miguel Lopez de Legaspi, 1565.
After Magellan's death his expedition wandered aimlessly for months.
El Cano commanding Victoria (Magellan) Expedition
Magellan 1521
Equator
Vilalobos
1542
Mota 1542
Pires 1517
Alvares
1513
Goes 1602-1607
Serrão 1512
Abreu 1511
Sequeira 1509
Conti
Covilha
Covilha 1491?
Covilha ?
Cabral
Vasco da Gama 1498
Diogo Dias 1500
B. Dias 1487
Discovered by B. Dias 1488
CAPE OF GOOD HOPE
CAPE CROSS
Discovered by Diogo Cão 1485
Zaire and Mani Congo discovered by Diogo Cão 1482-1483
Mani Congo
Zaire
Sofala
Mozambique
Kilwa
Mombasa
Malindi
Aden
Red Sea
Alexandria
Cairo
Jerusalem
Damascus
Persian Gulf
Muscat
Ormuz
Basra
Baghdad
Ispahan
Tabriz
Tiflis
Derbend
Astrakhan
Kaffa
Black Sea
Venice
Mediterranean Sea
Conterini 1474
Caspian Sea
Jenkinson
Bokhara
Moscow
Volga
Archangel
Chancellor
NORTH CAPE
Hudson
Barents Sea
SPITS-BERGEN
NOVAYA ZEMLYA
Enisei
Ob
L. Baikal
(Discovered 1643)
Peking
Canton
Macau
Mandalay
Pegu
Malacca
Delhi
Agra
Goes
Ganges
Brahmaputra
Indus
Damão
Diu
Bassein
Chaul
Goa
Cananor
Calicut
Cochin
Vijayanagar
Mailapur
Colombo
Yakutsk
Poyarkov
Lena
Amur
Okhotsk
Nizhne
Kolyma R.
Atlassov 1697
Dezhnev 1648

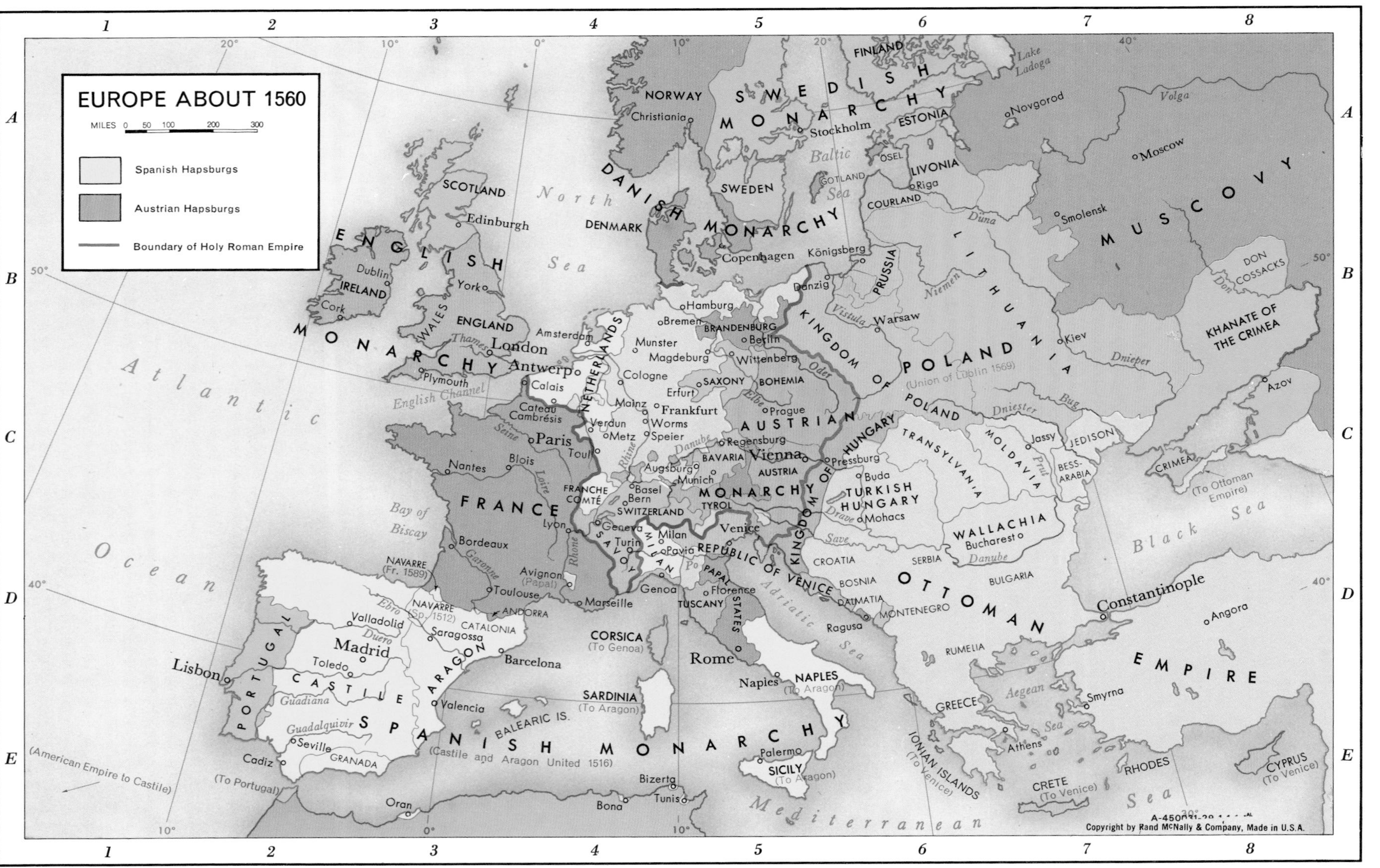
EUROPE ABOUT 1560
MILES 0 50 100 200 300
Spanish Hapsburgs
Austrian Hapsburgs
Boundary of Holy Roman Empire
SWEDISH MONARCHY
DANISH MONARCHY
ENGLISH MONARCHY
MUSCOVY
LITHUANIA
KINGDOM OF POLAND
AUSTRIAN MONARCHY
KINGDOM OF HUNGARY
OTTOMAN EMPIRE
SPANISH MONARCHY
FRANCE
REPUBLIC OF VENICE
KHANATE OF THE CRIMEA
Atlantic Ocean
North Sea
Baltic Sea
Black Sea
Mediterranean Sea
Adriatic Sea
Aegean Sea
Bay of Biscay
English Channel
Copyright by Rand McNally & Company, Made in U.S.A.

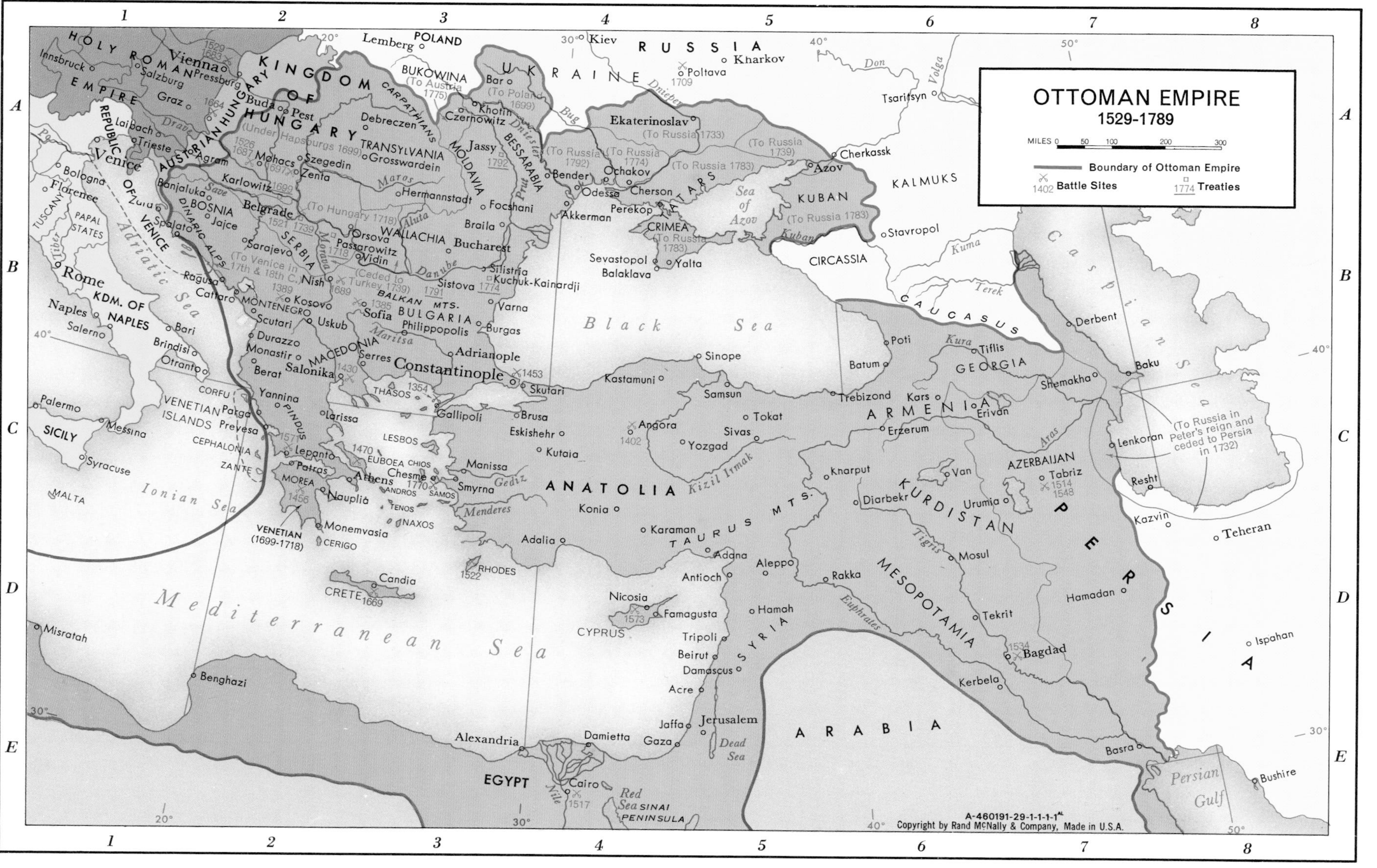
OTTOMAN EMPIRE
1529-1789
MILES 0 50 100 200 300
Boundary of Ottoman Empire
1402 Battle Sites
1774 Treaties
HOLY ROMAN EMPIRE
KINGDOM OF HUNGARY
AUSTRIAN HUNGARY
(Under Hapsburgs 1699)
REPUBLIC OF VENICE
POLAND
RUSSIA
UKRAINE
BUKOWINA (To Austria 1775)
KALMUKS
KUBAN (To Russia 1783)
CIRCASSIA
CAUCASUS
CRIMEA (To Russia 1783)
TATARS
BESSARABIA
MOLDAVIA
WALLACHIA
TRANSYLVANIA
CARPATHIANS
BOSNIA
SERBIA
MONTENEGRO
MACEDONIA
BULGARIA
BALKAN MTS.
DINARIC ALPS
KDM. OF NAPLES
PAPAL STATES
TUSCANY
SICILY
MALTA
VENETIAN ISLANDS
VENETIAN (1699-1718)
MOREA
ANATOLIA
TAURUS MTS.
ARMENIA
GEORGIA
AZERBAIJAN
KURDISTAN
MESOPOTAMIA
SYRIA
ARABIA
PERSIA
EGYPT
SINAI PENINSULA
CYPRUS
CRETE
RHODES
Black Sea
Sea of Azov
Caspian Sea
Mediterranean Sea
Adriatic Sea
Ionian Sea
Persian Gulf
Red Sea
Dead Sea
(To Russia in Peter's reign and ceded to Persia in 1732)
(To Russia 1733)
(To Russia 1739)
(To Russia 1774)
(To Russia 1783)
(To Russia 1792)
(To Poland 1699)
(To Hungary 1718)
(Ceded to Turkey 1739)
(To Venice in 17th & 18th C.)
Vienna
Pressburg
Salzburg
Innsbruck
Graz
Laibach
Trieste
Agram
Venice
Bologna
Florence
Rome
Naples
Salerno
Bari
Brindisi
Otranto
Palermo
Messina
Syracuse
Buda
Pest
Mohacs
Szegedin
Zenta
Karlowitz
Belgrade
Banjaluka
Jajce
Sarajevo
Spalato
Zara
Ragusa
Cattaro
Scutari
Durazzo
Monastir
Berat
Yannina
Corfu
Parga
Prevesa
Cephalonia
Zante
Lepanto
Patras
Nauplia
Monemvasia
Cerigo
Athens
Larissa
Salonika
Serres
Uskub
Kosovo
Nish
Sofia
Passarowitz
Orsova
Vidin
Sistova
Silistria
Kuchuk-Kainardji
Varna
Burgas
Philippopolis
Adrianople
Constantinople
Gallipoli
Thasos
Lesbos
Chios
Euboea
Andros
Tenos
Naxos
Samos
Chesme
Smyrna
Manissa
Debreczen
Grosswardein
Hermannstadt
Czernowitz
Khotin
Bar
Lemberg
Jassy
Focshani
Braila
Bucharest
Bender
Akkerman
Odessa
Ochakov
Cherson
Perekop
Ekaterinoslav
Kiev
Poltava
Kharkov
Sevastopol
Balaklava
Yalta
Azov
Cherkassk
Tsaritsyn
Stavropol
Derbent
Baku
Shemakha
Tiflis
Poti
Batum
Trebizond
Kars
Erivan
Erzerum
Sinope
Kastamuni
Samsun
Tokat
Sivas
Angora
Yozgad
Brusa
Eskishehr
Kutaia
Konia
Karaman
Adalia
Adana
Antioch
Aleppo
Hamah
Tripoli
Beirut
Damascus
Acre
Jaffa
Jerusalem
Gaza
Nicosia
Famagusta
Candia
Knarput
Diarbekr
Van
Urumia
Tabriz
Mosul
Rakka
Tekrit
Bagdad
Kerbela
Basra
Lenkoran
Resht
Kazvin
Teheran
Hamadan
Ispahan
Bushire
Alexandria
Damietta
Cairo
Benghazi
Misratah
Danube
Dniester
Dnieper
Bug
Prut
Don
Volga
Kuma
Terek
Kura
Aras
Tigris
Euphrates
Kizil Irmak
Nile
A-460191-29-1-1-1
Copyright by Rand McNally & Company, Made in U.S.A.

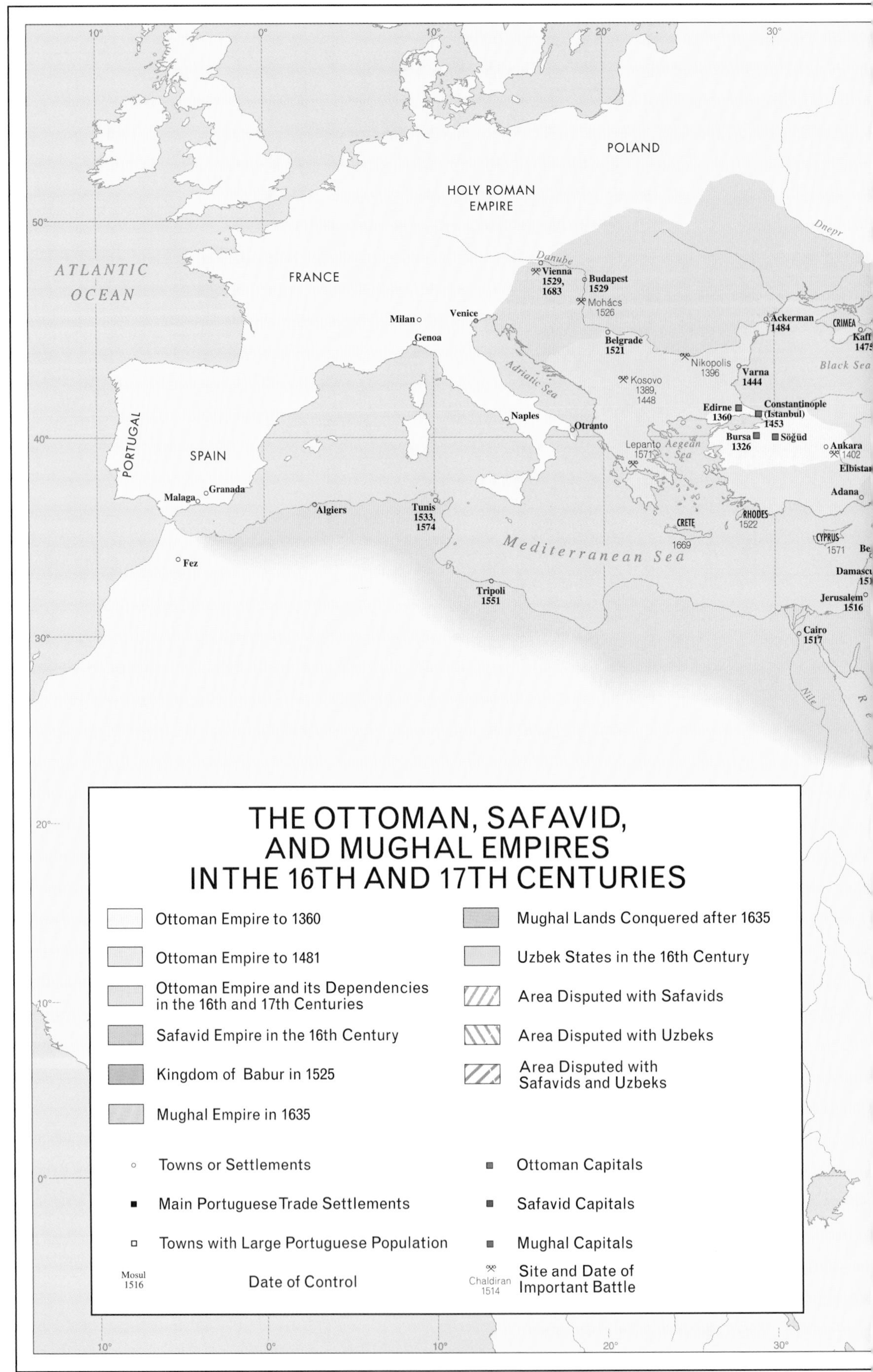
THE OTTOMAN, SAFAVID, AND MUGHAL EMPIRES IN THE 16TH AND 17TH CENTURIES
Ottoman Empire to 1360
Ottoman Empire to 1481
Ottoman Empire and its Dependencies in the 16th and 17th Centuries
Safavid Empire in the 16th Century
Kingdom of Babur in 1525
Mughal Empire in 1635
Mughal Lands Conquered after 1635
Uzbek States in the 16th Century
Area Disputed with Safavids
Area Disputed with Uzbeks
Area Disputed with Safavids and Uzbeks
Towns or Settlements
Main Portuguese Trade Settlements
Towns with Large Portuguese Population
Mosul 1516
Date of Control
Ottoman Capitals
Safavid Capitals
Mughal Capitals
Chaldiran 1514
Site and Date of Important Battle
ATLANTIC OCEAN
FRANCE
SPAIN
PORTUGAL
HOLY ROMAN EMPIRE
POLAND
Danube
Vienna 1529, 1683
Budapest 1529
Mohács 1526
Venice
Milan
Genoa
Belgrade 1521
Nikopolis 1396
Varna 1444
Ackerman 1484
CRIMEA
Black Sea
Kosovo 1389, 1448
Adriatic Sea
Naples
Otranto
Edirne 1360
Constantinople (Istanbul) 1453
Bursa 1326
Söğüd
Ankara 1402
Lepanto 1571
Aegean Sea
Malaga
Granada
Algiers
Tunis 1533, 1574
Fez
RHODES 1522
CRETE 1669
CYPRUS 1571
Mediterranean Sea
Tripoli 1551
Adana
Jerusalem 1516
Cairo 1517
Nile
Dnepr

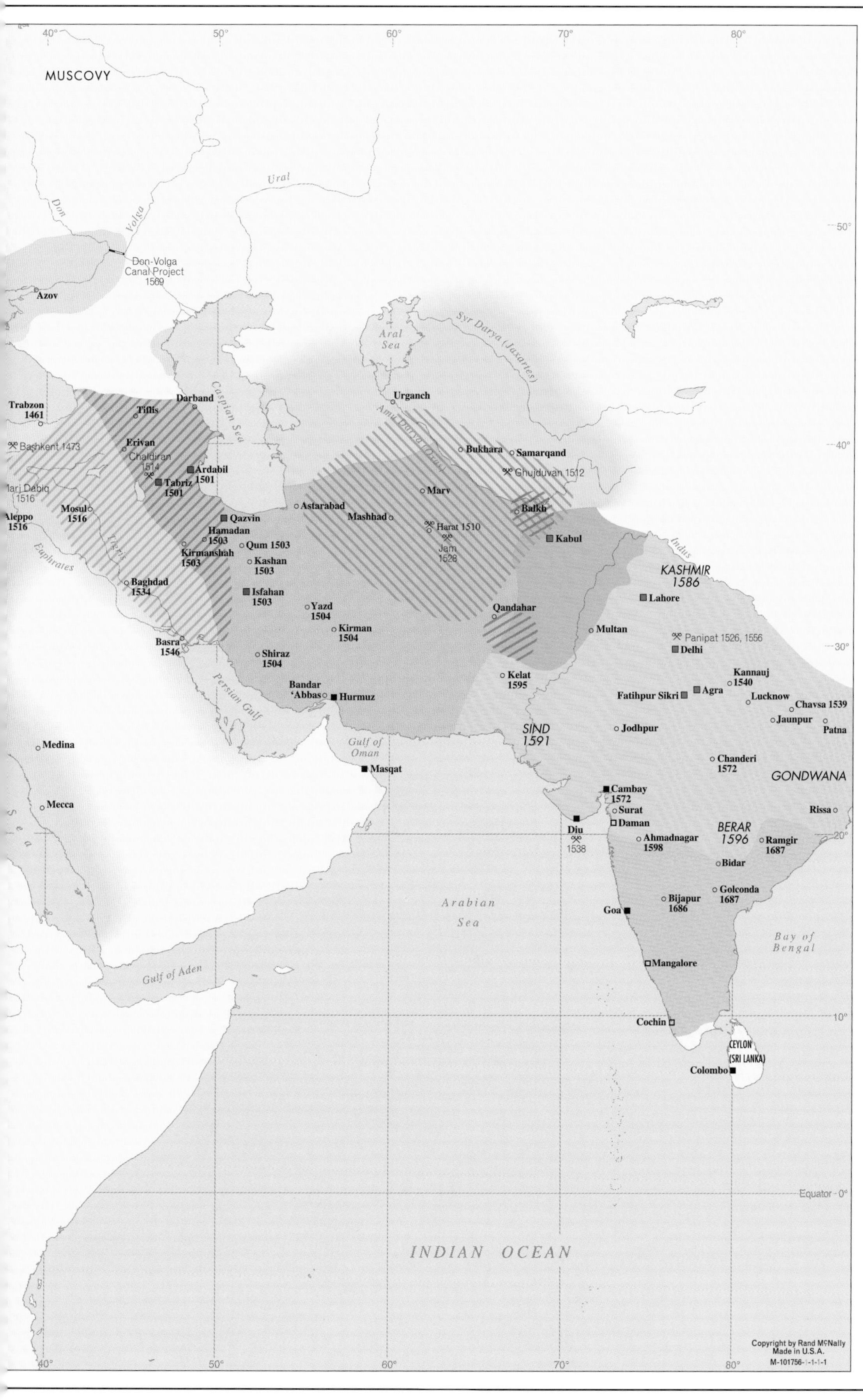
MUSCOVY
Ural
Don
Volga
Don-Volga Canal Project 1569
Azov
Aral Sea
Syr Darya (Jaxartes)
Caspian Sea
Urganch
Amu Darya (Oxus)
Trabzon 1461
Tiflis
Darband
Bashkent 1473
Erivan
Chaldiran 1514
Ardabil 1501
Tabriz 1501
Marj Dabiq 1516
Mosul 1516
Aleppo 1516
Bukhara
Samarqand
Ghujduvan 1512
Marv
Astarabad
Mashhad
Balkh
Qazvin
Hamadan 1503
Qum 1503
Kirmanshah 1503
Kashan 1503
Harat 1510
Jam 1528
Kabul
Tigris
Euphrates
Baghdad 1534
Isfahan 1503
Yazd 1504
Kirman 1504
Qandahar
Indus
KASHMIR 1586
Lahore
Multan
Panipat 1526, 1556
Delhi
Basra 1546
Shiraz 1504
Kelat 1595
Kannauj 1540
Agra
Fatihpur Sikri
Lucknow
Chavsa 1539
Jaunpur
Patna
Persian Gulf
Bandar 'Abbas
Hurmuz
SIND 1591
Jodhpur
Medina
Gulf of Oman
Masqat
Chanderi 1572
GONDWANA
Cambay 1572
Surat
Daman
Rissa
Mecca
Diu 1538
Ahmadnagar 1598
BERAR 1596
Ramgir 1687
Bidar
Golconda 1687
Bijapur 1686
Arabian Sea
Goa
Bay of Bengal
Mangalore
Gulf of Aden
Cochin
CEYLON (SRI LANKA)
Colombo
Equator 0°
INDIAN OCEAN
Copyright by Rand McNally
Made in U.S.A.
M-101756-1-1-1-1

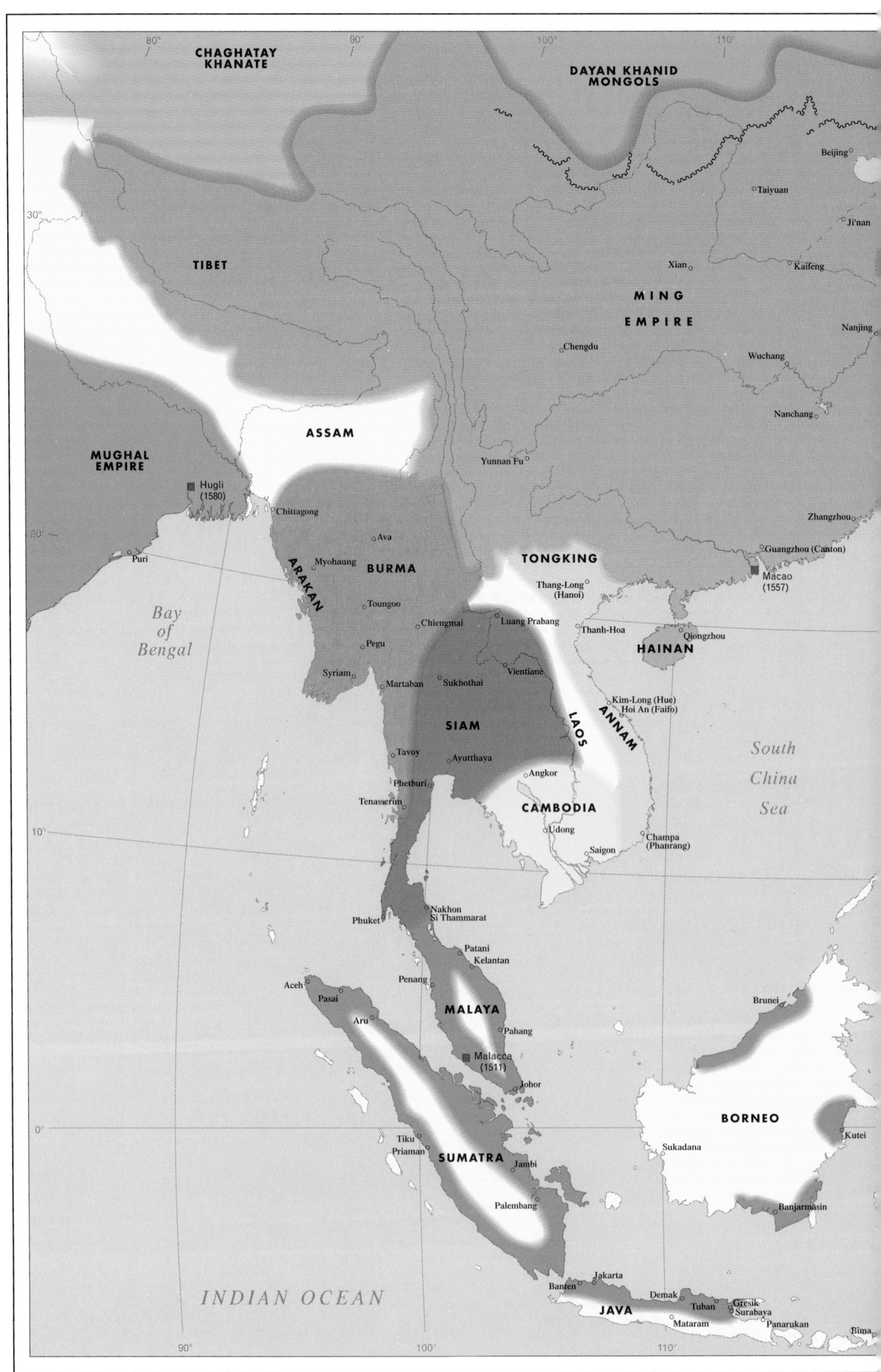
CHAGHATAY KHANATE
DAYAN KHANID MONGOLS
TIBET
MING EMPIRE
Beijing
Taiyuan
Ji'nan
Xian
Kaifeng
Nanjing
Chengdu
Wuchang
Nanchang
ASSAM
MUGHAL EMPIRE
Hugli (1580)
Yunnan Fu
Zhangzhou
Chittagong
Ava
Guangzhou (Canton)
Puri
Myohaung
ARAKAN
BURMA
TONGKING
Macao (1557)
Thang-Long (Hanoi)
Bay of Bengal
Toungoo
Chiengmai
Luang Prabang
Thanh-Hoa
Qiongzhou
Pegu
HAINAN
Syriam
Martaban
Sukhothai
Vientiane
Kim-Long (Hue)
Hoi An (Faifo)
LAOS
ANNAM
SIAM
Tavoy
Ayutthaya
South China Sea
Angkor
Phetburi
Tenasserim
CAMBODIA
Udong
Champa (Phanrang)
Saigon
Nakhon Si Thammarat
Phuket
Patani
Kelantan
Penang
Aceh
Pasai
Brunei
MALAYA
Aru
Pahang
Malacca (1511)
Johor
BORNEO
Kutei
Tiku
Priaman
Sukadana
SUMATRA
Jambi
Palembang
Banjarmasin
Jakarta
Banten
INDIAN OCEAN
Demak
Tuban
Gresik
Surabaya
JAVA
Mataram
Panarukan
Bima
80°
90°
100°
110°
30°
20°
10°
0°

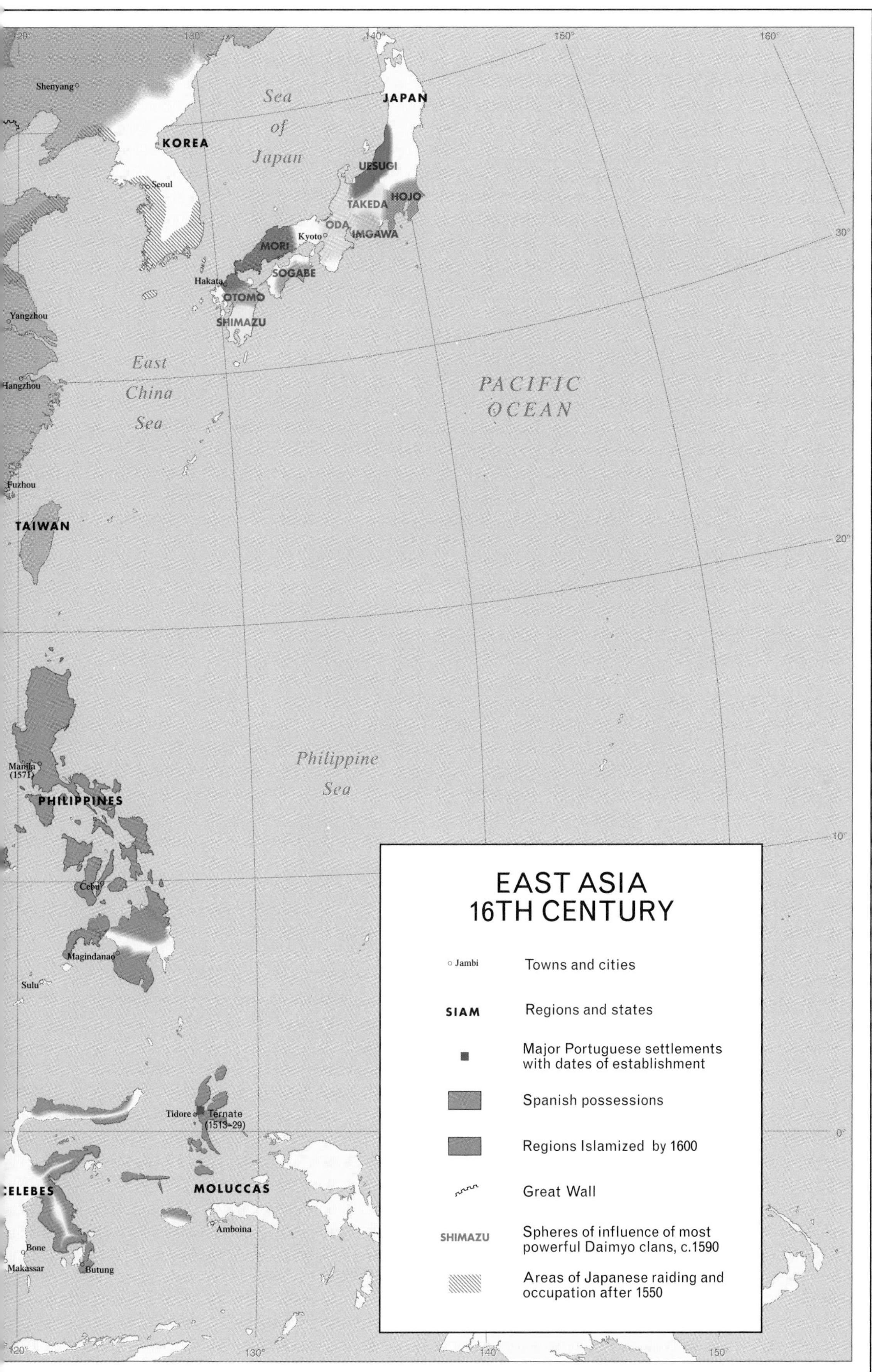
EAST ASIA
16TH CENTURY
Jambi
Towns and cities
SIAM
Regions and states
Major Portuguese settlements with dates of establishment
Spanish possessions
Regions Islamized by 1600
Great Wall
SHIMAZU
Spheres of influence of most powerful Daimyo clans, c.1590
Areas of Japanese raiding and occupation after 1550
Shenyang
KOREA
Seoul
Sea of Japan
JAPAN
UESUGI
TAKEDA
HOJO
ODA
IMAGAWA
Kyoto
MORI
SOGABE
Hakata
OTOMO
SHIMAZU
Yangzhou
Hangzhou
East China Sea
PACIFIC OCEAN
Fuzhou
TAIWAN
Philippine Sea
Manila (1571)
PHILIPPINES
Cebu
Magindanao
Sulu
Tidore
Ternate (1513–29)
CELEBES
MOLUCCAS
Amboina
Bone
Makassar
Butung
120°
130°
140°
150°
160°
30°
20°
10°
0°

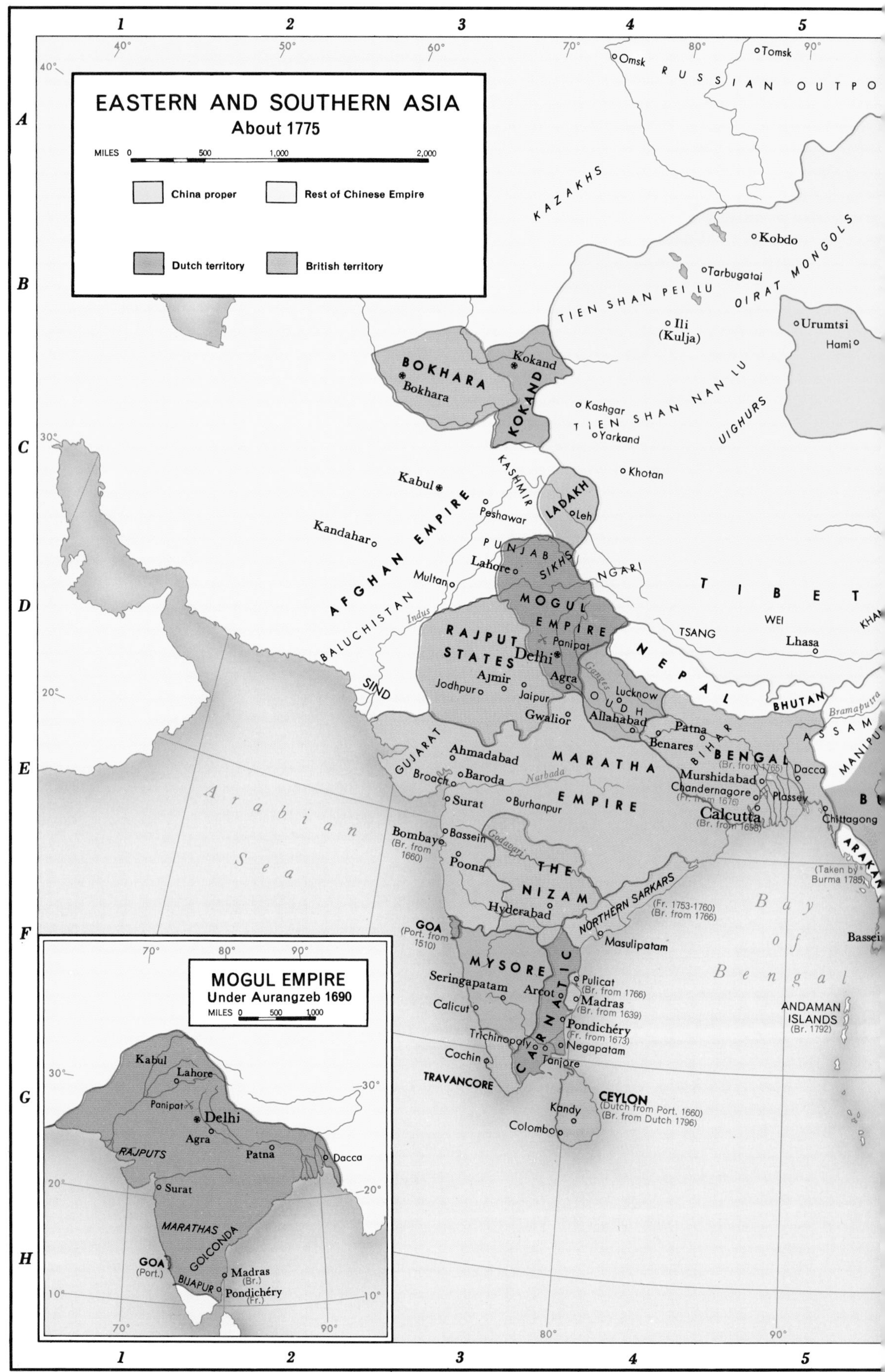

EASTERN AND SOUTHERN ASIA
About 1775
MILES 0 500 1,000 2,000
China proper
Rest of Chinese Empire
Dutch territory
British territory
RUSSIAN OUTPO
KAZAKHS
Omsk
Tomsk
Kobdo
Tarbugatai
OIRAT MONGOLS
TIEN SHAN PEI LU
Ili (Kulja)
Urumtsi
Hami
BOKHARA
Bokhara
KOKAND
Kokand
Kashgar
TIEN SHAN NAN LU
Yarkand
UIGHURS
Khotan
KASHMIR
LADAKH
Leh
Kabul
Peshawar
Kandahar
AFGHAN EMPIRE
PUNJAB
SIKHS
Lahore
Multan
NGARI
TIBET
BALUCHISTAN
Indus
MOGUL EMPIRE
Panipat
Delhi
Agra
TSANG
WEI
Lhasa
RAJPUT STATES
Ajmir
Jodhpur
Jaipur
Gwalior
NEPAL
BHUTAN
SIND
OUDH
Lucknow
Allahabad
Ganges
Patna
Benares
BIHAR
BENGAL
(Br. from 1765)
ASSAM
MANIPUR
Brahmaputra
GUJARAT
Ahmadabad
Broach
Baroda
MARATHA EMPIRE
Narbada
Surat
Burhanpur
Murshidabad
Chandernagore (Fr. from 1676)
Plassey
Dacca
Calcutta (Br. from 1656)
Chittagong
Arabian Sea
Bombay (Br. from 1660)
Bassein
Poona
Godavari
THE NIZAM
Hyderabad
ARAKAN
(Taken by Burma 1785)
NORTHERN SARKARS
(Fr. 1753-1760)
(Br. from 1766)
GOA (Port. from 1510)
Masulipatam
Bay of Bengal
Bassein
MYSORE
Seringapatam
Arcot
CARNATIC
Pulicat
(Br. from 1766)
Madras
(Br. from 1639)
Pondichéry
(Fr. from 1673)
Negapatam
Calicut
Trichinopoly
Tanjore
Cochin
ANDAMAN ISLANDS
(Br. 1792)
TRAVANCORE
CEYLON
(Dutch from Port. 1660)
(Br. from Dutch 1796)
Kandy
Colombo
MOGUL EMPIRE
Under Aurangzeb 1690
MILES 0 500 1,000
Kabul
Lahore
Panipat
Delhi
Agra
RAJPUTS
Patna
Dacca
Surat
MARATHAS
GOLCONDA
GOA (Port.)
BIJAPUR
Madras (Br.)
Pondichéry (Fr.)

6
7
8
9
10
A
B
C
D
E
F
G
H
Nerchinsk
Amur
Irkutsk
BURIAT MONGOLS
Kiakhta
MANCHURIA
Tsitsihar
Urga
Uliassutai
Kirin
OUTER MONGOLIA
KHALKHA MONGOLS
FORTY NINE MONGOL BANNERS OF INNER MONGOLIA
MANCHUS
Shengching (Mukden)
Jehol
CHAHAR MONGOLS
Kalgan
Peking
Great Wall
TORGUT MONGOLS
KANSU
DAM MONGOLS
KOKONOR MONGOLS
Lanchow
Huang
Paoting
Taiyüan
CHIHLI
SHANSI
Tsinan
SHANTUNG
Grand Canal
KIANGSU
SHENSI
Sian
Kaifeng
HONAN
ANWEI
Chiangning
Anking
Hangchow
HUPEH
Wuchang
Chengtu
SZECHWAN
Yangtze
Nanchang
CHEKIANG
Changsha
HUNAN
KIANGSI
FUKIEN
Foochow
Salween
Kweiyang
KWEICHOW
Kweilin
(Chinese repulsed 1766-1770)
Yünnan
YUNNAN
KWANGSI
KWANGTUNG
Kwangchow (Canton)
Hsi (West)
Macao
(Port, trading post from 1557)
Bhamo
Irrawaddy
Ava
TONGKING
Hanoi
Luang Prabang
Thanh Hoa
(Tongking, Annam and Cochin-China formed Vietnam Empire 1802)
Chiengsen
Toungoo
Prome
Chiengmai
Vientiane
Pegu
Sukhotai
(Laos states of Luang Prabang and Vientiane, under Siamese Suzerainty from 1778)
Rangoon
Syriam
Martaban
Hué
ANNAM
Mekong
Lopburi
SIAM
Ayuthia
(Destroyed by Burmese in 1767)
Tavoy
Bangkok
(Built 1780's)
Siemreap
CAMBODIA
Mergui
Phnom Penh
COCHIN-CHINA
Saigon
(Taken by Annam 1776)
Ligor
Patani
KEDAH
PERAK
PAHANG
Acheh
Pedir
ACHEH
Penang
(Br. from 1786)
SELANGOR
SUMATRA
(Dutch 1641-1795, 1818-1824)
(Br. 1795-1818, since 1824)
Malacca
JOHORE
RIAU ARCH
(Center of Bugis power)
Siak
MINANGKABAU
Padang
Jambi
Palembang
BANGKA
BILLITON
100°
110°
120°
130°
140°
150°
40°
30°
20°
10°
0°
YEZO
KOREA
Seoul
JAPAN
HONSHU
Yedo
Kyoto
Osaka
Sakai
SHIKOKU
KYUSHU
Nagasaki
(Dutch trading post of Deshima from 1641)
LIUCHIU
Pacific Ocean
Zelandia Castel
(Dutch, 1624-1662)
FORMOSA
China Sea
PHILIPPINE ISLANDS
(Spain)
Manila
BRUNEI
BORNEO
Succadana
Banjermassin
CELEBES
Macassar
Menado
MOLUCCAS
HALMAHERA
CERAM
Amboina
A-469036-29-1-1-1
Copyright by Rand McNally & Company, Made in U.S.A.

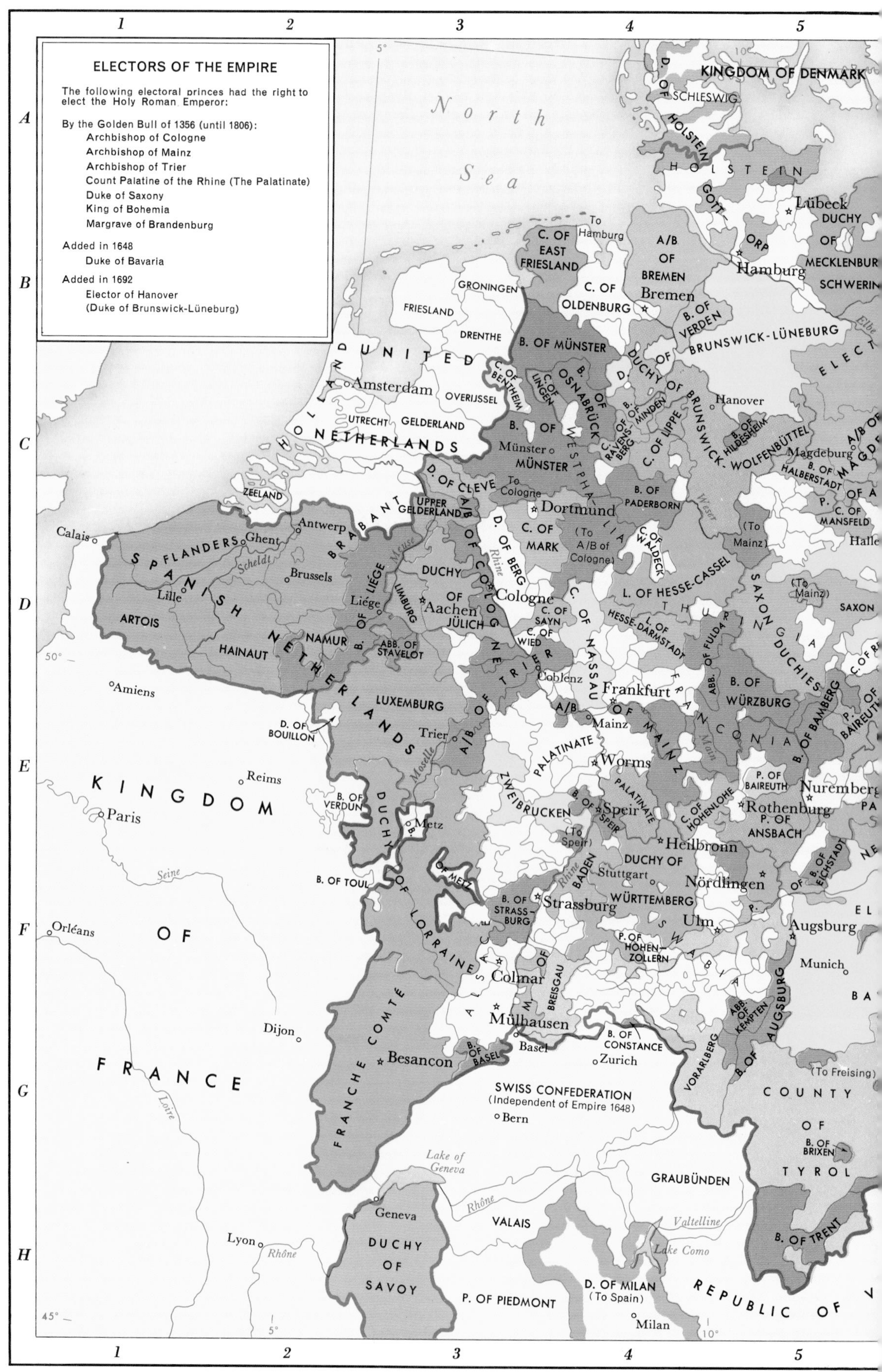
ELECTORS OF THE EMPIRE
The following electoral princes had the right to elect the Holy Roman Emperor:
By the Golden Bull of 1356 (until 1806):
Archbishop of Cologne
Archbishop of Mainz
Archbishop of Trier
Count Palatine of the Rhine (The Palatinate)
Duke of Saxony
King of Bohemia
Margrave of Brandenburg
Added in 1648
Duke of Bavaria
Added in 1692
Elector of Hanover
(Duke of Brunswick-Lüneburg)
1
2
3
4
5
A
B
C
D
E
F
G
H
North Sea
KINGDOM OF DENMARK
D. OF SCHLESWIG
D. OF HOLSTEIN
HOLSTEIN
GOTTORP
Lübeck
DUCHY OF MECKLENBURG SCHWERIN
Hamburg
To Hamburg
C. OF EAST FRIESLAND
A/B OF BREMEN
Bremen
C. OF OLDENBURG
B. OF VERDEN
BRUNSWICK-LÜNEBURG
GRONINGEN
FRIESLAND
DRENTHE
UNITED NETHERLANDS
HOLLAND
Amsterdam
OVERIJSSEL
UTRECHT
GELDERLAND
ZEELAND
C. OF BENTHEIM
B. OF MÜNSTER
C. OF LINGEN
B. OF OSNABRÜCK
DUCHY OF BRUNSWICK-WOLFENBÜTTEL
Hanover
B. OF MINDEN
C. OF RAVENSBERG
C. OF LIPPE
B. OF HILDESHEIM
Magdeburg
A/B OF MAGDEBURG
B. OF HALBERSTADT
Münster
WESTPHALIA
D. OF CLEVE
To Cologne
UPPER GELDERLAND
Dortmund
B. OF PADERBORN
C. OF MARK
(To A/B of Cologne)
C. OF WALDECK
C. OF MANSFELD
(To Mainz)
Halle
Calais
Ghent
Antwerp
BRABANT
FLANDERS
SPANISH NETHERLANDS
Brussels
Lille
ARTOIS
HAINAUT
NAMUR
B. OF LIÉGE
Liége
LIMBURG
DUCHY OF JÜLICH
Aachen
A/B OF COLOGNE
D. OF BERG
Cologne
C. OF SAYN
C. OF WIED
C. OF NASSAU
L. OF HESSE-CASSEL
L. OF HESSE-DARMSTADT
THURINGIA
SAXON DUCHIES
ABB. OF FULDA
ABB. OF STAVELOT
Coblenz
A/B OF TRIER
Frankfurt
A/B OF MAINZ
Mainz
FRANCONIA
B. OF WÜRZBURG
B. OF BAMBERG
P. OF BAIREUTH
Amiens
LUXEMBURG
D. OF BOUILLON
Trier
PALATINATE
Worms
KINGDOM OF FRANCE
Reims
Paris
B. OF VERDUN
DUCHY
Metz
B. OF METZ
ZWEIBRUCKEN
B. OF SPEIR
Speir
(To Speir)
P. OF HOHENLOHE
Rothenburg
P. OF ANSBACH
Nuremberg
Heilbronn
DUCHY OF WÜRTTEMBERG
BADEN
Stuttgart
Nördlingen
B. OF EICHSTADT
B. OF TOUL
DUCHY OF LORRAINE
B. OF STRASSBURG
Strassburg
Ulm
SWABIA
Augsburg
Orléans
P. OF HOHENZOLLERN
Munich
ALSACE
Colmar
BREISGAU
Mülhausen
B. OF AUGSBURG
ABB. OF KEMPTEN
Dijon
FRANCHE COMTÉ
Besancon
B. OF BASEL
Basel
B. OF CONSTANCE
Zurich
VORARLBERG
(To Freising)
SWISS CONFEDERATION
(Independent of Empire 1648)
Bern
COUNTY OF TYROL
B. OF BRIXEN
Seine
Loire
Rhine
Meuse
Scheldt
Moselle
Main
Weser
Elbe
Lake of Geneva
Geneva
GRAUBÜNDEN
Rhône
VALAIS
Valtelline
Lake Como
B. OF TRENT
Lyon
DUCHY OF SAVOY
P. OF PIEDMONT
D. OF MILAN
(To Spain)
Milan
REPUBLIC OF
50°
45°
5°
10°

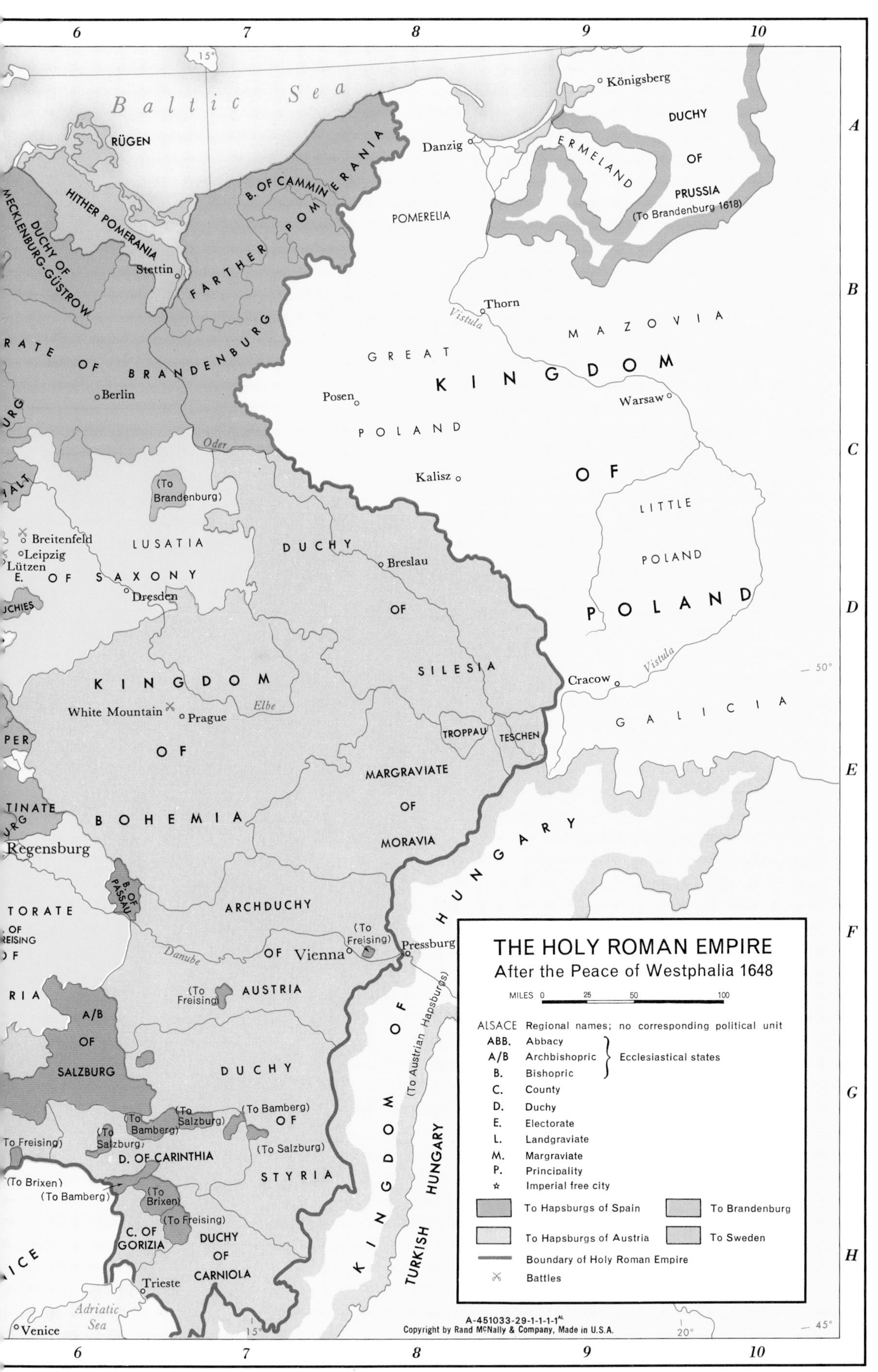
THE HOLY ROMAN EMPIRE
After the Peace of Westphalia 1648
MILES 0 25 50 100
ALSACE Regional names; no corresponding political unit
ABB. Abbacy
A/B Archbishopric
B. Bishopric
Ecclesiastical states
C. County
D. Duchy
E. Electorate
L. Landgraviate
M. Margraviate
P. Principality
☆ Imperial free city
To Hapsburgs of Spain
To Brandenburg
To Hapsburgs of Austria
To Sweden
Boundary of Holy Roman Empire
Battles
Baltic Sea
RÜGEN
Königsberg
DUCHY OF PRUSSIA (To Brandenburg 1618)
ERMELAND
Danzig
POMERELIA
B. OF CAMMIN
POMERANIA
FARTHER POMERANIA
HITHER POMERANIA
DUCHY OF MECKLENBURG-GÜSTROW
Stettin
Thorn
Vistula
MAZOVIA
GREAT POLAND
KINGDOM OF POLAND
OF BRANDENBURG
Berlin
Posen
Warsaw
Oder
Kalisz
LITTLE POLAND
(To Brandenburg)
Breitenfeld
Leipzig
Lützen
LUSATIA
E. OF SAXONY
Dresden
DUCHY OF SILESIA
Breslau
Cracow
GALICIA
KINGDOM OF BOHEMIA
White Mountain
Prague
Elbe
TROPPAU
TESCHEN
MARGRAVIATE OF MORAVIA
HUNGARY
Regensburg
B. OF PASSAU
ARCHDUCHY OF AUSTRIA
(To Freising)
Vienna
Pressburg
Danube
A/B OF SALZBURG
DUCHY OF STYRIA
(To Bamberg)
(To Salzburg)
D. OF CARINTHIA
(To Freising)
(To Brixen)
C. OF GORIZIA
DUCHY OF CARNIOLA
Trieste
Adriatic Sea
Venice
KINGDOM OF HUNGARY
(To Austrian Hapsburgs)
TURKISH HUNGARY
A-451033-29-1-1-1-1
Copyright by Rand McNally & Company, Made in U.S.A.

EUROPE IN 1721
After the treaty of Utrecht, 1713, and Associated Treaties
Miles 0 50 100 200 300
Boundary of Holy Roman Empire
× × Dutch Barrier Forts
SHETLAND ISLANDS
ORKNEY ISLANDS
HEBRIDES
SCOTLAND
Aberdeen
KINGDOM OF GREAT BRITAIN
Edinburgh
Glasgow
Belfast
IRELAND
Dublin
Cork
York
Liverpool
Nottingham
WALES
ENGLAND
Norwich
Cambridge
Oxford
Bristol
Thames
London
Plymouth
Portsmouth
BEACHY HEAD
English Channel
North Sea
Atlantic Ocean
Bergen
Stavanger
DENM
(To Hanover 1720)
THE UNITED NETHERLANDS
Bremen
Amsterdam
Utrecht
The Hague
Ryswick
Münster
Antwerp
Dunkirk
AUSTRIAN NETHERLANDS (1714)
Oudenarde
Neerwinden
Cologne
Lille
Ramillies
Aachen
Fontenoy
Malplaquet
Rhine
Mainz
LA HOGUE
Rouen
Reims
Rastatt
Brest
St. Malo
Paris
Seine
Nancy
LORRAINE
Strassburg
Lorient
Orléans
Loire
Nantes
Tours
Besançon
Basel
Bern
SWITZE
Bay of Biscay
FRANCE
Rochefort
Limoges
Angoulême
Lyon
Geneva
SAVOY
Turin
PIEDMONT
Bordeaux
Garonne
Rhone
CAPE FINISTERRE
Bayonne
Toulouse
Avignon
(To the Pope)
Montpellier
Marseille
Toulon
PYRENEES
Oporto
Burgos
Valladolid
Duero
Ebro
CATALONIA
Saragossa
CORSICA
(To Genoa)
PORTUGAL
Madrid
SPAIN
Barcelona
Tagus
Alcantara
Toledo
(To Bourbons, 1713)
Lisbon
Valencia
SARDINIA
(To Hapsburgs 1714)
(To Savoy 1720)
Guadiana
BALEARIC ISLANDS
MINORCA
(To Great Britain 1713)
MAJORCA
CAPE ST. VINCENT
Guadalquivir
Seville
Granada
Cartagena
Mediterranean
Cadiz
CAPE TRAFALGAR
Gibraltar
(To Great Britain 1713)
Algiers

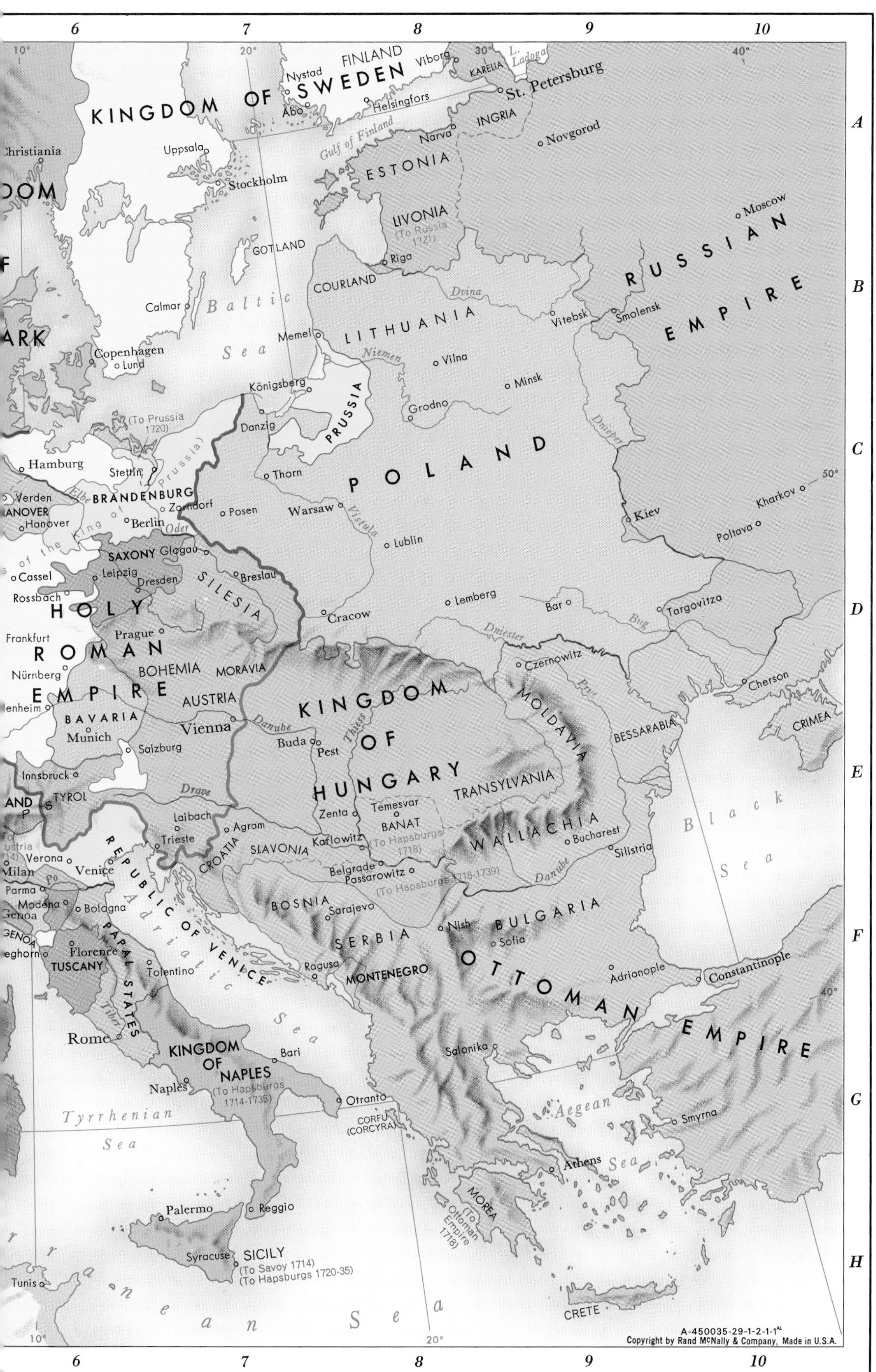
6
7
8
9
10
A
B
C
D
E
F
G
H
10°
20°
30°
40°
50°
FINLAND
Nystad
Viborg
KARELIA
L. Ladoga
KINGDOM OF SWEDEN
St. Petersburg
Abo
Helsingfors
INGRIA
Gulf of Finland
Narva
Novgorod
Uppsala
Stockholm
ESTONIA
LIVONIA
(To Russia 1721)
Moscow
GOTLAND
Riga
RUSSIAN EMPIRE
COURLAND
Dvina
Calmar
Baltic Sea
Vitebsk
Smolensk
Memel
LITHUANIA
Copenhagen
Lund
Niemen
Vilna
Minsk
Königsberg
PRUSSIA
Grodno
(To Prussia 1720)
Danzig
Dnieper
Hamburg
Stettin
Prussia
POLAND
Thorn
Verden
BRANDENBURG
Elbe
Zorndorf
Posen
Warsaw
Vistula
Kiev
Kharkov
Hanover
Berlin
Oder
Poltava
Lublin
of the King of Prussia
SAXONY
Glogau
Cassel
Leipzig
Dresden
Breslau
SILESIA
Rossbach
Lemberg
Bar
Targovitza
HOLY ROMAN EMPIRE
Bug
Cracow
Frankfurt
Prague
Dniester
Nürnberg
BOHEMIA
MORAVIA
Czernowitz
Prut
Cherson
KINGDOM OF HUNGARY
MOLDAVIA
AUSTRIA
BAVARIA
Vienna
Danube
Munich
Buda
Pest
Thiess
BESSARABIA
CRIMEA
Salzburg
Innsbruck
TRANSYLVANIA
TYROL
Drave
Temesvar
Zenta
BANAT
(To Hapsburgs 1718)
Laibach
Agram
Karlowitz
WALLACHIA
Bucharest
Silistria
Black Sea
Trieste
SLAVONIA
CROATIA
Verona
Venice
Belgrade
Passarowitz
(To Hapsburgs 1718-1739)
Danube
REPUBLIC OF VENICE
Po
Parma
Modena
Bologna
BOSNIA
Sarajevo
Adriatic Sea
Nish
BULGARIA
Sofia
SERBIA
Florence
TUSCANY
PAPAL STATES
Tolentino
Ragusa
MONTENEGRO
OTTOMAN EMPIRE
Adrianople
Constantinople
Tiber
Rome
Salonika
KINGDOM OF NAPLES
(To Hapsburgs 1714-1735)
Bari
Naples
Otranto
Aegean Sea
Smyrna
Tyrrhenian Sea
CORFU (CORCYRA)
Athens
MOREA
(To Ottoman Empire 1718)
Palermo
Reggio
SICILY
Syracuse
(To Savoy 1714)
(To Hapsburgs 1720-35)
Tunis
Mediterranean Sea
CRETE
A-450035-29-1-2-1-1
Copyright by Rand McNally & Company, Made in U.S.A.

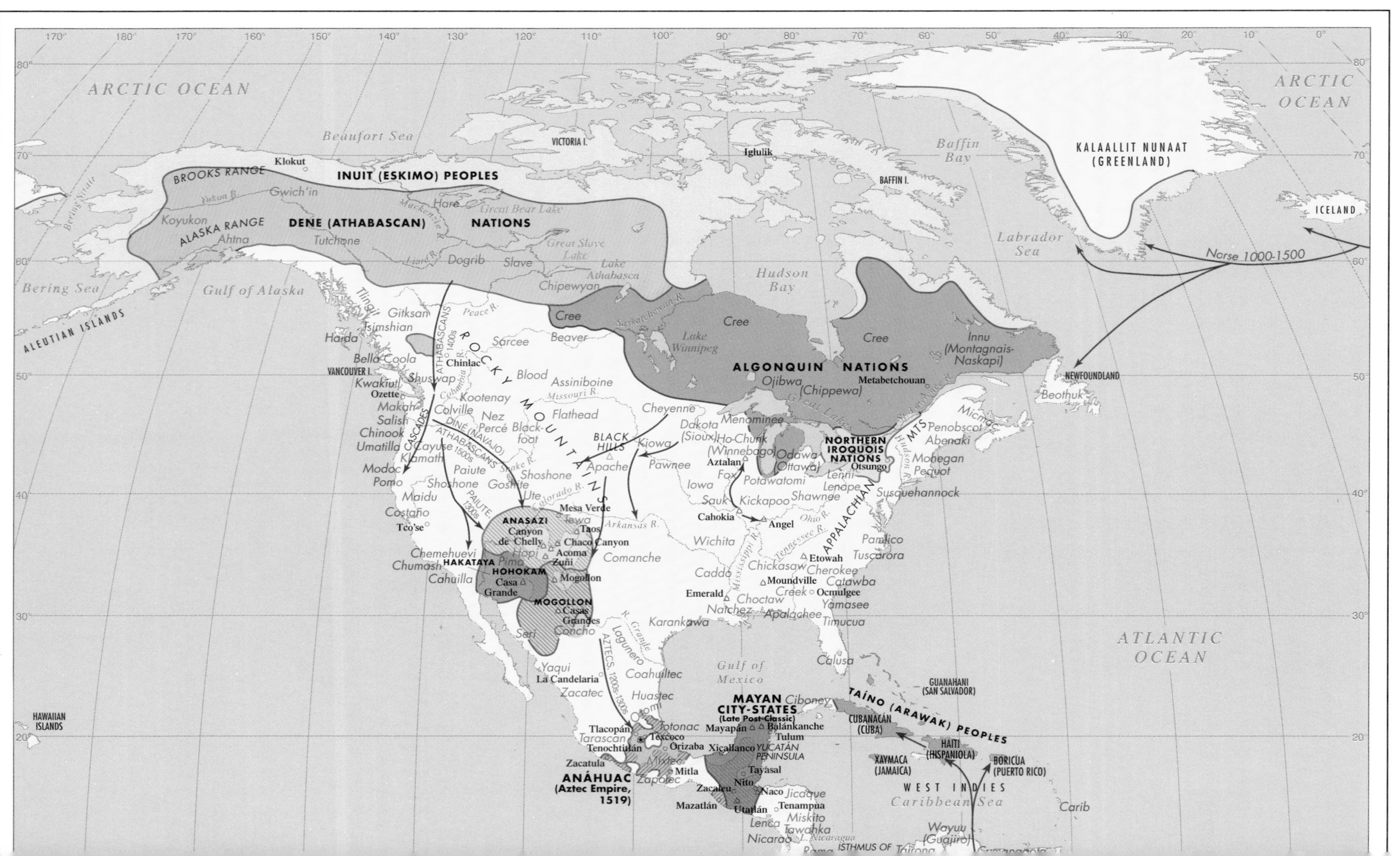
ARCTIC OCEAN
Beaufort Sea
VICTORIA I.
Iglulik
BAFFIN I.
Baffin Bay
KALAALLIT NUNAAT (GREENLAND)
ICELAND
Labrador Sea
Norse 1000-1500
Hudson Bay
Klokut
BROOKS RANGE
INUIT (ESKIMO) PEOPLES
Gwich'in
Koyukon
ALASKA RANGE
Ahtna
DENE (ATHABASCAN) NATIONS
Hare
Great Bear Lake
Tutchone
Great Slave Lake
Dogrib
Slave
Lake Athabasca
Chipewyan
Bering Sea
Gulf of Alaska
ALEUTIAN ISLANDS
Tlingit
Gitksan
Tsimshian
Haida
Bella Coola
VANCOUVER I.
Kwakiutl
Ozette
Makah
Salish
Chinook
Umatilla
Modoc
Pomo
Maidu
Costano
Tco'se
Chemehuevi
Chumash
Cahuilla
ATHABASCANS 1400s
Chinlac
Shuswap
Kootenay
Colville
Nez Percé
Cayuse
Klamath
CASCADES
DINÉ (NAVAJO)
ATHABASCANS 1500s
Paiute
Shoshone
Goshute
PAIUTE 1300s
ROCKY MOUNTAINS
Sarcee
Beaver
Blood
Assiniboine
Flathead
Blackfoot
Shoshone
Ute
Cree
Lake Winnipeg
ALGONQUIN NATIONS
Ojibwa (Chippewa)
Metabetchouan
Innu (Montagnais-Naskapi)
NEWFOUNDLAND
Beothuk
Micmac
Penobscot
Abenaki
Mohegan
Pequot
Susquehannock
NORTHERN IROQUOIS NATIONS
Otsungo
Lenni Lenape
APPALACHIAN MTS.
Cheyenne
Dakota (Sioux)
Menominee
Ho-Chunk (Winnebago)
Odawa (Ottawa)
Aztalan
Fox
Potawatomi
BLACK HILLS
Kiowa
Pawnee
Apache
Iowa
Sauk
Kickapoo
Shawnee
Cahokia
Angel
Mesa Verde
Tewa
Taos
ANASAZI
Canyon de Chelly
Chaco Canyon
Hopi
Acoma
Zuñi
HAKATAYA
Pima
HOHOKAM
Casa Grande
Mogollon
MOGOLLON
Casas Grandes
Concho
Seri
Comanche
Wichita
Caddo
Emerald
Natchez
Choctaw
Chickasaw
Etowah
Cherokee
Moundville
Creek
Ocmulgee
Catawba
Pamlico
Tuscarora
Yamasee
Apalachee
Timucua
Karankawa
Calusa
Gulf of Mexico
ATLANTIC OCEAN
Yaqui
La Candelaria
Zacatec
Lagunero
AZTECS, 1200s-1300s
Coahuiltec
Huastec
Otomi
Totonac
Tlacopán
Texcoco
Tarascan
Tenochtitlán
Orizaba
Zacatula
Mixtec
Mitla
Zapotec
ANÁHUAC (Aztec Empire, 1519)
MAYAN CITY-STATES (Late Post-Classic)
Mayapán
Balánkanche
Tulum
Xicallanco
YUCATÁN PENINSULA
Tayasal
Nito
Zacaleu
Naco
Mazatlán
Utatlán
Jicaque
Tenampua
Lenca
Miskito
Tawahka
Nicarao
Ciboney
TAÍNO (ARAWAK) PEOPLES
GUANAHANI (SAN SALVADOR)
CUBANACÁN (CUBA)
HAITI (HISPANIOLA)
XAYMACA (JAMAICA)
BORICUA (PUERTO RICO)
WEST INDIES
Caribbean Sea
Carib
Wayuu (Guajiro)
ISTHMUS OF
HAWAIIAN ISLANDS

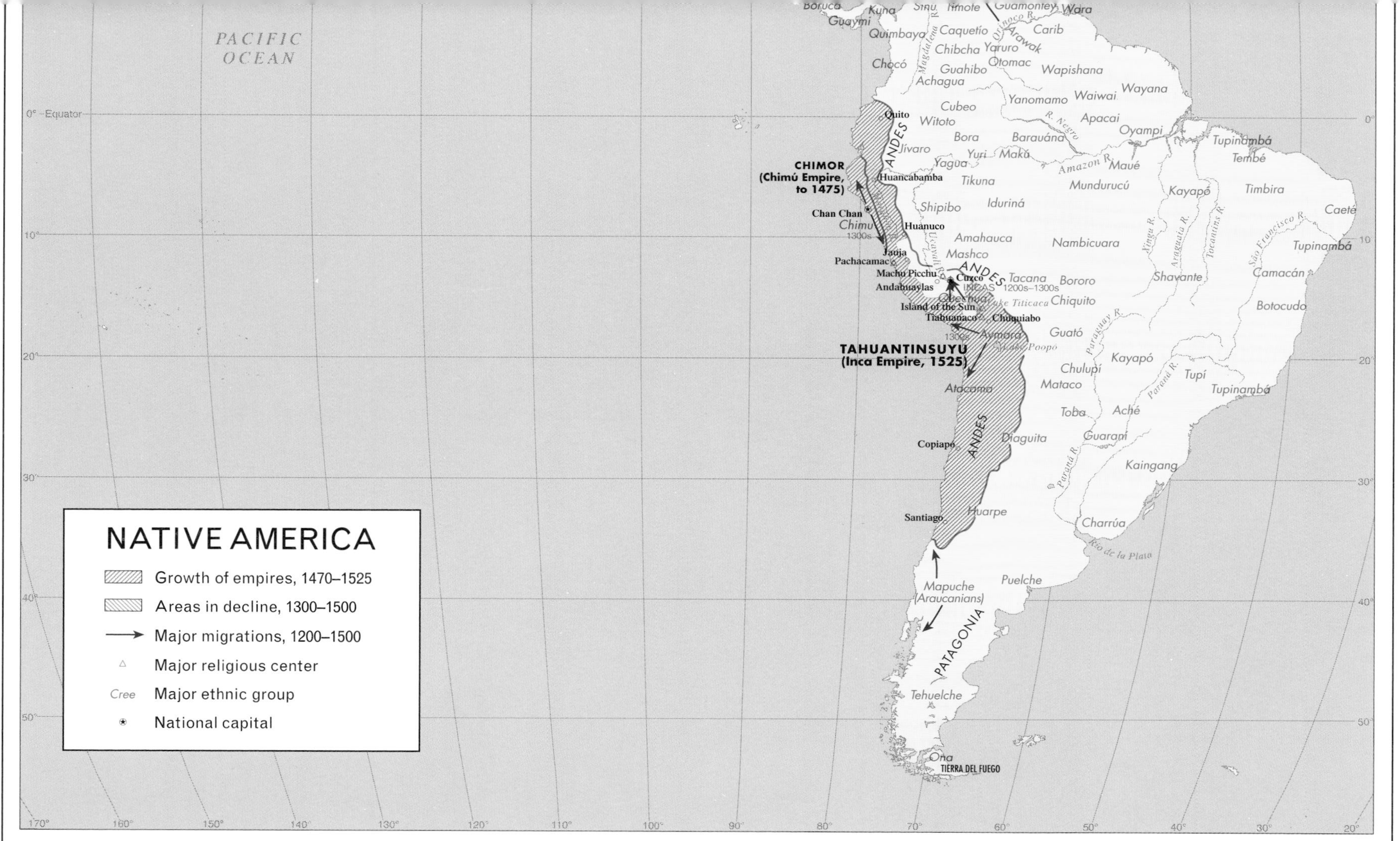

NATIVE AMERICA
Growth of empires, 1470–1525
Areas in decline, 1300–1500
Major migrations, 1200–1500
Major religious center
Cree
Major ethnic group
National capital
PACIFIC OCEAN
0° Equator
CHIMOR (Chimú Empire, to 1475)
TAHUANTINSUYU (Inca Empire, 1525)
ANDES
PATAGONIA
TIERRA DEL FUEGO
Quito
Huancabamba
Chan Chan
Chimu 1300s
Huanuco
Jauja
Pachacamac
Machu Picchu
Andahuaylas
Cuzco
INCAS 1200s–1300s
Quechua
Island of the Sun
Tiahuanaco
Chuquiabo
Aymara 1300s
Atacama
Copiapó
Santiago
Diaguita
Huarpe
Mapuche (Araucanians)
Puelche
Tehuelche
Ona
Boruca
Guaymi
Kuna
Quimbaya
Caquetío
Chibcha
Yaruro
Otomac
Carib
Arawak
Wara
Chocó
Guahibo
Achagua
Wapishana
Yanomamo
Waiwai
Wayana
Cubeo
Witoto
Apacai
Oyampi
Bora
Barauána
Jívaro
Yagua
Yuri
Makú
Maué
Tikuna
Mundurucú
Shipibo
Iduriná
Amahauca
Mashco
Nambicuara
Tacana
Bororo
Chiquito
Guató
Chulupí
Mataco
Toba
Kayapó
Tupí
Aché
Guaraní
Kaingang
Charrúa
Shavante
Tupinambá
Tembé
Timbira
Caeté
Camacán
Botocudo
Amazon R.
R. Negro
Lake Titicaca
Río de la Plata
Paraná R.
São Francisco R.

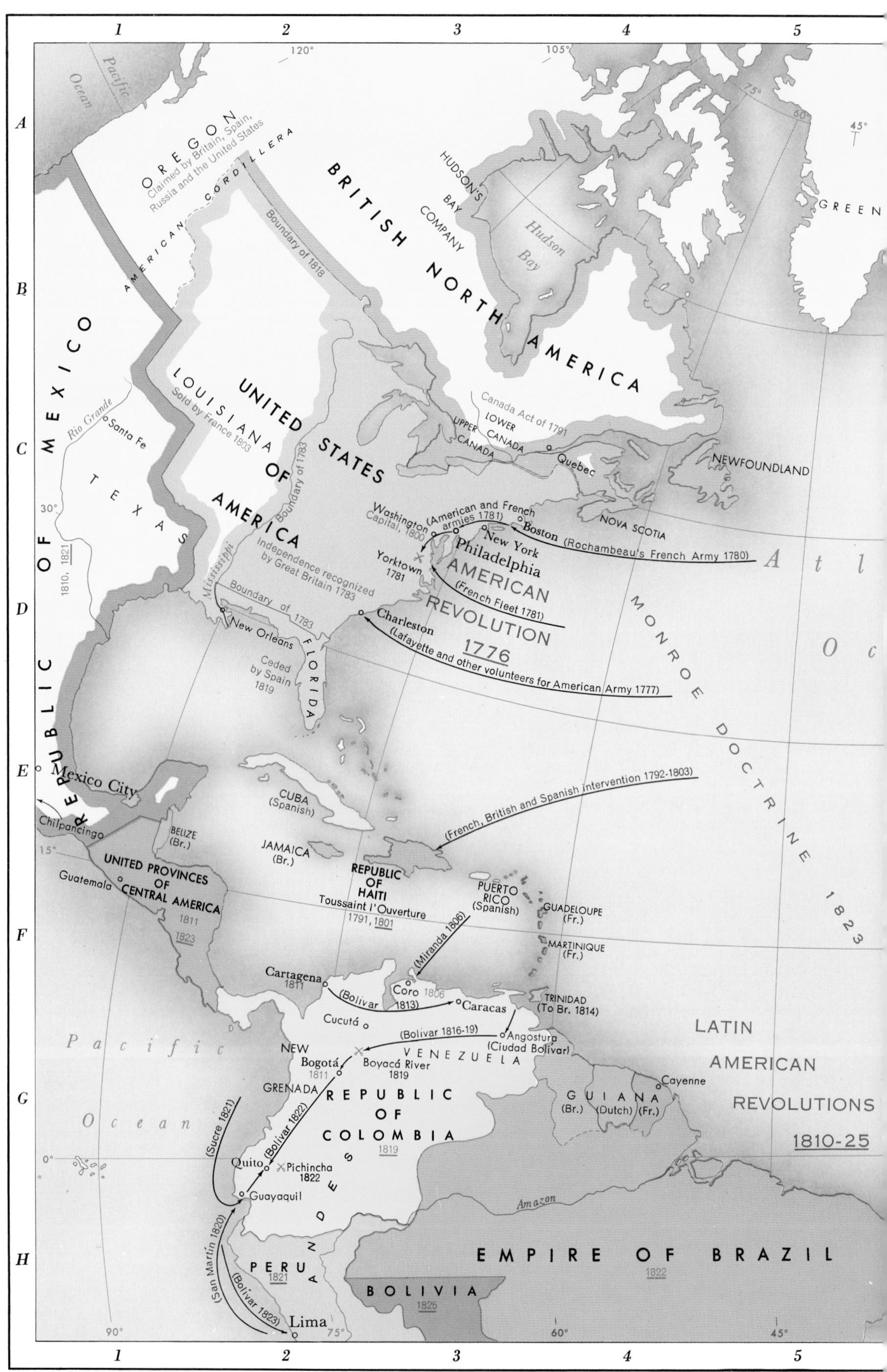

LATIN AMERICAN REVOLUTIONS 1810-25
AMERICAN REVOLUTION 1776
Pacific Ocean
OREGON
Claimed by Britain, Spain, Russia and the United States
AMERICAN CORDILLERA
BRITISH NORTH AMERICA
HUDSON'S BAY COMPANY
Hudson Bay
GREEN
Boundary of 1818
UNITED STATES OF AMERICA
LOUISIANA
Sold by France 1803
Boundary of 1783
Canada Act of 1791
UPPER CANADA
LOWER CANADA
Quebec
NEWFOUNDLAND
NOVA SCOTIA
REPUBLIC OF MEXICO
1810, 1821
Rio Grande
Santa Fe
TEXAS
Washington Capital, 1800
(American and French armies 1781)
Boston
(Rochambeau's French Army 1780)
New York
Philadelphia
Yorktown 1781
(French Fleet 1781)
Independence recognized by Great Britain 1783
Mississippi
Boundary of 1783
New Orleans
Charleston
(Lafayette and other volunteers for American Army 1777)
FLORIDA
Ceded by Spain 1819
MONROE DOCTRINE 1823
Atl
Oc
Mexico City
Chilpancingo
CUBA (Spanish)
(French, British and Spanish intervention 1792-1803)
BELIZE (Br.)
JAMAICA (Br.)
REPUBLIC OF HAITI
Toussaint l'Ouverture 1791, 1801
UNITED PROVINCES OF CENTRAL AMERICA
1811
1823
Guatemala
PUERTO RICO (Spanish)
GUADELOUPE (Fr.)
MARTINIQUE (Fr.)
(Miranda 1806)
Cartagena 1811
Coro 1806
(Bolivar 1813)
Caracas
TRINIDAD (To Br. 1814)
Cucutá
(Bolivar 1816-19)
Angostura (Ciudad Bolivar)
VENEZUELA
NEW GRENADA
Bogotá 1811
Boyacá River 1819
REPUBLIC OF COLOMBIA
1819
GUIANA
(Br.) (Dutch) (Fr.)
Cayenne
Pacific Ocean
(Sucre 1821)
(Bolivar 1822)
Quito
Pichincha 1822
Guayaquil
ANDES
Amazon
(San Martín 1820)
(Bolivar 1823)
PERU
1821
Lima
EMPIRE OF BRAZIL
1822
BOLIVIA
1825
120°
105°
75°
60°
45°
30°
15°
0°
90°
A
B
C
D
E
F
G
H
1
2
3
4
5

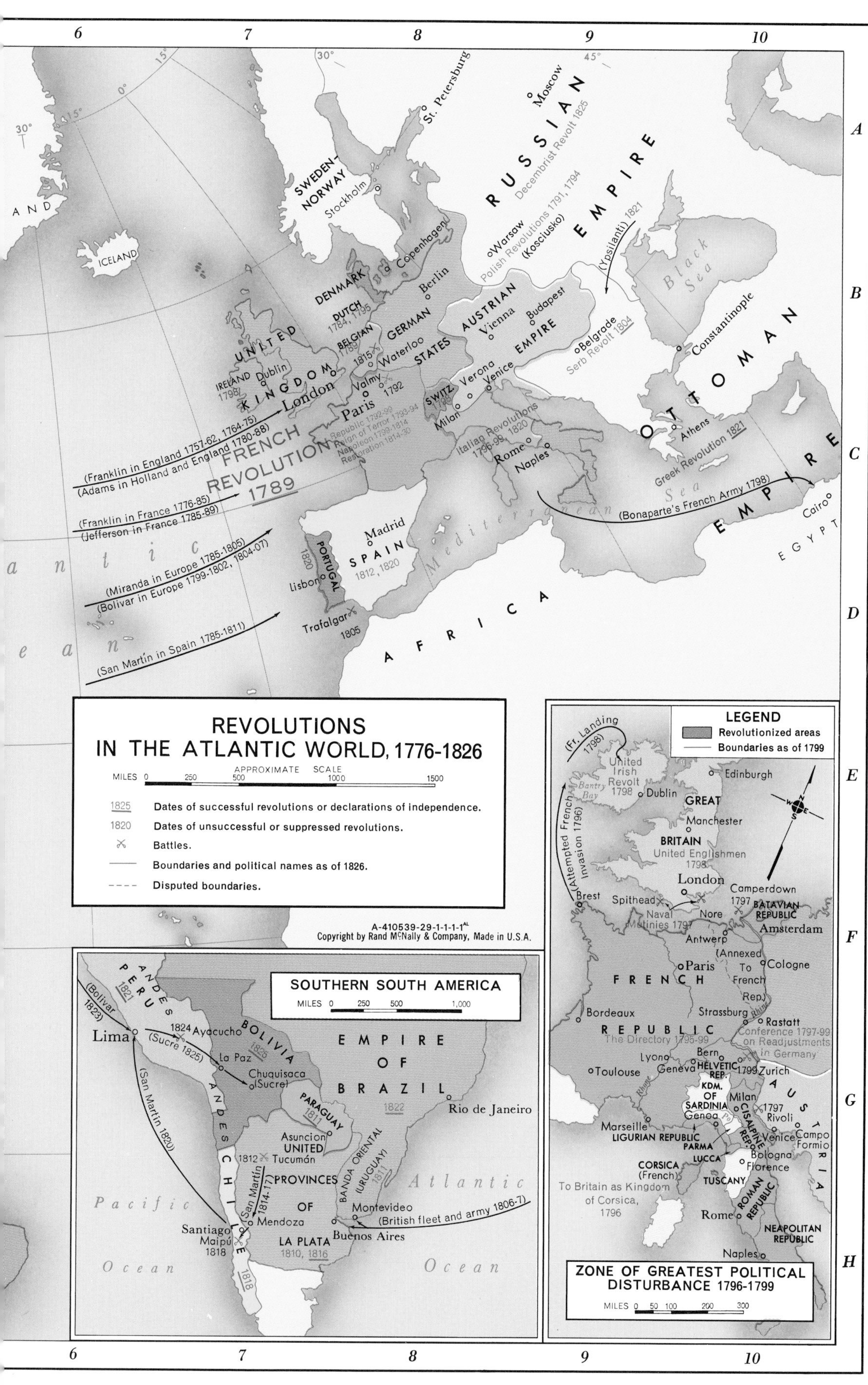

REVOLUTIONS IN THE ATLANTIC WORLD, 1776-1826
MILES 0 250 500 1000 1500
APPROXIMATE SCALE
1825 Dates of successful revolutions or declarations of independence.
1820 Dates of unsuccessful or suppressed revolutions.
Battles.
Boundaries and political names as of 1826.
Disputed boundaries.
A-410539-29-1-1-1-1
Copyright by Rand McNally & Company, Made in U.S.A.
RUSSIAN EMPIRE
Decembrist Revolt 1825
Polish Revolutions 1791, 1794 (Kosciusko)
Moscow
St. Petersburg
SWEDEN-NORWAY
Stockholm
Warsaw
(Ypsilanti) 1821
Black Sea
ICELAND
DENMARK
Copenhagen
Berlin
DUTCH 1784, 1795
BELGIAN 1789
1815 Waterloo
GERMAN STATES
AUSTRIAN EMPIRE
Vienna
Budapest
Belgrade
Serb Revolt 1804
Constantinople
OTTOMAN EMPIRE
UNITED KINGDOM
IRELAND 1798
Dublin
London
Valmy 1792
Paris
FRENCH REVOLUTION 1789
Republic 1792-99
Reign of Terror 1793-94
Napoleon 1799-1814
Restoration 1814-30
SWITZ. 1798
Verona
Venice
Milan
Italian Revolutions 1796-99, 1820
Rome
Naples
Athens
Greek Revolution 1821
(Bonaparte's French Army 1798)
Mediterranean Sea
Cairo
EGYPT
(Franklin in England 1757-62, 1764-75)
(Adams in Holland and England 1780-88)
(Franklin in France 1776-85)
(Jefferson in France 1785-89)
(Miranda in Europe 1785-1805)
(Bolivar in Europe 1799-1802, 1804-07)
(San Martín in Spain 1785-1811)
Madrid
SPAIN 1812, 1820
PORTUGAL 1820
Lisbon
Trafalgar 1805
AFRICA
Atlantic Ocean
SOUTHERN SOUTH AMERICA
MILES 0 250 500 1,000
ANDES
PERU 1821
(Bolivar 1823)
Lima
1824 Ayacucho
(Sucre 1825)
BOLIVIA 1825
La Paz
Chuquisaca (Sucre)
EMPIRE OF BRAZIL 1822
Rio de Janeiro
PARAGUAY 1811
Asuncion
(San Martin 1820)
1812 Tucumán
UNITED PROVINCES OF LA PLATA 1810, 1816
BANDA ORIENTAL (URUGUAY) 1811
CHILE 1818
(San Martin 1814-17)
Mendoza
Santiago
Maipú 1818
Montevideo
(British fleet and army 1806-7)
Buenos Aires
Pacific Ocean
Atlantic Ocean
LEGEND
Revolutionized areas
Boundaries as of 1799
(Fr. Landing 1798)
United Irish Revolt 1798
Bantry Bay
Dublin
Edinburgh
GREAT BRITAIN
Manchester
United Englishmen 1798
London
(Attempted French Invasion 1796)
Brest
Spithead
Naval Mutinies 1797
Nore
Camperdown 1797
BATAVIAN REPUBLIC
Amsterdam
Antwerp
(Annexed To French Rep.)
Cologne
Paris
FRENCH REPUBLIC
The Directory 1795-99
Bordeaux
Strassburg
Rastatt Conference 1797-99 on Readjustments in Germany
Lyon
Toulouse
Geneva
Bern
HELVETIC REP.
1799 Zurich
KDM. OF SARDINIA
Milan
Genoa
CISALPINE REP.
1797 Rivoli
Campo Formio
Venice
Marseille
LIGURIAN REPUBLIC
PARMA
LUCCA
Bologna
Florence
TUSCANY
CORSICA (French)
To Britain as Kingdom of Corsica, 1796
ROMAN REPUBLIC
Rome
NEAPOLITAN REPUBLIC
Naples
AUSTRIA
ZONE OF GREATEST POLITICAL DISTURBANCE 1796-1799
MILES 0 50 100 200 300

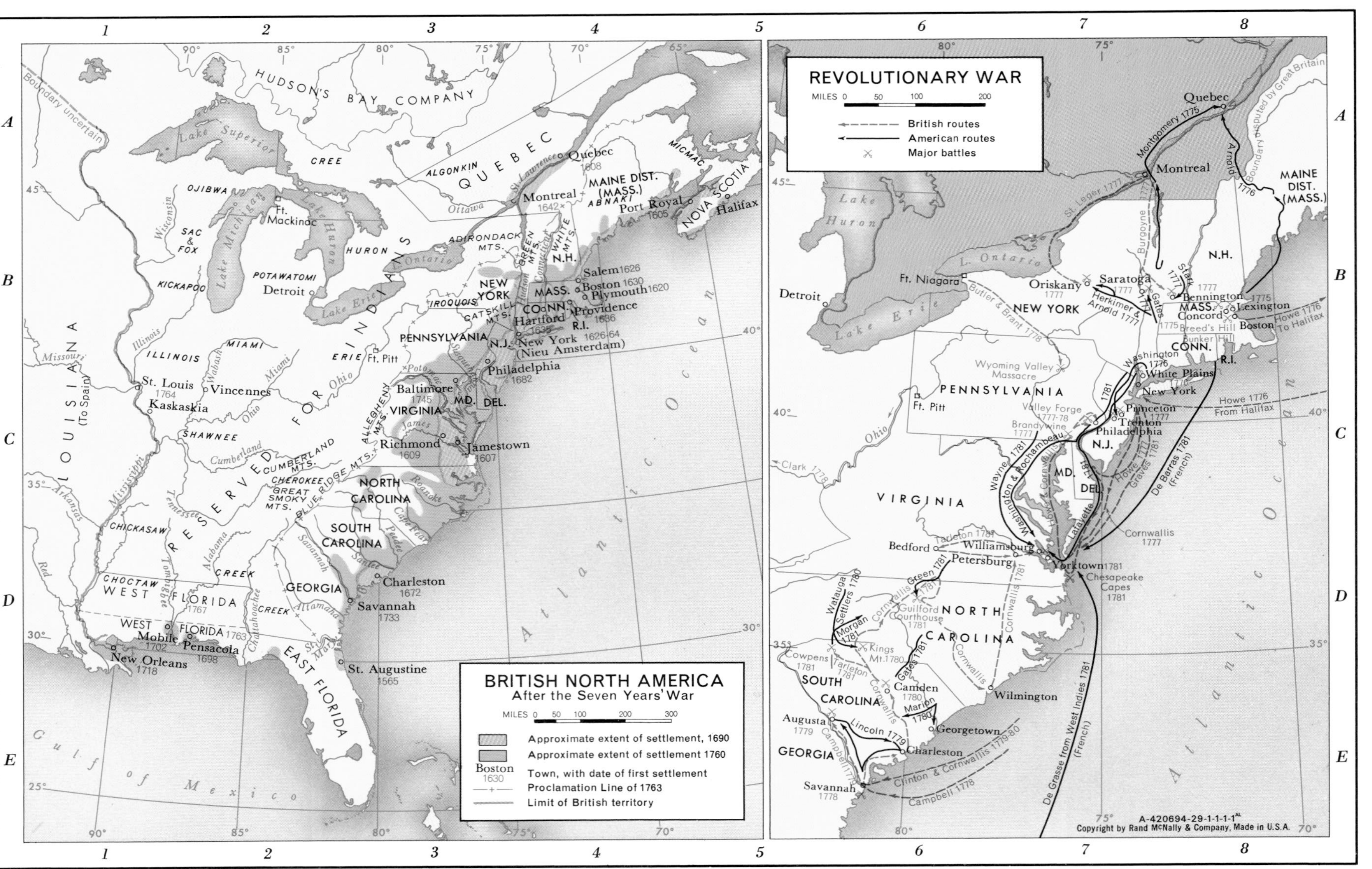
BRITISH NORTH AMERICA
After the Seven Years' War
MILES 0 50 100 200 300
Approximate extent of settlement, 1690
Approximate extent of settlement 1760
Boston 1630 Town, with date of first settlement
Proclamation Line of 1763
Limit of British territory
REVOLUTIONARY WAR
MILES 0 50 100 200
British routes
American routes
Major battles
A-420694-29-1-1-1
Copyright by Rand McNally & Company, Made in U.S.A.

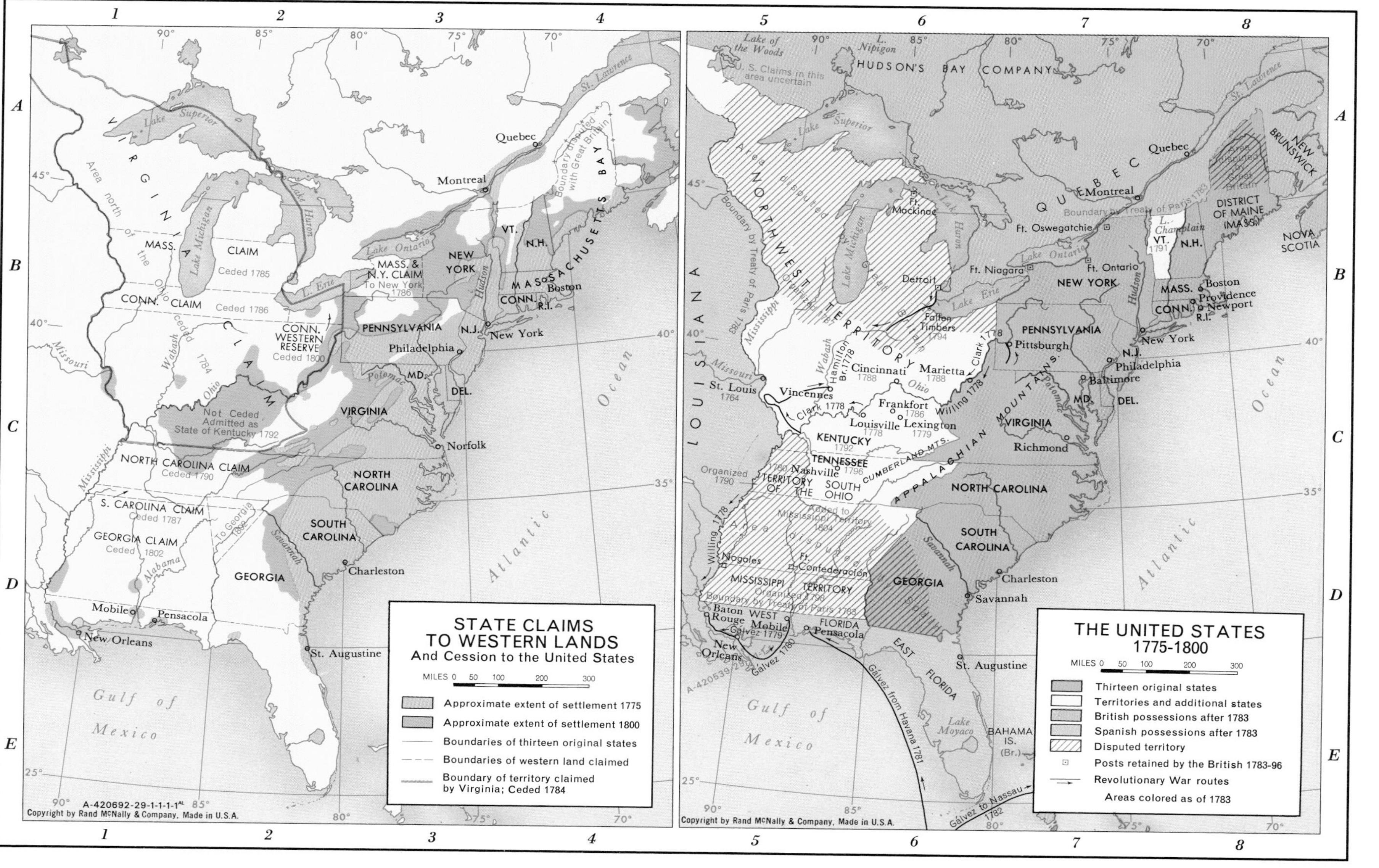
STATE CLAIMS TO WESTERN LANDS
And Cession to the United States
MILES 0 50 100 200 300
Approximate extent of settlement 1775
Approximate extent of settlement 1800
Boundaries of thirteen original states
Boundaries of western land claimed
Boundary of territory claimed by Virginia; Ceded 1784
VIRGINIA CLAIM
Area north of the Ohio ceded 1784
MASS. CLAIM Ceded 1785
CONN. CLAIM Ceded 1786
CONN. WESTERN RESERVE Ceded 1800
MASS. & N.Y. CLAIM To New York 1786
Not Ceded Admitted as State of Kentucky 1792
NORTH CAROLINA CLAIM Ceded 1790
S. CAROLINA CLAIM Ceded 1787
GEORGIA CLAIM Ceded 1802
To Georgia 1802
MASSACHUSETTS BAY
Boundary disputed with Great Britain
Gulf of Mexico
Atlantic Ocean
A-420692-29-1-1-1
Copyright by Rand McNally & Company, Made in U.S.A.
THE UNITED STATES 1775-1800
MILES 0 50 100 200 300
Thirteen original states
Territories and additional states
British possessions after 1783
Spanish possessions after 1783
Disputed territory
Posts retained by the British 1783-96
Revolutionary War routes
Areas colored as of 1783
HUDSON'S BAY COMPANY
QUEBEC
U. S. Claims in this area uncertain
NORTHWEST TERRITORY
Area disputed
Boundary by Treaty of Paris 1783
LOUISIANA
DISTRICT OF MAINE (MASS.)
NEW BRUNSWICK
NOVA SCOTIA
Area disputed by Great Britain
KENTUCKY 1792
TENNESSEE 1796
TERRITORY SOUTH OF THE OHIO 1790
MISSISSIPPI TERRITORY Organized 1798
Added to Mississippi Territory 1804
WEST FLORIDA
EAST FLORIDA
APPALACHIAN MOUNTAINS
CUMBERLAND MTS.
Clark 1778
Willing 1778
Gálvez 1779
Gálvez 1780
Gálvez from Havana 1781
Gálvez to Nassau 1782
Fallen Timbers 1794
Copyright by Rand McNally & Company, Made in U.S.A.

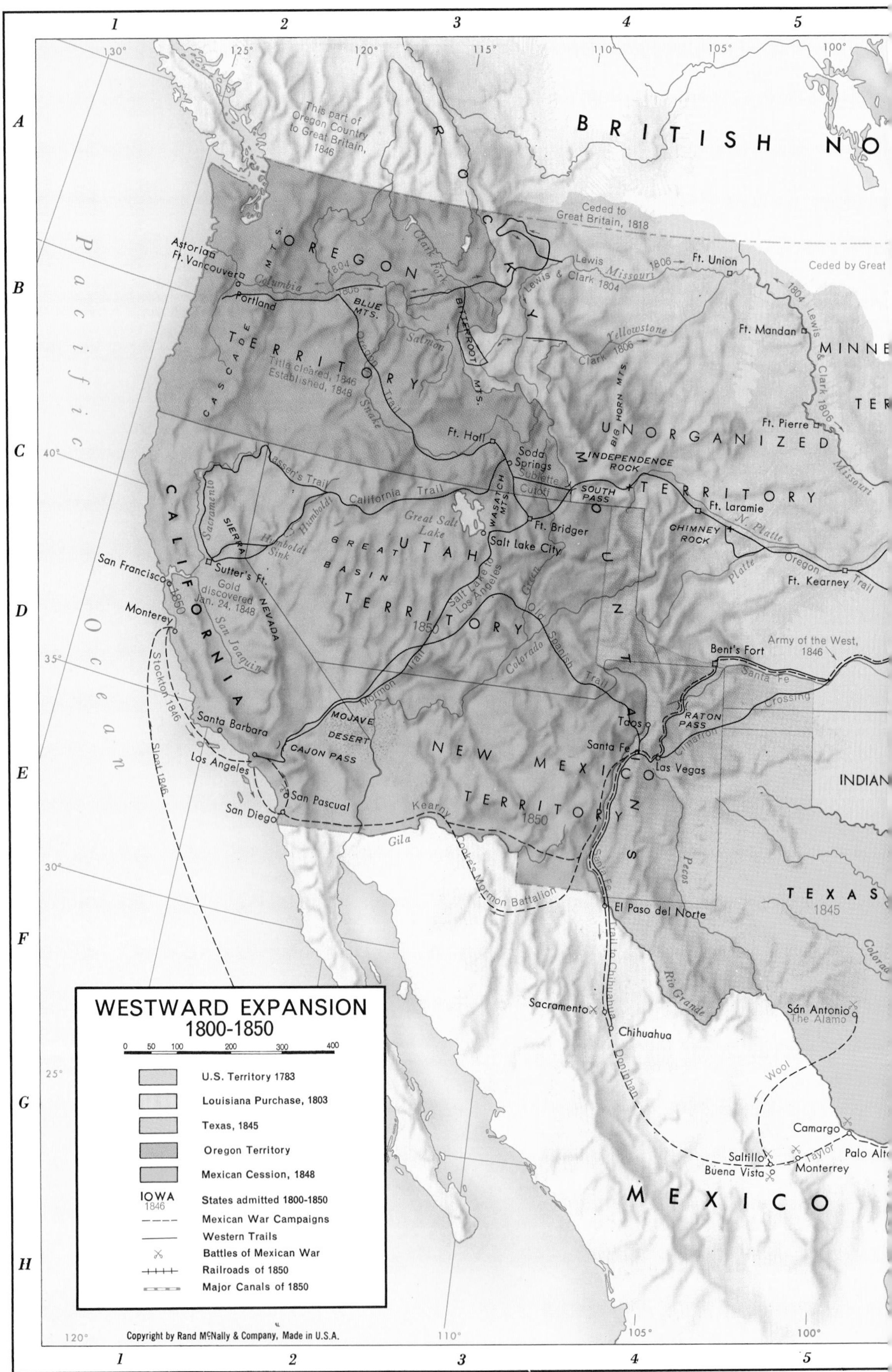

WESTWARD EXPANSION
1800-1850
0 50 100 200 300 400
U.S. Territory 1783
Louisiana Purchase, 1803
Texas, 1845
Oregon Territory
Mexican Cession, 1848
IOWA 1846
States admitted 1800-1850
Mexican War Campaigns
Western Trails
Battles of Mexican War
Railroads of 1850
Major Canals of 1850
Copyright by Rand McNally & Company, Made in U.S.A.
BRITISH NO
This part of Oregon Country to Great Britain, 1846
Ceded to Great Britain, 1818
Ceded by Great
OREGON TERRITORY
Title cleared, 1846
Established, 1848
Astoria
Ft. Vancouver
Portland
Columbia
BLUE MTS.
CASCADE MTS.
BITTERROOT
ROCKY MTS.
Lewis & Clark 1804
Clark 1806
Ft. Union
Ft. Mandan
Ft. Pierre
Ft. Hall
Soda Springs
INDEPENDENCE ROCK
SOUTH PASS
UNORGANIZED TERRITORY
Ft. Laramie
CHIMNEY ROCK
Ft. Kearney
Oregon Trail
Ft. Bridger
Salt Lake City
Great Salt Lake
WASATCH MTS.
California Trail
Lassen's Trail
Humboldt
Humboldt Sink
UTAH TERRITORY
1850
GREAT BASIN
CALIFORNIA
1850
SIERRA NEVADA
Sutter's Ft.
Gold discovered Jan. 24, 1848
San Francisco
Monterey
San Joaquin
Sacramento
Santa Barbara
Los Angeles
San Pascual
San Diego
Stockton 1846
Sloat 1846
MOJAVE DESERT
CAJON PASS
Mormon Trail
Old Spanish Trail
Colorado
NEW MEXICO TERRITORY
1850
Kearny
Gila
Cooke's Mormon Battalion
Taos
Santa Fe
Las Vegas
RATON PASS
Cimarron
Bent's Fort
Army of the West, 1846
Santa Fe Crossing
El Paso del Norte
Trail to Chihuahua
Sacramento
Chihuahua
Doniphan
Rio Grande
Pecos
TEXAS
1845
INDIAN
MINNE
TER
Sán Antonio
The Alamo
Wool
Camargo
Saltillo
Buena Vista
Monterrey
Taylor
Palo Alto
MEXICO
Pacific Ocean

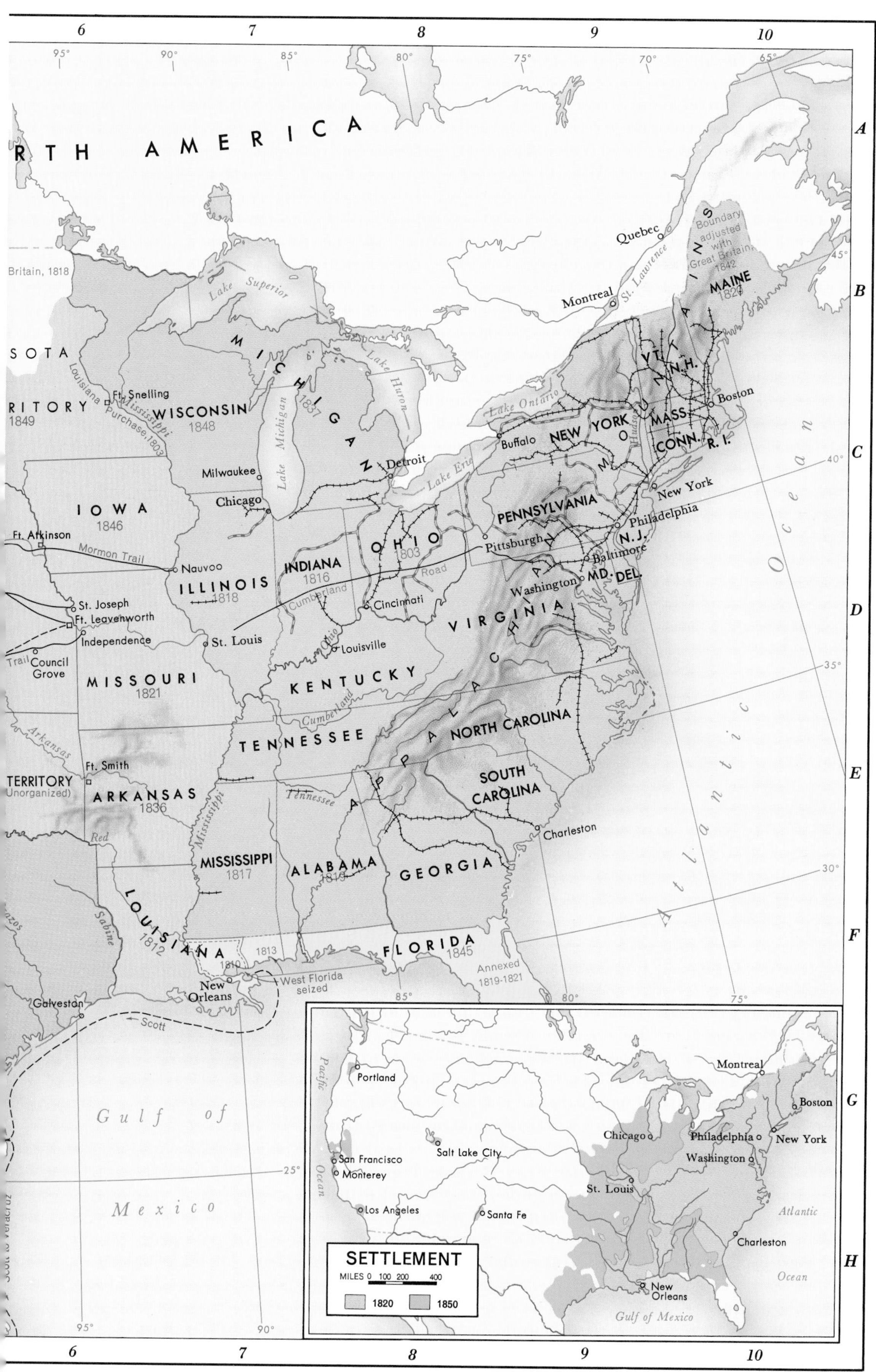

6
7
8
9
10
A
B
C
D
E
F
G
H
RTH AMERICA
Britain, 1818
SOTA
RITORY
1849
Louisiana Purchase, 1803
Ft. Snelling
Mississippi
WISCONSIN
1848
MICHIGAN
1837
Lake Superior
Lake Michigan
Lake Huron
Lake Ontario
Lake Erie
Quebec
Montreal
St. Lawrence
Boundary adjusted with Great Britain, 1842
MAINE
1820
VT.
N.H.
MASS.
Boston
CONN.
R. I.
NEW YORK
Hudson
Buffalo
Detroit
Milwaukee
Chicago
IOWA
1846
Ft. Atkinson
Mormon Trail
Nauvoo
ILLINOIS
1818
INDIANA
1816
OHIO
1803
Cumberland Road
PENNSYLVANIA
Pittsburgh
New York
Philadelphia
N.J.
Baltimore
Washington
MD.
DEL.
St. Joseph
Ft. Leavenworth
Independence
Council Grove
Trail
St. Louis
Cincinnati
Louisville
Ohio
VIRGINIA
APPALACHIAN MTS.
MISSOURI
1821
KENTUCKY
Cumberland
TENNESSEE
NORTH CAROLINA
SOUTH CAROLINA
Charleston
Arkansas
Ft. Smith
TERRITORY
(Unorganized)
ARKANSAS
1836
Red
Mississippi
Tennessee
MISSISSIPPI
1817
ALABAMA
1819
GEORGIA
LOUISIANA
1812
Sabine
1813
1810
FLORIDA
1845
Annexed 1819-1821
West Florida seized
New Orleans
Galveston
Scott
Atlantic Ocean
Gulf of Mexico
95°
90°
85°
80°
75°
70°
65°
45°
40°
35°
30°
25°
SETTLEMENT
MILES 0 100 200 400
1820
1850
Portland
Pacific Ocean
San Francisco
Monterey
Los Angeles
Salt Lake City
Santa Fe
Montreal
Boston
Chicago
Philadelphia
New York
Washington
St. Louis
Charleston
New Orleans
Atlantic Ocean
Gulf of Mexico

BRITISH NORTH AMERICA
UNITED STATES OF AMERICA
Atlantic Ocean
Pacific Ocean
Gulf of Mexico
Caribbean Sea
Tropic of Cancer
Disputed by Spain, Russia, and England
Claimed by Spain, but unoccupied
Disputed with U.S. 1783-1795
VICEROYALTY OF NEW SPAIN
VICEROYALTY OF NEW GRANADA
INTENDANCY OF NUEVA CALIFORNIA
WESTERN INTERIOR PROVINCES
INTENDANCY OF VIEJA CALIFORNIA
INTENDANCY OF NUEVO MEXICO
PRESIDENCY
INTENDANCY OF SONORA
AUDIENCIA OF GUADALAJARA
INTENDANCY OF DURANGO
EASTERN INTERIOR PROVINCES
INTENDANCY OF ZACATECAS
INTENDANCY OF GUADALAJARE
INTENDANCY OF VALLADOLID
INTENDANCY OF MEXICO
AUDIENCIA OF MEXICO
INTENDANCY OF SAN LUIS POTOSI
INTENDANCY OF VERA CRUZ
INTENDANCY OF OAXACA
CHIAPAS
INTENDANCY OF YUCATAN
CAPTAINCY-GENERAL (AUDIENCIA) OF GUATEMALA
CAPTAINCY-GENERAL OF LOUISIANA
WEST FLORIDA
EAST FLORIDA
CAPTAINCY-GENERAL OF CUBA
CAPTAINCY-GENERAL OF SANTO DOMINGO
Ceded to France 1795
PUERTO RICO
JAMAICA Br. 1655
TRINIDAD
Ceded to Great Britain, 1802
CAPTAINCY-GENERAL OF CARACAS
AUDIENCIA OF SANTA FE
Established 1717, Restored 1740
PRESIDENCY (AUDIENCIA) OF QUITO
GALAPAGOS IS.
Claimed by Spain, but unoccupied
DUTCH GUIANA
Dutch in 1790
FRENCH GUIANA
CAPTAINCY OF PARÁ
CAPTAINCY OF RIO NEGRO
San Francisco 1776
Monterey 1770
Santa Barbara 1782
San Luis Obispo 1772
Los Angeles 1781
San Diego 1769
San Juan 1776
La Paz 1535
Santa Fé 1609
El Paso del Norte 1659
Chihuahua 1704
Culiacán 1531
San Antonio 1718
Laredo 1755
Saltillo
Queretaro 1550
Mexico City 1325
Vera Cruz 1519
Guatemala
San Salvador 1525
Granada 1524
León 1525
San José 1738
Cartago 1564
Portobelo 1584
Panamá 1519
Cartagena 1533
Santa Marta 1525
La Guaira 1588
Caracas 1567
Bogotá
Quito
Guayaquil 1535
St. Louis 1764
New Orleans 1718
Pensacola 1698
St. Augustine 1565
Habana 1515
Santiago 1514
Port au Prince 1749
Santo Domingo 1496
San Juan 1511
Belice
Stabroek (Georgetown) Approx. 1740
Paramaribo 1640
Cayenne 1664
Belem 1616
São Luis 1612
Fortaleza
Barcelos 1658
Barra do Rio Negro 1660
Tabatinga
Amazon
Negro
Orinoco
Magdalena
Maracaibo
Napo
Putumayo
Yapurá
Marañon
Nootka Sound

LATIN AMERICA ABOUT 1790
MILES 0 250 500 1,000
European Colonies
Spain
Great Britain
Netherlands
Portugal
France
Seat of Government
1535 Lima Dates indicate year of founding
VICEROYALTY OF BRAZIL
Definitively established 1714
VICEROYALTY OF LA PLATA
(Established 1776)
VICEROYALTY OF PERU
Established 1542
CAPTAINCY GENERAL (AUDIENCIA) OF CHILE
Loosely joined to Peru
AUDIENCIA OF LIMA
PRESIDENCY (AUDIENCIA) OF CHARCAS
PRESIDENCY (AUDIENCIA) OF CUZCO
AUDIENCIA OF BUENOS AIRES
BANDA ORIENTAL
PARAGUAY
Abandoned Jesuit Missions
PATAGONIA
MARANHÃO
PIAUI
CAPTAINCY OF MATO GROSSO
CAPTAINCY OF GOIAZ
CAPTAINCY OF MINAS GERAIS
CAPTAINCY OF SÃO PAULO
CAPTAINCY OF SANTA CATARINA
CAPTAINCY OF RIO GRANDE DO SUL
CAPTAINCY OF RIO DE JANEIRO
CAPTAINCY OF ESPIRITO SANTO
CAPTAINCY OF BAÍA
CAPTAINCY OF SERGIPE
CAPTAINCY OF PERNAMBUCO
Recife (Pernambuco) 1561
Salvador (Baía) 1549
Tijuco (Diamantina)
Ouro Preto 1698
Rio de Janeiro 1567
Santos 1536
São Paulo 1554
Porto Alegre 1743
Rio Grande 1737
Montevideo 1724
Colonia 1680
Buenos Aires 1580
Asunción 1537
Santa Fé 1573
Córdoba 1573
Mendoza 1561
Santiago 1541
Valparaíso 1544
Concepción 1550
Valdivia 1552
La Serena 1544
Tucumán 1585
Salta 1612
Potosí 1545
Chuquisaca 1538
La Paz 1548
L. Titicaca
Cuzco
Lima 1535
Callao 1537
Trujillo 1535
Principe da Beira 1760
Villa Bella (Mato Grosso) 1752
Santa Anna (Goiaz) 1736
Purús
Madeira
Ucayali
Pilcomayo
Paraná
Uruguay
Río de la Plata
MALVINAS (FALKLAND ISLANDS)
TIERRA DEL FUEGO
CAPE HORN
CHILOE I.
Drake Passage
Tropic of Capricorn
Ocean
A-440037-29-1-1-1
Copyright by Rand McNally & Company, Made in U.S.A.

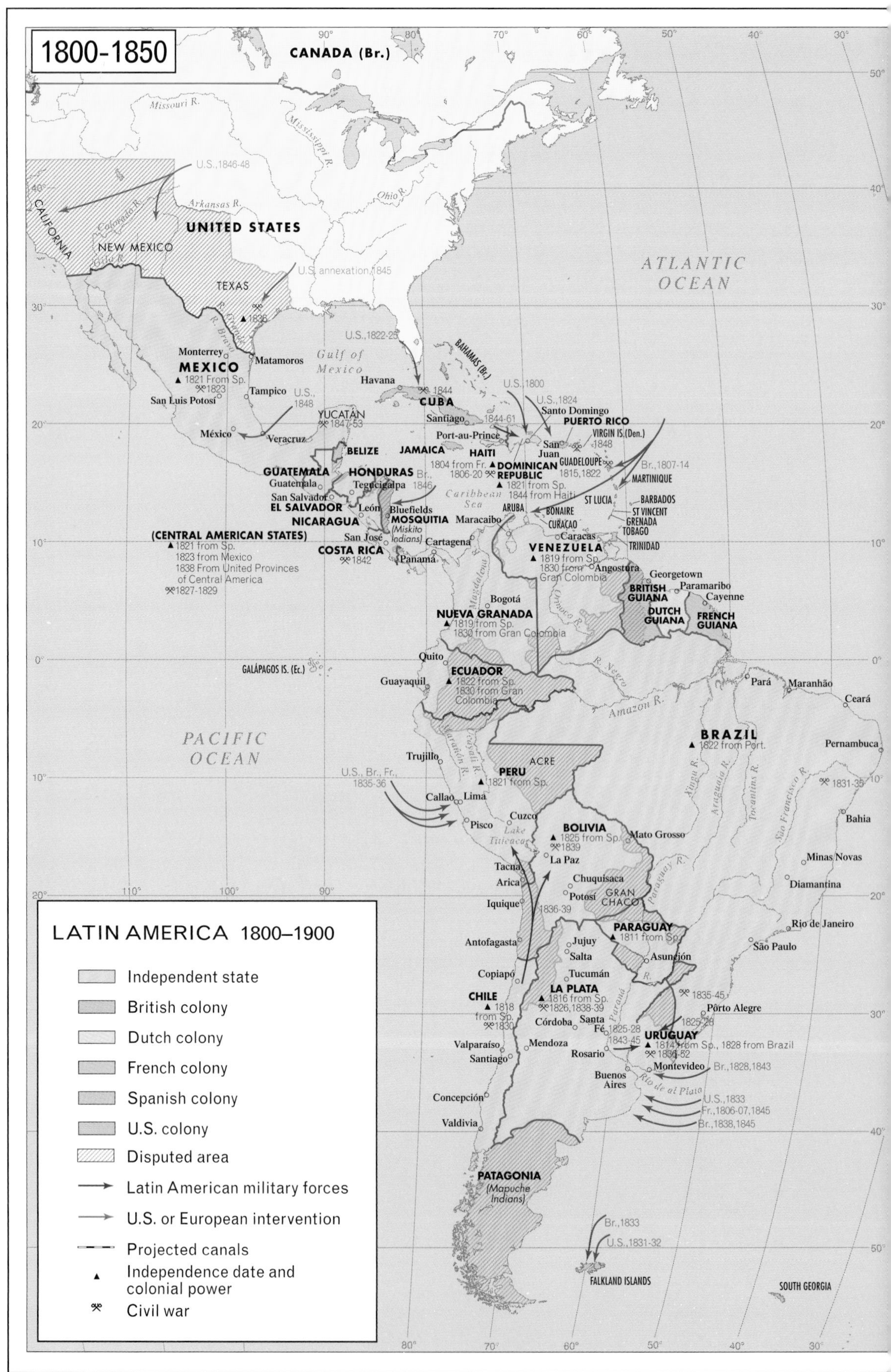
1800-1850
CANADA (Br.)
Missouri R.
Mississippi R.
Ohio R.
Arkansas R.
U.S.,1846-48
CALIFORNIA
NEW MEXICO
UNITED STATES
TEXAS
▲1836
U.S. annexation,1845
ATLANTIC
OCEAN
U.S.,1822-25
BAHAMAS (Br.)
Monterrey
Matamoros
MEXICO
▲ 1821 From Sp.
1823
San Luis Potosí
Tampico
U.S., 1848
Gulf of Mexico
Havana
1844
CUBA
U.S.,1800
U.S.,1824
Santo Domingo
PUERTO RICO
YUCATÁN
1847-53
México
Veracruz
Santiago
1844-61
Port-au-Prince
San Juan
VIRGIN IS.(Den.)
1848
BELIZE
JAMAICA
HAITI
1804 from Fr.
1806-20
▲DOMINICAN REPUBLIC
▲ 1821 from Sp.
1844 from Haiti
GUADELOUPE
1815,1822
Br.,1807-14
MARTINIQUE
GUATEMALA
Guatemala
HONDURAS
Br., 1846
Tegucigalpa
Caribbean Sea
ST LUCIA
BARBADOS
ST VINCENT
GRENADA
TOBAGO
San Salvador
EL SALVADOR
León
Bluefields
ARUBA
BONAIRE
CURAÇAO
NICARAGUA
MOSQUITIA
(Miskito Indians)
Maracaibo
Caracas
(CENTRAL AMERICAN STATES)
▲1821 from Sp.
1823 from Mexico
1838 From United Provinces of Central America
1827-1829
San José
COSTA RICA
1842
Cartagena
Panamá
VENEZUELA
▲ 1819 from Sp.
1830 from Gran Colombia
Angostura
TRINIDAD
Georgetown
BRITISH GUIANA
Paramaribo
Cayenne
DUTCH GUIANA
FRENCH GUIANA
Bogotá
NUEVA GRANADA
▲1819 from Sp.
1830 from Gran Colombia
Magdalena
Orinoco R.
Quito
GALÁPAGOS IS. (Ec.)
ECUADOR
▲ 1822 from Sp.
1830 from Gran Colombia
Guayaquil
R. Negro
Amazon R.
Pará
Maranhão
Ceará
PACIFIC
OCEAN
BRAZIL
▲ 1822 from Port.
Pernambuca
Trujillo
ACRE
PERU
▲1821 from Sp.
U.S., Br., Fr., 1835-36
Callao
Lima
1831-35
Bahia
Pisco
Cuzco
Lake Titicaca
BOLIVIA
▲ 1825 from Sp.
1839
Mato Grosso
La Paz
Minas Novas
Tacna
Arica
Chuquisaca
Potosí
GRAN CHACO
Diamantina
Iquique
1836-39
LATIN AMERICA 1800–1900
Independent state
British colony
Dutch colony
French colony
Spanish colony
U.S. colony
Disputed area
Latin American military forces
U.S. or European intervention
Projected canals
Independence date and colonial power
Civil war
Antofagasta
Jujuy
Salta
PARAGUAY
▲ 1811 from Sp.
Rio de Janeiro
São Paulo
Asunción
Copiapó
Tucumán
LA PLATA
▲ 1816 from Sp.
1826,1838-39
1835-45
CHILE
▲ 1818 from Sp.
1830
Córdoba
Santa Fé
Porto Alegre
1825-28
1825-28
1843-45
URUGUAY
▲ 1814 from Sp., 1828 from Brazil
1836-52
Valparaíso
Santiago
Mendoza
Rosario
Montevideo
Br.,1828,1843
Buenos Aires
Rio de al Plata
U.S.,1833
Fr.,1806-07,1845
Br.,1838,1845
Concepción
Valdivia
PATAGONIA
(Mapuche Indians)
Br.,1833
U.S.,1831-32
FALKLAND ISLANDS
SOUTH GEORGIA

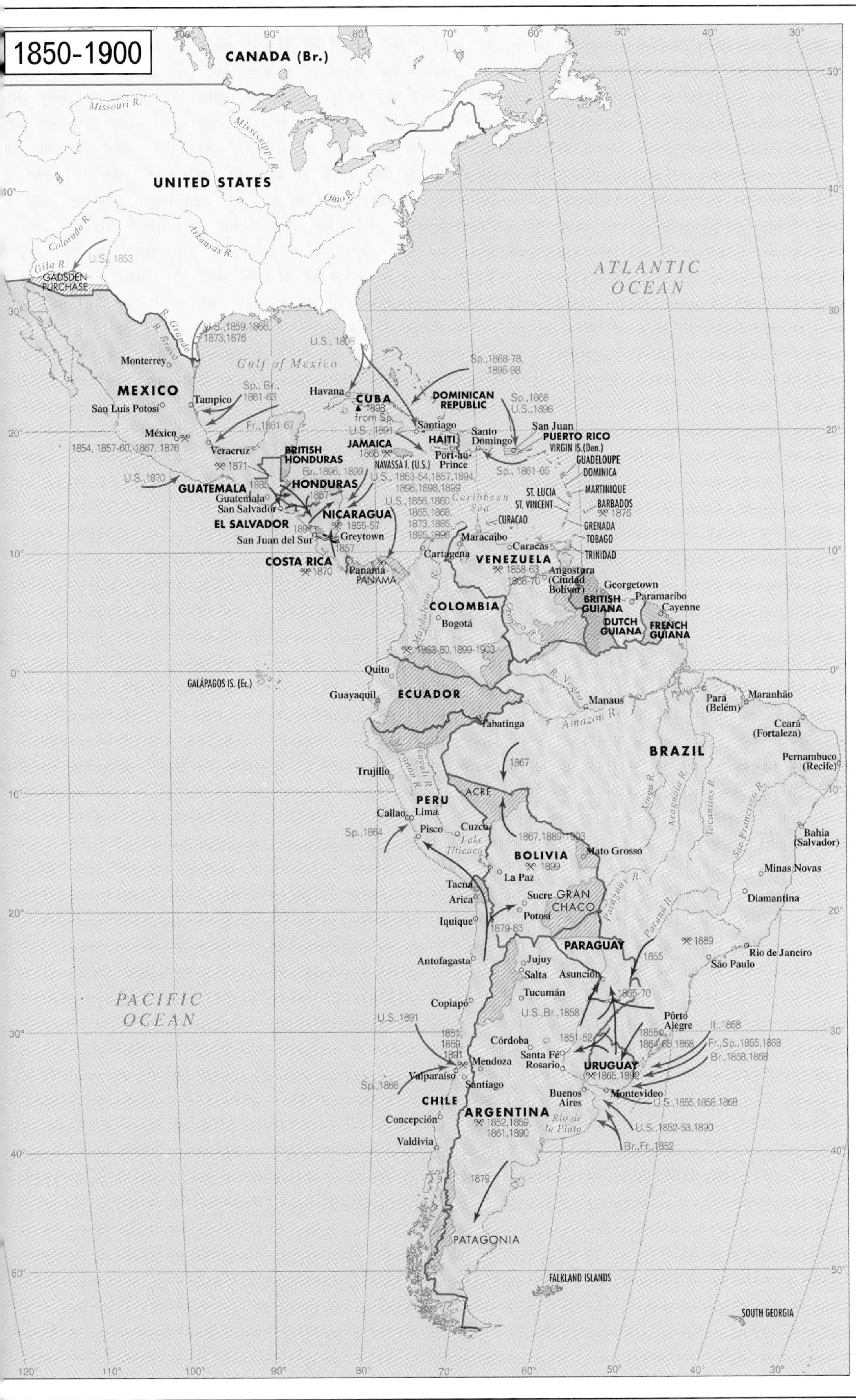
1850-1900
CANADA (Br.)
UNITED STATES
Missouri R.
Mississippi R.
Ohio R.
Arkansas R.
Colorado R.
Gila R.
GADSDEN PURCHASE
U.S., 1853
R. Grande
R. Bravo
U.S.,1859,1866, 1873,1876
ATLANTIC OCEAN
U.S., 1898
Gulf of Mexico
Sp.,1868-78, 1895-98
Monterrey
MEXICO
Tampico
Sp., Br., 1861-63
Havana
CUBA
1898 from Sp.
DOMINICAN REPUBLIC
Sp.,1868 U.S.,1898
San Luis Potosí
Fr.,1861-67
U.S., 1891
Santiago
San Juan
PUERTO RICO
México
1854, 1857-60, 1867, 1876
Veracruz
BRITISH HONDURAS
JAMAICA
1865
HAITI
Santo Domingo
Port-au-Prince
VIRGIN IS.(Den.)
GUADELOUPE
DOMINICA
1871
Br.,1896, 1899
NAVASSA I. (U.S.)
Sp., 1861-65
MARTINIQUE
U.S.,1870
GUATEMALA
1885
HONDURAS
U.S., 1853-54,1857,1894, 1896,1898,1899
ST. LUCIA
ST. VINCENT
BARBADOS
1876
Guatemala
San Salvador
1857
U.S.,1856,1860, 1865,1868, 1873,1885, 1895,1896
Caribbean Sea
CURAÇAO
EL SALVADOR
NICARAGUA
1855-57
GRENADA
San Juan del Sur
Greytown
Maracaibo
Caracas
TOBAGO
TRINIDAD
COSTA RICA
1870
Panamá
PANAMA
Cartagena
VENEZUELA
1858-63, 1868-70
Angostura (Ciudad Bolívar)
Georgetown
BRITISH GUIANA
Paramaribo
Cayenne
COLOMBIA
Bogotá
DUTCH GUIANA
FRENCH GUIANA
Magdalena R.
Orinoco R.
1863-80, 1899-1903
Quito
GALÁPAGOS IS. (Ec.)
ECUADOR
Guayaquil
R. Negro
Manaus
Pará (Belém)
Maranhão
Amazon R.
Tabatinga
Ceará (Fortaleza)
BRAZIL
1867
Pernambuco (Recife)
Trujillo
Marañón R.
Ucayali R.
ACRE
PERU
Callao
Lima
Xingu R.
Araguaia R.
Tocantins R.
São Francisco R.
Sp.,1864
Pisco
Cuzco
1867,1889-1903
Bahia (Salvador)
Lake Titicaca
BOLIVIA
Mato Grosso
1899
Minas Novas
La Paz
Tacna
Arica
Sucre
GRAN CHACO
Paraguay R.
Paraná R.
Diamantina
Potosí
Iquique
1879-83
PARAGUAY
1889
Rio de Janeiro
Antofagasta
Jujuy
1855
São Paulo
Salta
Asunción
PACIFIC OCEAN
Tucumán
1865-70
Copiapó
U.S.,Br.,1858
Pôrto Alegre
U.S.,1891
It.,1868
1851, 1859, 1891
Córdoba
1851-52
1855, 1864-65,1868
Fr.,Sp.,1855,1868
Br.,1858,1868
Mendoza
Santa Fé
Rosario
URUGUAY
1865,1892
Valparaíso
Santiago
Sp.,1866
Buenos Aires
Montevideo
U.S.,1855,1858,1868
CHILE
ARGENTINA
1852,1859, 1861,1890
Río de la Plata
U.S.,1852-53,1890
Concepción
Br.,Fr.,1852
Valdivia
1879
PATAGONIA
FALKLAND ISLANDS
SOUTH GEORGIA

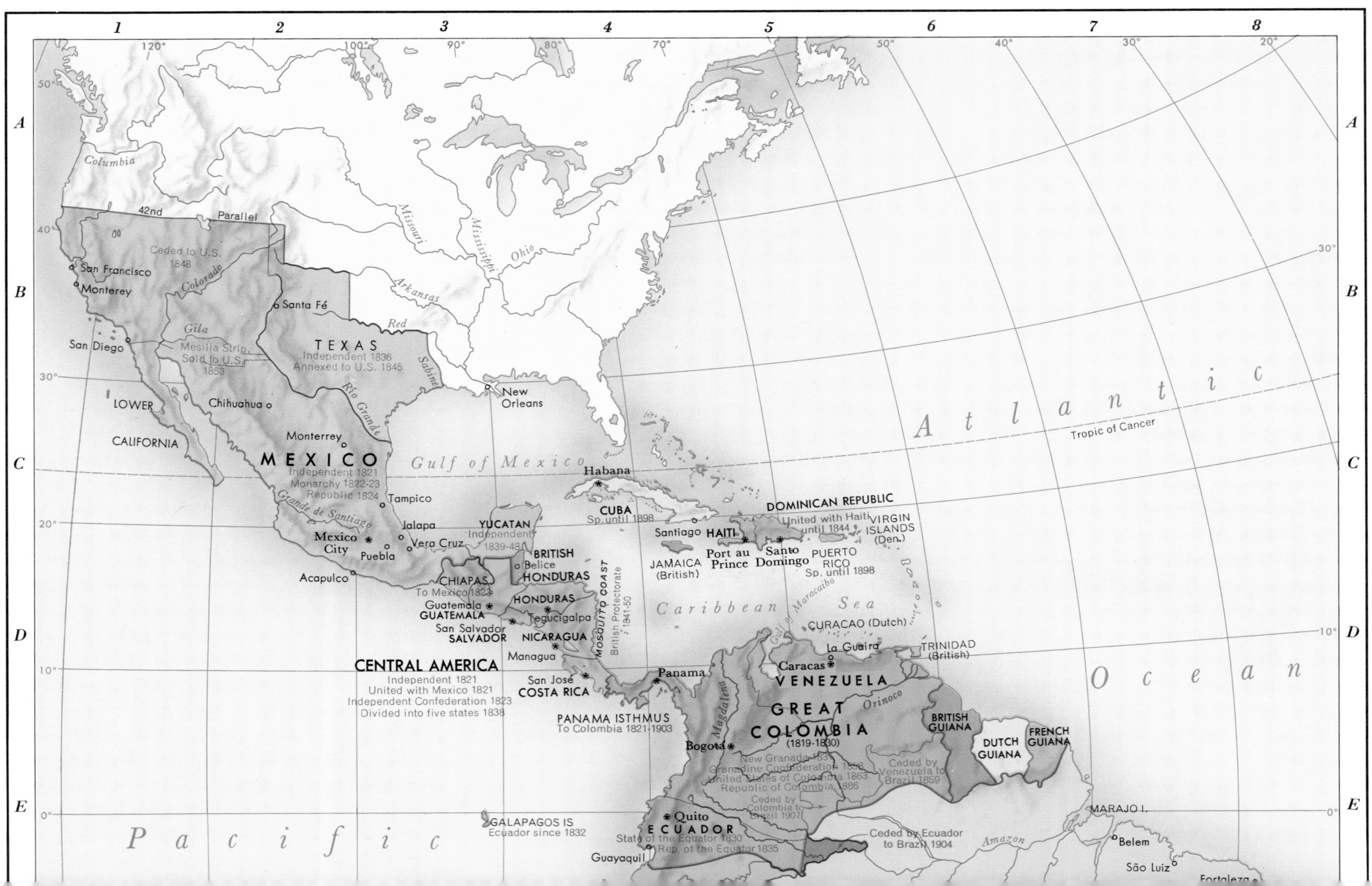
A t l a n t i c
O c e a n
P a c i f i c
Gulf of Mexico
Caribbean Sea
Tropic of Cancer
MEXICO
Independent 1821
Monarchy 1822-23
Republic 1824
TEXAS
Independent 1836
Annexed to U.S. 1845
Ceded to U.S. 1848
Mesilla Strip Sold to U.S. 1853
42nd Parallel
LOWER CALIFORNIA
CENTRAL AMERICA
Independent 1821
United with Mexico 1821
Independent Confederation 1823
Divided into five states 1838
CHIAPAS
To Mexico 1823
YUCATAN
Independent 1839-48
BRITISH HONDURAS
GUATEMALA
SALVADOR
HONDURAS
NICARAGUA
COSTA RICA
MOSQUITO COAST
British Protectorate 1841-50
PANAMA ISTHMUS
To Colombia 1821-1903
CUBA
Sp. until 1898
HAITI
DOMINICAN REPUBLIC
United with Haiti until 1844
PUERTO RICO
Sp. until 1898
VIRGIN ISLANDS (Den.)
JAMAICA (British)
CURACAO (Dutch)
TRINIDAD (British)
VENEZUELA
GREAT COLOMBIA
(1819-1830)
New Granada 1831
Granadine Confederation 1858
United States of Colombia 1863
Republic of Colombia 1886
Ceded by Colombia to Brazil 1907
Ceded by Venezuela to Brazil 1859
ECUADOR
State of the Equator 1830
Rep. of the Equator 1835
Ceded by Ecuador to Brazil 1904
GALAPAGOS IS
Ecuador since 1832
BRITISH GUIANA
DUTCH GUIANA
FRENCH GUIANA
MARAJO I.
San Francisco
Monterey
San Diego
Santa Fé
Chihuahua
Monterrey
Tampico
Jalapa
Vera Cruz
Mexico City
Puebla
Acapulco
New Orleans
Habana
Santiago
Port au Prince
Santo Domingo
Belice
Guatemala
San Salvador
Tegucigalpa
Managua
San José
Panama
Caracas
La Guaira
Bogotá
Quito
Guayaquil
Belem
São Luiz
Fortaleza
Columbia
Colorado
Gila
Rio Grande
Grande de Santiago
Red
Sabine
Arkansas
Missouri
Mississippi
Ohio
Magdalena
Orinoco
Amazon
Gulf of Maracaibo
1
2
3
4
5
6
7
8
A
B
C
D
E
120°
100°
90°
80°
70°
50°
40°
30°
20°
10°
0°

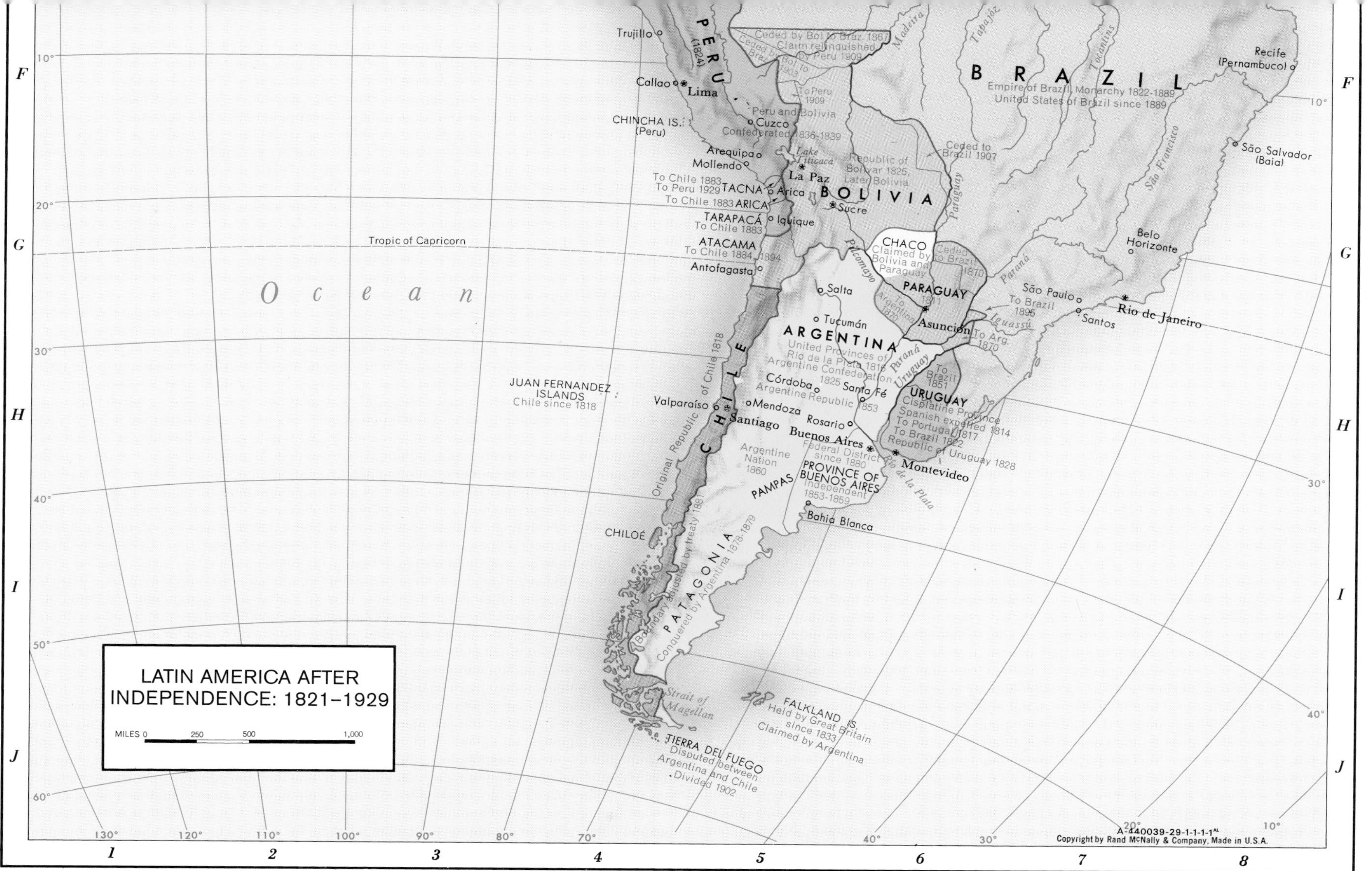

LATIN AMERICA AFTER INDEPENDENCE: 1821–1929
MILES 0 250 500 1,000
Ocean
Tropic of Capricorn
PERU (1824)
Trujillo
Callao
Lima
CHINCHA IS. (Peru)
Cuzco
Peru and Bolivia Confederated 1836-1839
Arequipa
Mollendo
To Chile 1883 To Peru 1929 TACNA
To Chile 1883 ARICA
Arica
TARAPACÁ To Chile 1883
Iquique
ATACAMA To Chile 1884, 1894
Antofagasta
Ceded by Bol to Braz. 1867 Claim relinquished by Peru 1909
Ceded by Bol to Braz. 1903
To Peru 1909
Lake Titicaca
La Paz
Republic of Bolivar 1825, Later Bolivia
BOLIVIA
Sucre
Ceded to Brazil 1907
BRAZIL
Empire of Brazil, Monarchy 1822-1889 United States of Brazil since 1889
Madeira
Tapajóz
Tocantins
São Francisco
Paraguay
Paraná
Recife (Pernambuco)
São Salvador (Baia)
Belo Horizonte
São Paulo
To Brazil 1895
Santos
Rio de Janeiro
Iguassú
CHACO Claimed by Bolivia and Paraguay
Ceded to Brazil 1870
PARAGUAY 1811
To Argentina 1870
Asunción
To Arg. 1870
Pilcomayo
Salta
Tucumán
ARGENTINA
United Provinces of Rio de la Plata 1816 Argentine Confederation 1825
Córdoba
Argentine Republic 1853
Santa Fé
Mendoza
Rosario
Buenos Aires
Federal District since 1880
PROVINCE OF BUENOS AIRES Independent 1853-1859
Argentine Nation 1860
PAMPAS
Bahia Blanca
Uruguay
To Brazil 1851
URUGUAY
Cisplatine Province Spanish expelled 1814 To Portugal 1817 To Brazil 1822 Republic of Uruguay 1828
Montevideo
Rio de la Plata
JUAN FERNANDEZ ISLANDS Chile since 1818
Valparaíso
Santiago
CHILE
Original Republic of Chile 1818
CHILOÉ
Boundary adjusted by treaty 1881
PATAGONIA
Conquered by Argentina 1878-1879
Strait of Magellan
FALKLAND IS. Held by Great Britain since 1833 Claimed by Argentina
TIERRA DEL FUEGO Disputed between Argentina and Chile Divided 1902
A-440039-29-1-1-1-1
Copyright by Rand McNally & Company, Made in U.S.A.

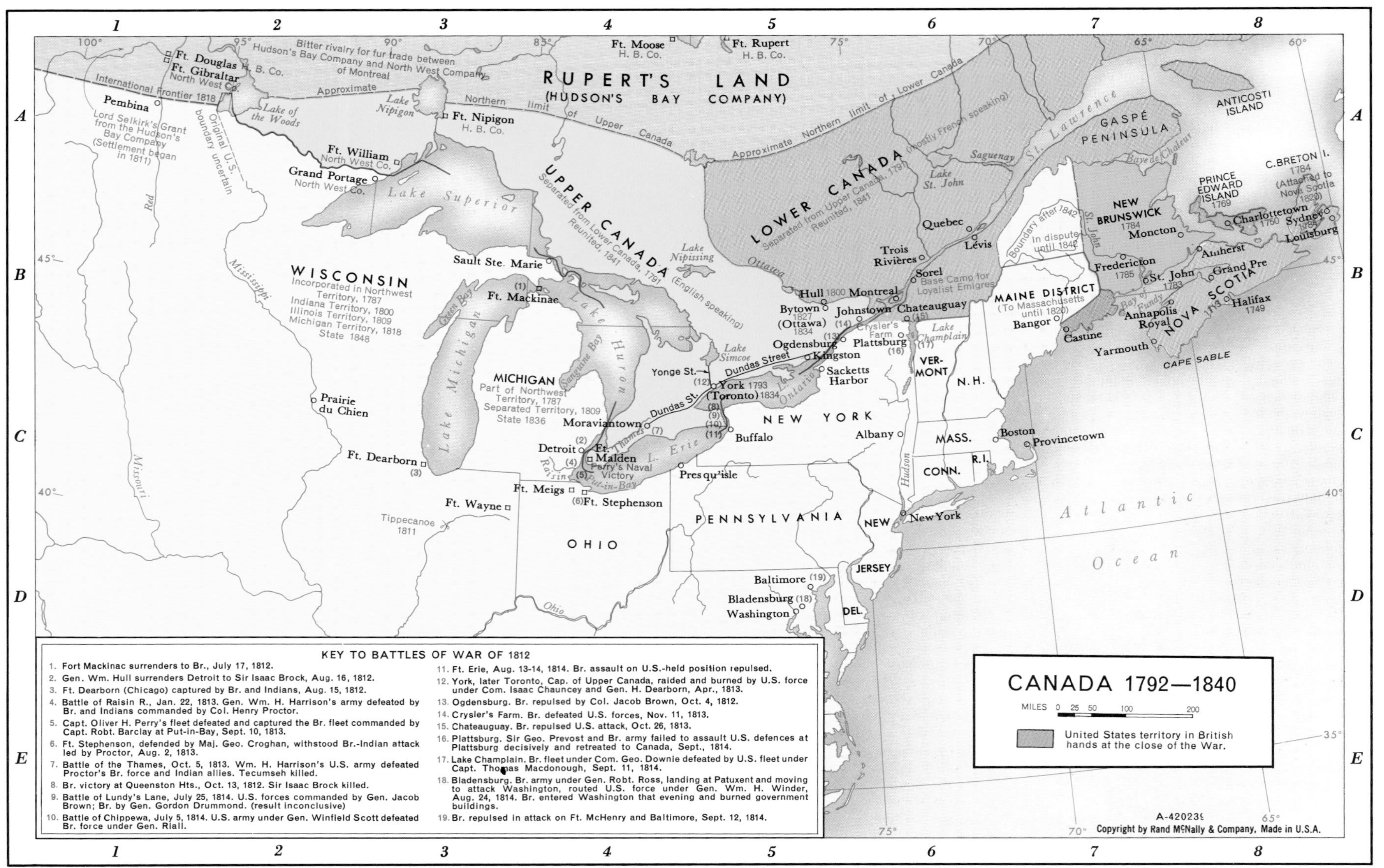
CANADA 1792—1840
MILES 0 25 50 100 200
United States territory in British hands at the close of the War.
KEY TO BATTLES OF WAR OF 1812
1. Fort Mackinac surrenders to Br., July 17, 1812.
2. Gen. Wm. Hull surrenders Detroit to Sir Isaac Brock, Aug. 16, 1812.
3. Ft. Dearborn (Chicago) captured by Br. and Indians, Aug. 15, 1812.
4. Battle of Raisin R., Jan. 22, 1813. Gen. Wm. H. Harrison's army defeated by Br. and Indians commanded by Col. Henry Proctor.
5. Capt. Oliver H. Perry's fleet defeated and captured the Br. fleet commanded by Capt. Robt. Barclay at Put-in-Bay, Sept. 10, 1813.
6. Ft. Stephenson, defended by Maj. Geo. Croghan, withstood Br.-Indian attack led by Proctor, Aug. 2, 1813.
7. Battle of the Thames, Oct. 5, 1813. Wm. H. Harrison's U.S. army defeated Proctor's Br. force and Indian allies. Tecumseh killed.
8. Br. victory at Queenston Hts., Oct. 13, 1812. Sir Isaac Brock killed.
9. Battle of Lundy's Lane, July 25, 1814. U.S. forces commanded by Gen. Jacob Brown; Br. by Gen. Gordon Drummond. (result inconclusive)
10. Battle of Chippewa, July 5, 1814. U.S. army under Gen. Winfield Scott defeated Br. force under Gen. Riall.
11. Ft. Erie, Aug. 13-14, 1814. Br. assault on U.S.-held position repulsed.
12. York, later Toronto, Cap. of Upper Canada, raided and burned by U.S. force under Com. Isaac Chauncey and Gen. H. Dearborn, Apr., 1813.
13. Ogdensburg. Br. repulsed by Col. Jacob Brown, Oct. 4, 1812.
14. Crysler's Farm. Br. defeated U.S. forces, Nov. 11, 1813.
15. Chateauguay. Br. repulsed U.S. attack, Oct. 26, 1813.
16. Plattsburg. Sir Geo. Prevost and Br. army failed to assault U.S. defences at Plattsburg decisively and retreated to Canada, Sept., 1814.
17. Lake Champlain. Br. fleet under Com. Geo. Downie defeated by U.S. fleet under Capt. Thomas Macdonough, Sept. 11, 1814.
18. Bladensburg. Br. army under Gen. Robt. Ross, landing at Patuxent and moving to attack Washington, routed U.S. force under Gen. Wm. H. Winder, Aug. 24, 1814. Br. entered Washington that evening and burned government buildings.
19. Br. repulsed in attack on Ft. McHenry and Baltimore, Sept. 12, 1814.
RUPERT'S LAND
(HUDSON'S BAY COMPANY)
Bitter rivalry for fur trade between Hudson's Bay Company and North West Company of Montreal
UPPER CANADA
Separated from Lower Canada, 1791
Reunited, 1841
(English speaking)
LOWER CANADA
Separated from Upper Canada, 1791
Reunited, 1841
(Mostly French speaking)
Approximate Northern limit of Upper Canada
Approximate Northern limit of Lower Canada
International Frontier 1818
Original U.S. boundary uncertain
Lord Selkirk's Grant from the Hudson's Bay Company (Settlement began in 1811)
WISCONSIN
Incorporated in Northwest Territory, 1787
Indiana Territory, 1800
Illinois Territory, 1809
Michigan Territory, 1818
State 1848
MICHIGAN
Part of Northwest Territory, 1787
Separated Territory, 1809
State 1836
OHIO
PENNSYLVANIA
NEW YORK
NEW JERSEY
DEL.
VER-MONT
N.H.
MASS.
CONN.
R.I.
MAINE DISTRICT
(To Massachusetts until 1820)
In dispute until 1842
Boundary after 1842
NEW BRUNSWICK 1784
NOVA SCOTIA 1713
PRINCE EDWARD ISLAND 1769
C.BRETON I. 1784 (Attached to Nova Scotia 1820)
GASPÉ PENINSULA
ANTICOSTI ISLAND
CAPE SABLE
Atlantic Ocean
Ft. Moose H. B. Co.
Ft. Rupert H. B. Co.
Ft. Nipigon H. B. Co.
Ft. Douglas
Ft. Gibraltar North West Co.
Pembina
Ft. William North West Co.
Grand Portage North West Co.
Sault Ste. Marie
Ft. Mackinac
Prairie du Chien
Ft. Dearborn
Ft. Wayne
Tippecanoe 1811
Ft. Meigs
Ft. Stephenson
Detroit
Ft. Malden
Perry's Naval Victory
Moraviantown
Dundas St.
Yonge St.
Dundas Street
York 1793 (Toronto) 1834
Buffalo
Pres qu'isle
Kingston
Sacketts Harbor
Ogdensburg
Bytown 1827 (Ottawa) 1834
Hull 1800
Montreal
Johnstown
Chateauguay
Crysler's Farm
Plattsburg
Sorel
Base Camp for Loyalist Emigres
Trois Rivières
Quebec
Lévis
Albany
New York
Boston
Provincetown
Bangor
Castine
Fredericton 1785
St. John 1783
Moncton
Amherst
Grand Pre
Annapolis Royal
Yarmouth
Halifax 1749
Charlottetown 1750
Sydney 1784
Louisburg
Baltimore
Bladensburg
Washington
A-42023
Copyright by Rand McNally & Company, Made in U.S.A.

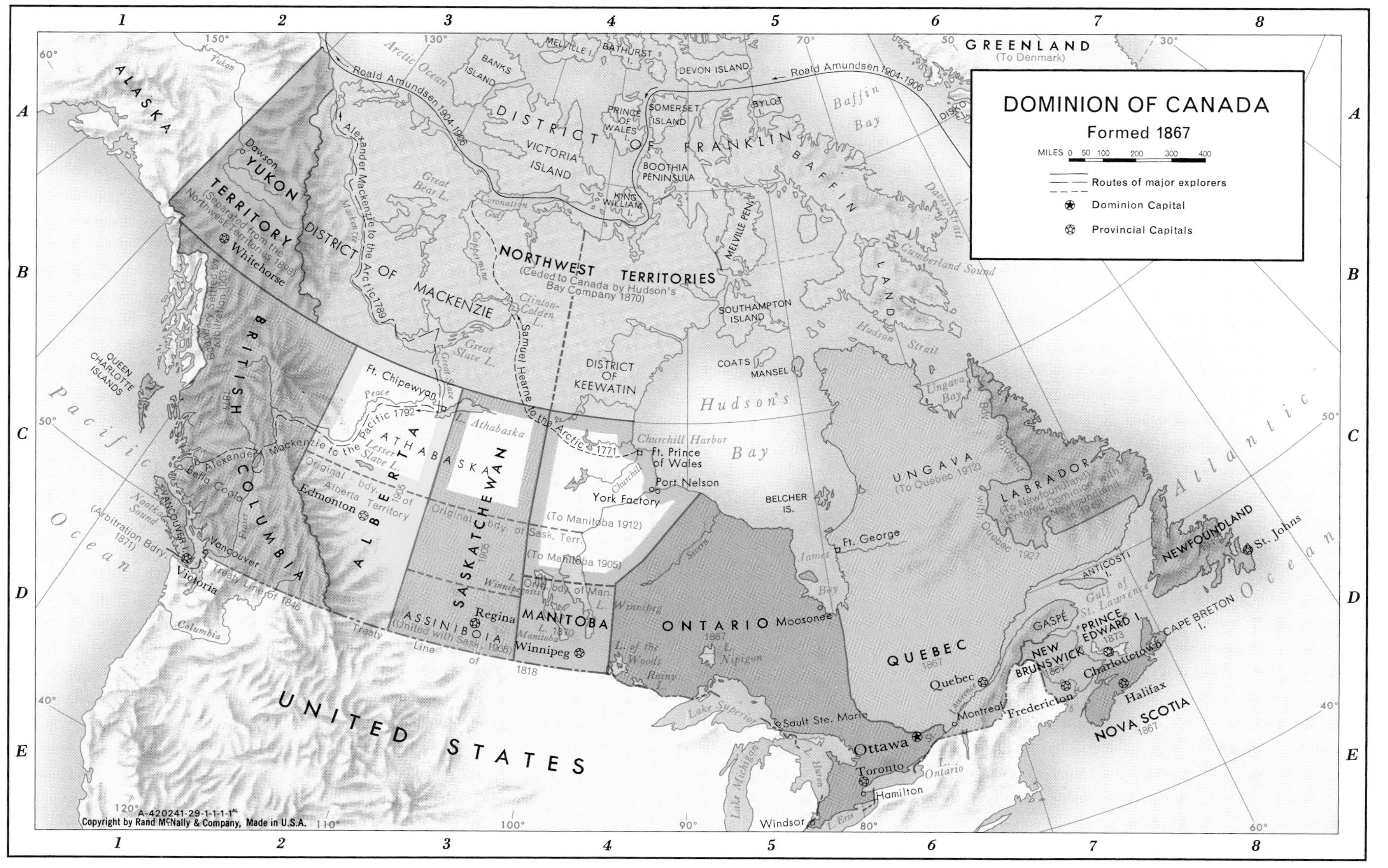
DOMINION OF CANADA
Formed 1867
MILES 0 50 100 200 300 400
Routes of major explorers
Dominion Capital
Provincial Capitals
GREENLAND
(To Denmark)
ALASKA
YUKON
TERRITORY
(Separated from the Northwest Territories 1898)
Dawson
Whitehorse
Boundary Settled by Arbitration 1903
BRITISH COLUMBIA
1871
QUEEN CHARLOTTE ISLANDS
VANCOUVER I.
Vancouver
Victoria
Bella Coola
Alexander Mackenzie to the Pacific 1792
Alexander Mackenzie to the Arctic 1789
Roald Amundsen 1904-1906
Samuel Hearne to the Arctic 1771
DISTRICT OF MACKENZIE
DISTRICT OF FRANKLIN
DISTRICT OF KEEWATIN
NORTHWEST TERRITORIES
(Ceded to Canada by Hudson's Bay Company 1870)
BANKS ISLAND
MELVILLE I.
BATHURST I.
DEVON ISLAND
BYLOT I.
PRINCE OF WALES I.
SOMERSET ISLAND
BOOTHIA PENINSULA
KING WILLIAM I.
VICTORIA ISLAND
MELVILLE PEN.
BAFFIN LAND
SOUTHAMPTON ISLAND
COATS I.
MANSEL I.
BELCHER IS.
Baffin Bay
Davis Strait
Cumberland Sound
Hudson Strait
Ungava Bay
Hudson's Bay
James Bay
Great Bear L.
Great Slave L.
Coronation Gulf
Coppermine
Clinton-Colden L.
L. Athabaska
Lesser Slave L.
Peace
Ft. Chipewyan
ALBERTA
Edmonton
Original bdy. of Alberta Territory
1905
ATHABASKA
SASKATCHEWAN
1905
Original bdy. of Sask. Terr.
ASSINIBOIA
(United with Sask. 1905)
Regina
(To Manitoba 1912)
(To Manitoba 1905)
MANITOBA
L. Manitoba
1870
Orig. bdy. of Man.
Winnipeg
L. Winnipegosis
L. Winnipeg
Treaty Line of 1818
Treaty Line of 1846
(Arbitration Bdry. 1871)
Churchill Harbor
Ft. Prince of Wales
Churchill
Port Nelson
York Factory
Severn
ONTARIO
1867
L. Nipigon
L. of the Woods
Rainy L.
Moosonee
Ft. George
Sault Ste. Marie
Lake Superior
Lake Michigan
L. Huron
L. Erie
L. Ontario
Ottawa
Toronto
Hamilton
Windsor
UNGAVA
(To Quebec 1912)
LABRADOR
(To Newfoundland)
(Entered Dominion with Newfoundland in 1949)
Bdy. adjusted with Quebec 1927
QUEBEC
1867
Quebec
Montreal
St. Lawrence
GASPÉ
ANTICOSTI I.
Gulf of St. Lawrence
NEW BRUNSWICK
1867
Fredericton
PRINCE EDWARD I.
1873
Charlottetown
CAPE BRETON I.
NOVA SCOTIA
1867
Halifax
NEWFOUNDLAND
1949
St. Johns
Pacific Ocean
Atlantic Ocean
Arctic Ocean
Nootka Sound
Columbia
Fraser
Yukon
Mackenzie
UNITED STATES
A-420241-29-1-1-1
Copyright by Rand McNally & Company, Made in U.S.A.

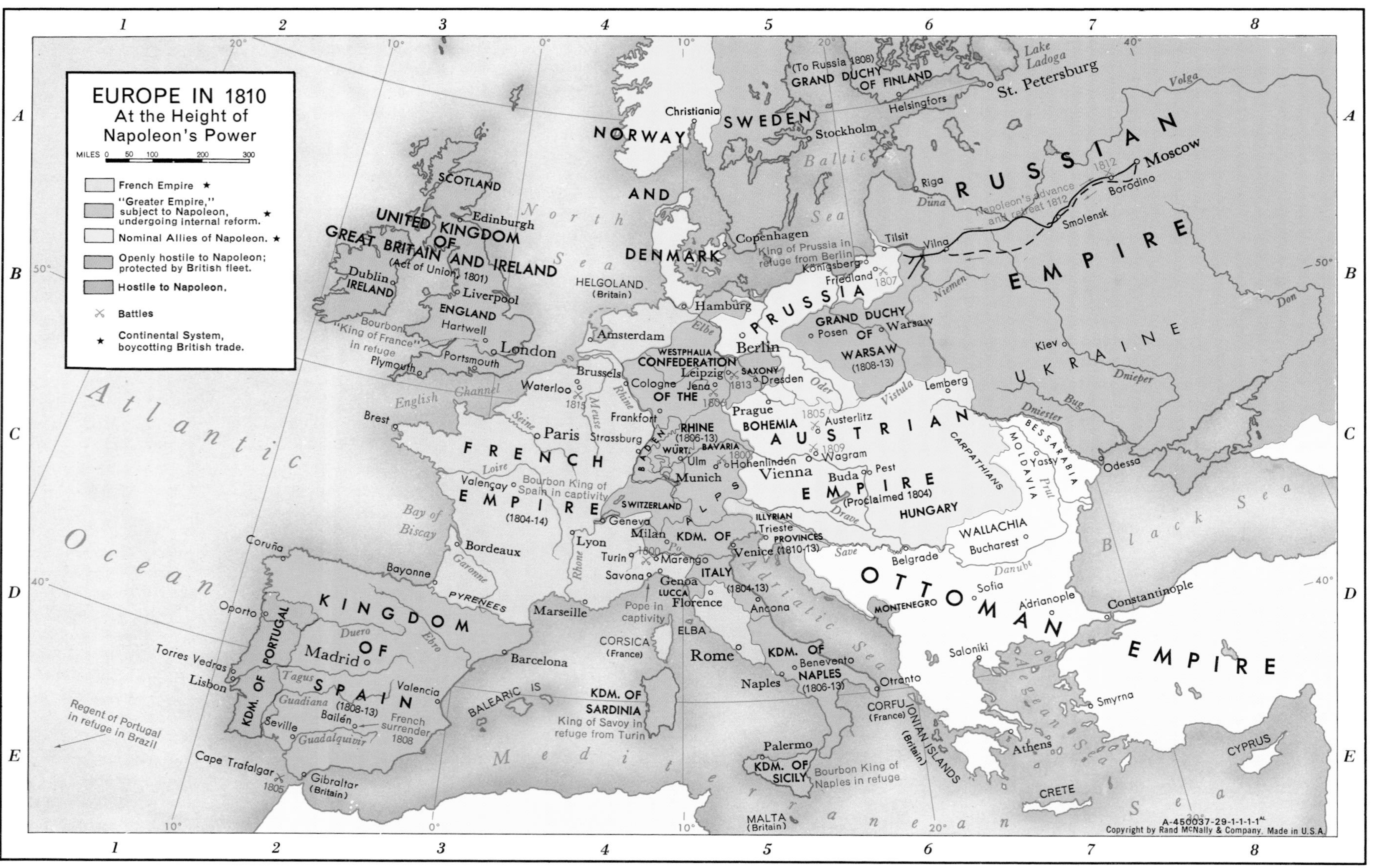
EUROPE IN 1810
At the Height of
Napoleon's Power
MILES 0 50 100 200 300
French Empire ★
"Greater Empire," subject to Napoleon, undergoing internal reform. ★
Nominal Allies of Napoleon. ★
Openly hostile to Napoleon; protected by British fleet.
Hostile to Napoleon.
Battles
Continental System, boycotting British trade.
NORWAY AND DENMARK
SWEDEN
(To Russia 1808) GRAND DUCHY OF FINLAND
RUSSIAN EMPIRE
UKRAINE
UNITED KINGDOM OF GREAT BRITAIN AND IRELAND (Act of Union, 1801)
SCOTLAND
ENGLAND
IRELAND
FRENCH EMPIRE (1804-14)
CONFEDERATION OF THE RHINE (1806-13)
PRUSSIA
GRAND DUCHY OF WARSAW (1808-13)
AUSTRIAN EMPIRE (Proclaimed 1804)
HUNGARY
BOHEMIA
ILLYRIAN PROVINCES (1810-13)
KDM. OF ITALY (1804-13)
SWITZERLAND
KINGDOM OF SPAIN (1808-13)
KDM. OF PORTUGAL
KDM. OF NAPLES (1806-13)
KDM. OF SARDINIA
KDM. OF SICILY
OTTOMAN EMPIRE
WALLACHIA
MOLDAVIA
BESSARABIA
MONTENEGRO
IONIAN ISLANDS (Britain)
CORFU (France)
CORSICA (France)
HELGOLAND (Britain)
MALTA (Britain)
Gibraltar (Britain)
Napoleon's advance and retreat 1812
King of Prussia in refuge from Berlin
Bourbon "King of France" in refuge
Bourbon King of Spain in captivity
Pope in captivity
King of Savoy in refuge from Turin
Bourbon King of Naples in refuge
Regent of Portugal in refuge in Brazil
French surrender 1808
Atlantic Ocean
North Sea
Baltic Sea
Black Sea
Mediterranean Sea
Adriatic Sea
Aegean Sea
Bay of Biscay
English Channel
A-450037-29-1-1-1-1
Copyright by Rand McNally & Company. Made in U.S.A.

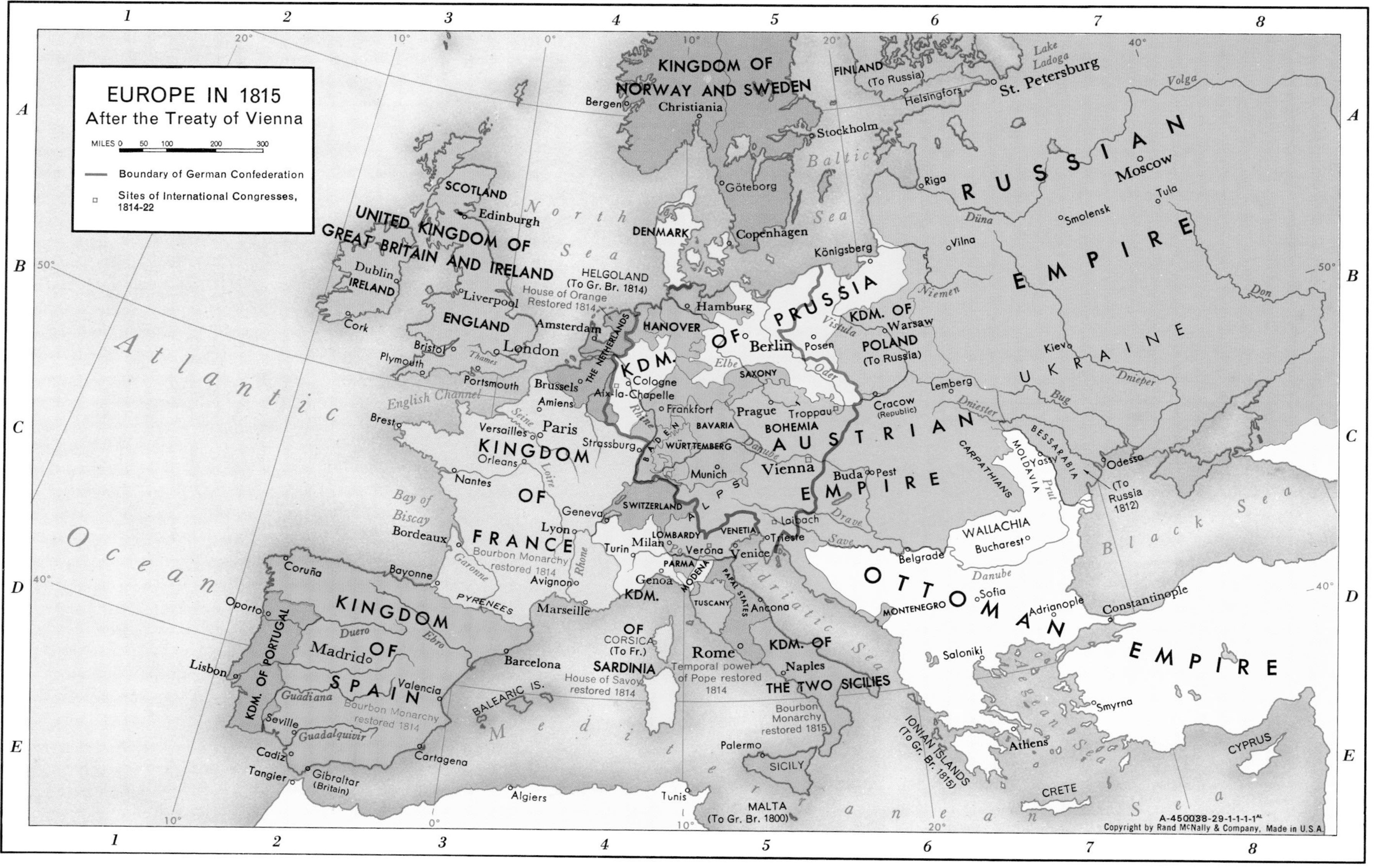
EUROPE IN 1815
After the Treaty of Vienna
MILES 0 50 100 200 300
Boundary of German Confederation
Sites of International Congresses, 1814-22
KINGDOM OF NORWAY AND SWEDEN
Bergen
Christiania
Stockholm
Göteborg
Copenhagen
DENMARK
FINLAND (To Russia)
Helsingfors
St. Petersburg
Lake Ladoga
Volga
RUSSIAN EMPIRE
Moscow
Tula
Smolensk
Riga
Düna
Vilna
Niemen
Don
UKRAINE
Kiev
Dnieper
Bug
Dniester
Lemberg
Königsberg
Baltic Sea
North Sea
SCOTLAND
Edinburgh
UNITED KINGDOM OF GREAT BRITAIN AND IRELAND
Dublin
IRELAND
Cork
Liverpool
ENGLAND
London
Thames
Bristol
Plymouth
Portsmouth
English Channel
HELGOLAND (To Gr. Br. 1814)
House of Orange Restored 1814
Amsterdam
THE NETHERLANDS
Brussels
Amiens
HANOVER
Hamburg
PRUSSIA
KDM. OF PRUSSIA
Berlin
Elbe
Posen
Vistula
Oder
KDM. OF POLAND (To Russia)
Warsaw
SAXONY
Cologne
Aix-la-Chapelle
Frankfort
Rhine
BADEN
BAVARIA
WÜRTTEMBERG
Prague
Troppau
BOHEMIA
Cracow (Republic)
AUSTRIAN EMPIRE
Vienna
Danube
Munich
ALPS
Buda
Pest
CARPATHIANS
MOLDAVIA
Yassy
Prut
BESSARABIA
Odessa
(To Russia 1812)
Black Sea
WALLACHIA
Bucharest
Drave
Save
Laibach
Trieste
Belgrade
OTTOMAN EMPIRE
Sofia
MONTENEGRO
Adrianople
Constantinople
Saloniki
Smyrna
Athens
Aegean Sea
CRETE
CYPRUS
IONIAN ISLANDS (To Gr. Br. 1815)
Atlantic Ocean
Brest
Versailles
Paris
Seine
KINGDOM OF FRANCE
Orleans
Loire
Nantes
Strassburg
Bay of Biscay
Bordeaux
Garonne
Bourbon Monarchy restored 1814
Lyon
Geneva
Rhone
Avignon
Marseille
PYRENEES
SWITZERLAND
LOMBARDY
Milan
Turin
VENETIA
Verona
Venice
PARMA
MODENA
Genoa
KDM. OF SARDINIA
CORSICA (To Fr.)
House of Savoy restored 1814
TUSCANY
PAPAL STATES
Ancona
Adriatic Sea
Rome
Temporal power of Pope restored 1814
KDM. OF THE TWO SICILIES
Naples
Bourbon Monarchy restored 1815
Palermo
SICILY
MALTA (To Gr. Br. 1800)
Tunis
Algiers
Mediterranean Sea
BALEARIC IS.
Barcelona
KINGDOM OF SPAIN
Coruña
Bayonne
Ebro
Duero
Madrid
Valencia
Guadiana
Guadalquivir
Seville
Cadiz
Gibraltar (Britain)
Tangier
Cartagena
KDM. OF PORTUGAL
Oporto
Lisbon
A-450038-29-1-1-1-1
Copyright by Rand McNally & Company, Made in U.S.A.

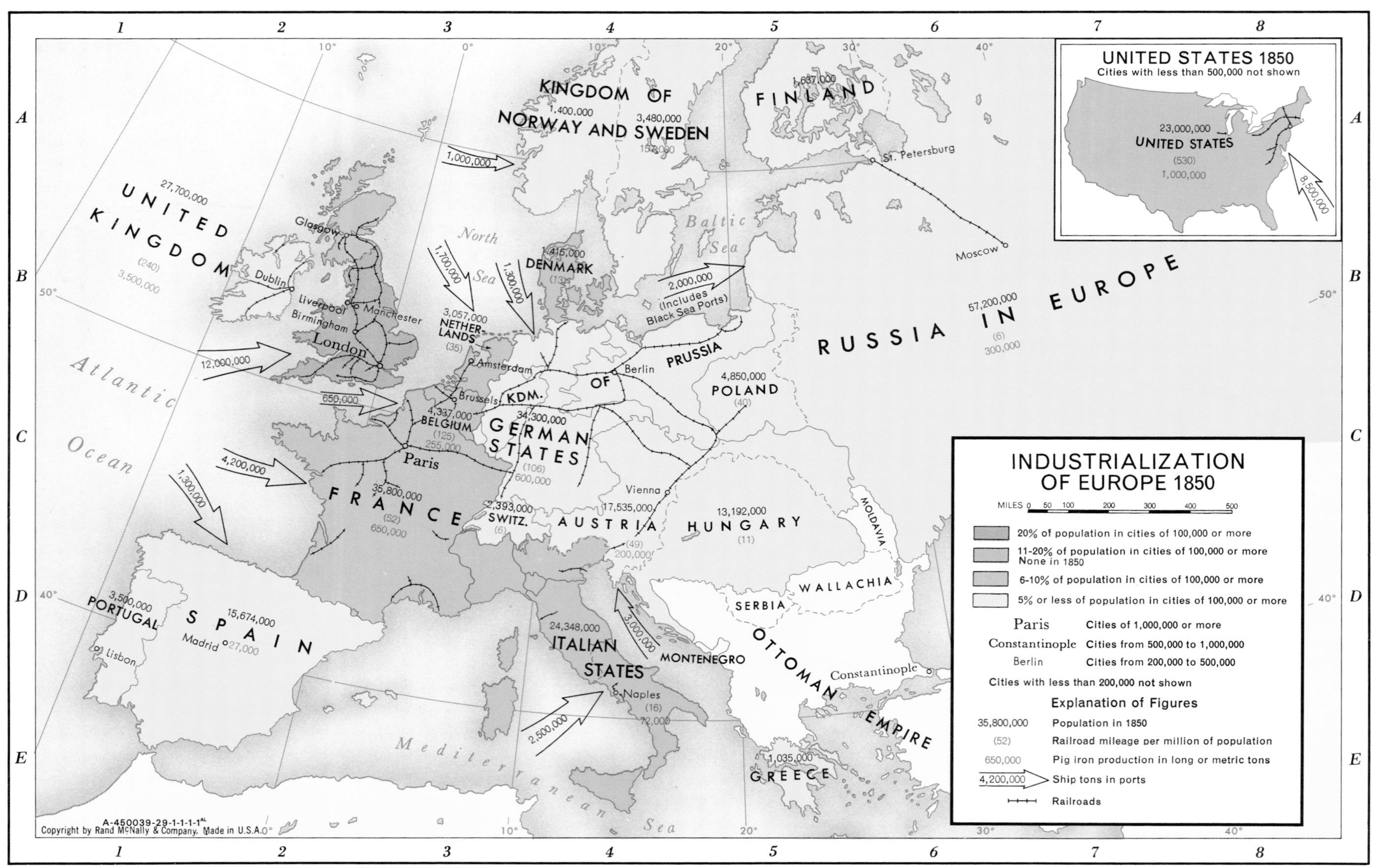

INDUSTRIALIZATION OF EUROPE 1850
MILES 0 50 100 200 300 400 500
20% of population in cities of 100,000 or more
11-20% of population in cities of 100,000 or more
None in 1850
6-10% of population in cities of 100,000 or more
5% or less of population in cities of 100,000 or more
Paris Cities of 1,000,000 or more
Constantinople Cities from 500,000 to 1,000,000
Berlin Cities from 200,000 to 500,000
Cities with less than 200,000 not shown
Explanation of Figures
35,800,000 Population in 1850
(52) Railroad mileage per million of population
650,000 Pig iron production in long or metric tons
4,200,000 Ship tons in ports
Railroads
UNITED STATES 1850
Cities with less than 500,000 not shown
23,000,000
UNITED STATES
(530)
1,000,000
8,500,000
UNITED KINGDOM
27,700,000
(240)
3,500,000
Glasgow
Dublin
Liverpool
Manchester
Birmingham
London
12,000,000
650,000
KINGDOM OF NORWAY AND SWEDEN
1,400,000
3,480,000
1,000,000
FINLAND
1,637,000
St. Petersburg
Moscow
RUSSIA IN EUROPE
57,200,000
(6)
300,000
DENMARK
1,415,000
North Sea
Baltic Sea
1,700,000
1,300,000
2,000,000
(Includes Black Sea Ports)
NETHERLANDS
3,057,000
(35)
Amsterdam
Brussels
BELGIUM
4,337,000
(125)
255,000
KDM. OF PRUSSIA
Berlin
GERMAN STATES
34,300,000
(106)
600,000
POLAND
4,850,000
(40)
Paris
FRANCE
35,800,000
(52)
650,000
4,200,000
1,300,000
SWITZ.
2,393,000
(6)
AUSTRIA
17,535,000
(49)
200,000
Vienna
HUNGARY
13,192,000
(11)
MOLDAVIA
WALLACHIA
SERBIA
MONTENEGRO
OTTOMAN EMPIRE
Constantinople
GREECE
1,035,000
ITALIAN STATES
24,348,000
Naples
(16)
72,000
3,000,000
2,500,000
PORTUGAL
3,500,000
Lisbon
SPAIN
15,674,000
Madrid
27,000
Atlantic Ocean
Mediterranean Sea
A-450039-29-1-1-1-1
Copyright by Rand McNally & Company. Made in U.S.A.

INDUSTRIALIZATION OF EUROPE 1910
MILES 0 50 100 200 300 400 500
20% of population in cities of 100,000 or more
11-20% of population in cities of 100,000 or more
6-10% of population in cities of 100,000 or more
5% or less of population in cities of 100,000 or more
Paris Cities of 1,000,000 or more
Lyon Cities from 500,000 to 1,000,000
Genoa Cities from 200,000 to 500,000
Cities with less than 200,000 not shown
Explanation of Figures
39,600,000 Population in 1910
(790) Railroad mileage per million of population
4,000,000 Pig iron production in long or metric tons
61,362,000 Ship tons in ports
UNITED STATES 1910
Cities with less than 500,000 not shown
92,000,000
UNITED STATES
(2720)
27,700,000
64,750,000
UNITED KINGDOM
45,800,000
(530)
10,200,000
NORWAY
2,400,000
(810)
SWEDEN
5,500,000
(1580)
604,000
FINLAND
3,100,000
(730)
DENMARK
2,800,000
(770)
NETHER-LANDS
5,900,000
(330)
BELGIUM
7,424,000
(730)
1,850,000
GERMANY
64,900,000
(600)
13,100,000
FRANCE
39,600,000
(790)
4,000,000
SWITZ.
3,753,000
(770)
AUSTRIA-HUNGARY
28,600,000
(490)
1,500,000
20,900,000
(620)
502,000
POLAND
12,100,000
(320)
RUSSIA IN EUROPE
119,000,000
(240)
3,040,000
SPAIN
19,200,000
(440)
370,000
PORTUGAL
5,960,000
(330)
ITALY
34,700,000
(310)
350,000
GREECE
2,631,000
(370)
RUMANIA
BULGARIA
SERBIA
BOSNIA
MONTENEGRO
OTTOMAN EMPIRE
10,245,000
30,848,000
49,460,000
27,814,000
(Includes Black Sea Ports)
138,909,000
31,803,000
61,362,000
41,403,000
7,609,000
51,958,000
Glasgow
Edinburgh
Belfast
Dublin
Newcastle
Bradford
Leeds
Hull
Liverpool
Manchester
Stoke
Sheffield
Birmingham
Nottingham
Leicester
Bristol
London
Portsmouth
Christiania
Stockholm
St. Petersburg
Riga
Moscow
Kiev
Kharkov
Odessa
Copenhagen
Kiel
Hamburg
Bremen
Amsterdam
The Hague
Rotterdam
Antwerp
Brussels
Lille
Düssel-dorf
Duisburg
Essen
Dortmund
Wuppertal
Cologne
Hanover
Berlin
Magdeburg
Stettin
Königsberg
Warsaw
Lodz
Leipzig
Dresden
Chemnitz
Breslau
Frankfurt
Prague
Lemberg
Nuremberg
Stuttgart
Munich
Vienna
Budapest
Bucharest
Trieste
Paris
Lyon
Bordeaux
Marseille
Turin
Milan
Genoa
Florence
Rome
Naples
Palermo
Catania
Madrid
Barcelona
Valencia
Lisbon
Constantinople
Smyrna
Atlantic Ocean
North Sea
Baltic Sea
Mediterranean Sea
A -450079-29-1-1-1-1AL
Copyright by Rand McNally & Company, Made in U.S.A.

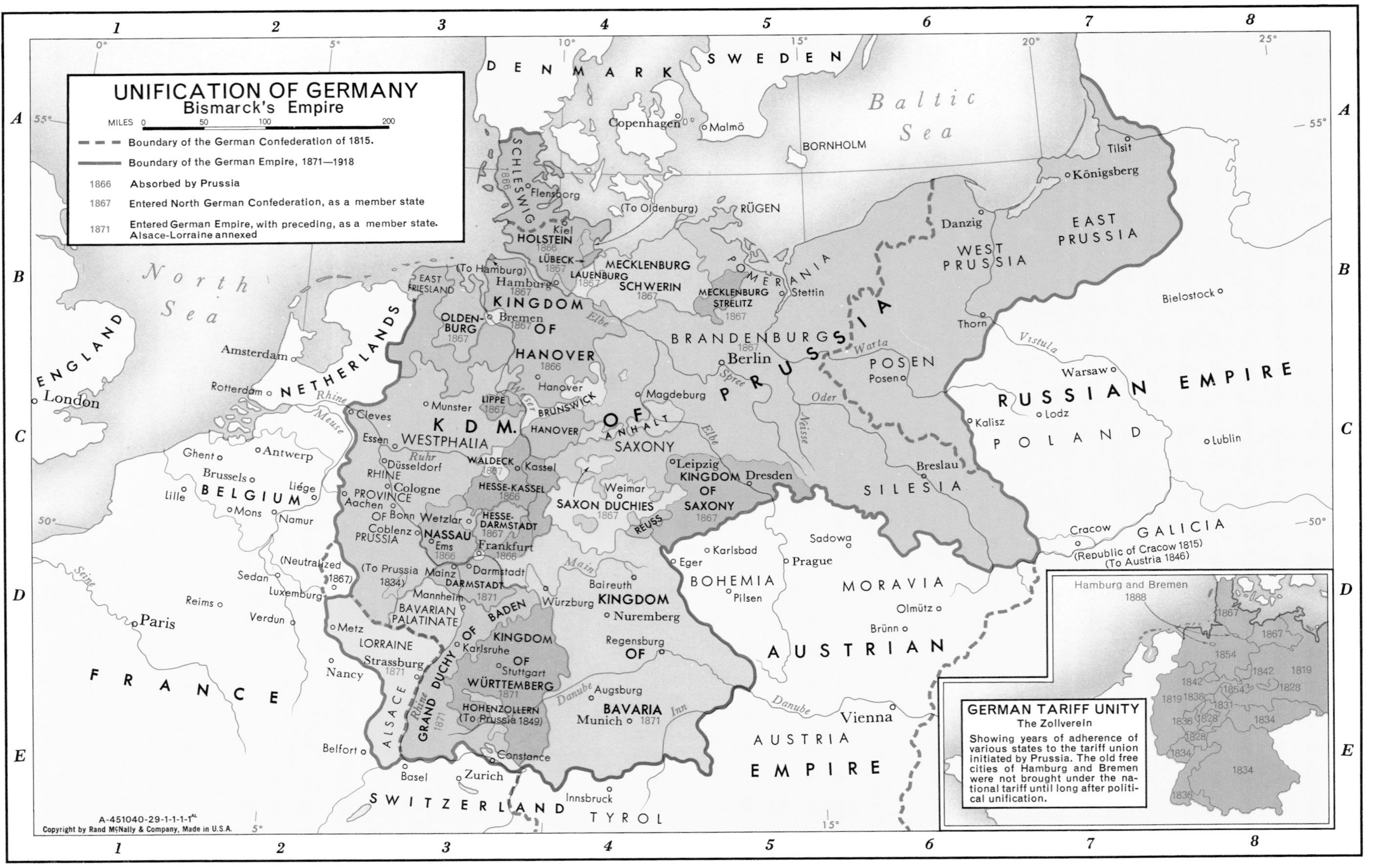
UNIFICATION OF GERMANY
Bismarck's Empire
MILES 0 50 100 200
Boundary of the German Confederation of 1815.
Boundary of the German Empire, 1871—1918
1866 Absorbed by Prussia
1867 Entered North German Confederation, as a member state
1871 Entered German Empire, with preceding, as a member state. Alsace-Lorraine annexed
DENMARK
SWEDEN
Baltic Sea
North Sea
BORNHOLM
RÜGEN
Copenhagen
Malmö
(To Oldenburg)
SCHLESWIG 1866
Flensborg
Kiel
HOLSTEIN 1866
LÜBECK 1867
LAUENBURG 1867
MECKLENBURG SCHWERIN 1867
MECKLENBURG STRELITZ 1867
POMERANIA
Stettin
Danzig
WEST PRUSSIA
EAST PRUSSIA
Königsberg
Tilsit
Thorn
Bielostock
(To Hamburg)
Hamburg 1867
EAST FRIESLAND
OLDEN-BURG 1867
Bremen 1867
KINGDOM OF HANOVER 1866
Hanover
Elbe
BRANDENBURG 1867
Berlin
Spree
PRUSSIA
POSEN
Posen
Warta
Oder
Neisse
Vistula
Warsaw
RUSSIAN EMPIRE
Kalisz
Lodz
POLAND
Lublin
ENGLAND
London
Amsterdam
Rotterdam
NETHERLANDS
Rhine
Meuse
Cleves
Munster
LIPPE 1867
BRUNSWICK
HANOVER
Magdeburg
KDM. OF SAXONY
ANHALT
Essen
WESTPHALIA
Ruhr
Düsseldorf
RHINE PROVINCE OF PRUSSIA
Cologne
Aachen
Bonn
Wetzlar
Coblenz
WALDECK 1867
Kassel
HESSE-KASSEL 1866
HESSE-DARMSTADT 1867
NASSAU
Ems 1866
Frankfurt 1866
Weimar
SAXON DUCHIES 1867
Leipzig
KINGDOM OF SAXONY 1867
Dresden
REUSS
Breslau
SILESIA
Ghent
Antwerp
Brussels
Liége
Lille
BELGIUM
Mons
Namur
(Neutralized 1867)
Luxemburg
(To Prussia 1834)
Mainz
Darmstadt
DARMSTADT 1871
Main
Mannheim
BAVARIAN PALATINATE
Sedan
Reims
Verdun
Paris
Seine
FRANCE
Metz
LORRAINE
Strassburg 1871
Nancy
ALSACE
Belfort
GRAND DUCHY OF BADEN 1871
Karlsruhe
KINGDOM OF WÜRTTEMBERG 1871
Stuttgart
HOHENZOLLERN (To Prussia 1849)
Würzburg
Baireuth
KINGDOM OF BAVARIA 1871
Nuremberg
Regensburg
Danube
Augsburg
Munich
Inn
Constance
Basel
Zurich
SWITZERLAND
Innsbruck
TYROL
Karlsbad
Eger
BOHEMIA
Pilsen
Prague
Sadowa
MORAVIA
Olmütz
Brünn
AUSTRIAN
Vienna
AUSTRIA
EMPIRE
Cracow
GALICIA
(Republic of Cracow 1815) (To Austria 1846)
Hamburg and Bremen 1888
GERMAN TARIFF UNITY
The Zollverein
Showing years of adherence of various states to the tariff union initiated by Prussia. The old free cities of Hamburg and Bremen were not brought under the national tariff until long after political unification.
A-451040-29-1-1-1
Copyright by Rand McNally & Company, Made in U.S.A.

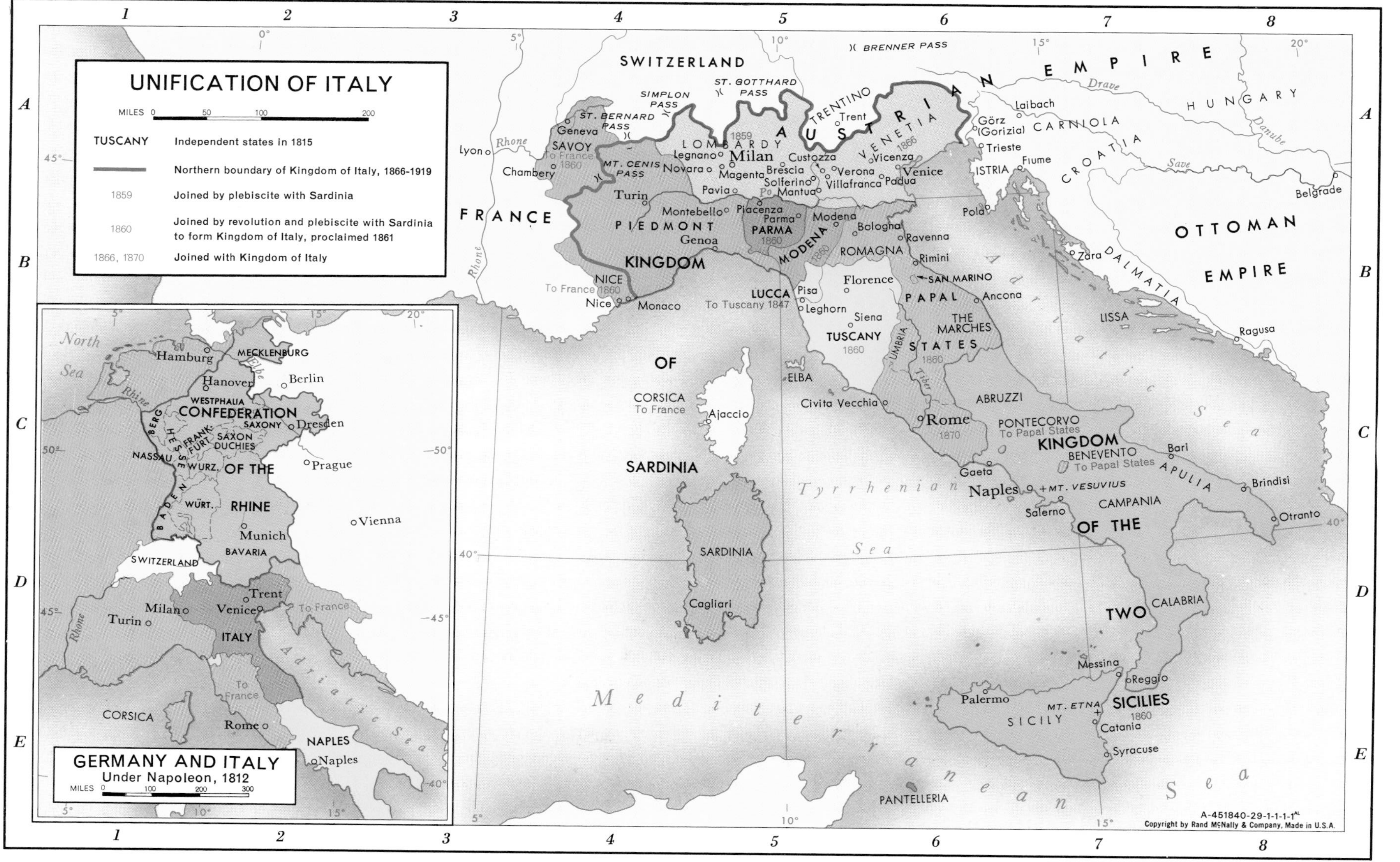
UNIFICATION OF ITALY
MILES 0 50 100 200
TUSCANY Independent states in 1815
Northern boundary of Kingdom of Italy, 1866-1919
1859 Joined by plebiscite with Sardinia
1860 Joined by revolution and plebiscite with Sardinia to form Kingdom of Italy, proclaimed 1861
1866, 1870 Joined with Kingdom of Italy
SWITZERLAND
BRENNER PASS
SIMPLON PASS
ST. GOTTHARD PASS
ST. BERNARD PASS
MT. CENIS PASS
AUSTRIAN EMPIRE
HUNGARY
Drave
Danube
Save
Laibach
Görz (Gorizia)
CARNIOLA
Trieste
Fiume
CROATIA
ISTRIA
Pola
Belgrade
OTTOMAN EMPIRE
Zara
DALMATIA
LISSA
Ragusa
TRENTINO
Trent
LOMBARDY
1859
Milan
Legnano
Novara
Magenta
Brescia
Custozza
Solferino
Mantua
Verona
Villafranca
VENETIA
1866
Vicenza
Venice
Padua
Po
Pavia
Geneva
SAVOY
To France 1860
Chambery
Lyon
Rhone
FRANCE
Turin
Montebello
Piacenza
Parma
PARMA
1860
Modena
MODENA
1860
Bologna
Ravenna
ROMAGNA
Rimini
SAN MARINO
PIEDMONT
Genoa
KINGDOM OF SARDINIA
NICE
To France 1860
Nice
Monaco
LUCCA
To Tuscany 1847
Pisa
Leghorn
Florence
Siena
TUSCANY
1860
PAPAL STATES
1860
Ancona
THE MARCHES
UMBRIA
Tiber
ELBA
CORSICA
To France
Ajaccio
Civita Vecchia
Rome
1870
ABRUZZI
PONTECORVO
To Papal States
BENEVENTO
To Papal States
Bari
APULIA
Brindisi
Otranto
Gaeta
Naples
MT. VESUVIUS
Salerno
CAMPANIA
KINGDOM OF THE TWO SICILIES
1860
CALABRIA
Adriatic Sea
Tyrrhenian Sea
SARDINIA
Cagliari
Messina
Reggio
Palermo
MT. ETNA
SICILY
Catania
Syracuse
PANTELLERIA
Mediterranean Sea
GERMANY AND ITALY
Under Napoleon, 1812
MILES 0 100 200 300
North Sea
Hamburg
MECKLENBURG
Elbe
Berlin
Hanover
Rhine
WESTPHALIA
CONFEDERATION OF THE RHINE
SAXONY
Dresden
BERG
HESSE
FRANK-FURT
SAXON DUCHIES
NASSAU
WURZ.
BADEN
WÜRT.
Prague
Vienna
Munich
BAVARIA
SWITZERLAND
Trent
Milano
Venice
Turin
ITALY
To France
Rhone
CORSICA
Rome
NAPLES
Naples
Adriatic Sea
A-451840-29-1-1-1-1
Copyright by Rand McNally & Company, Made in U.S.A.

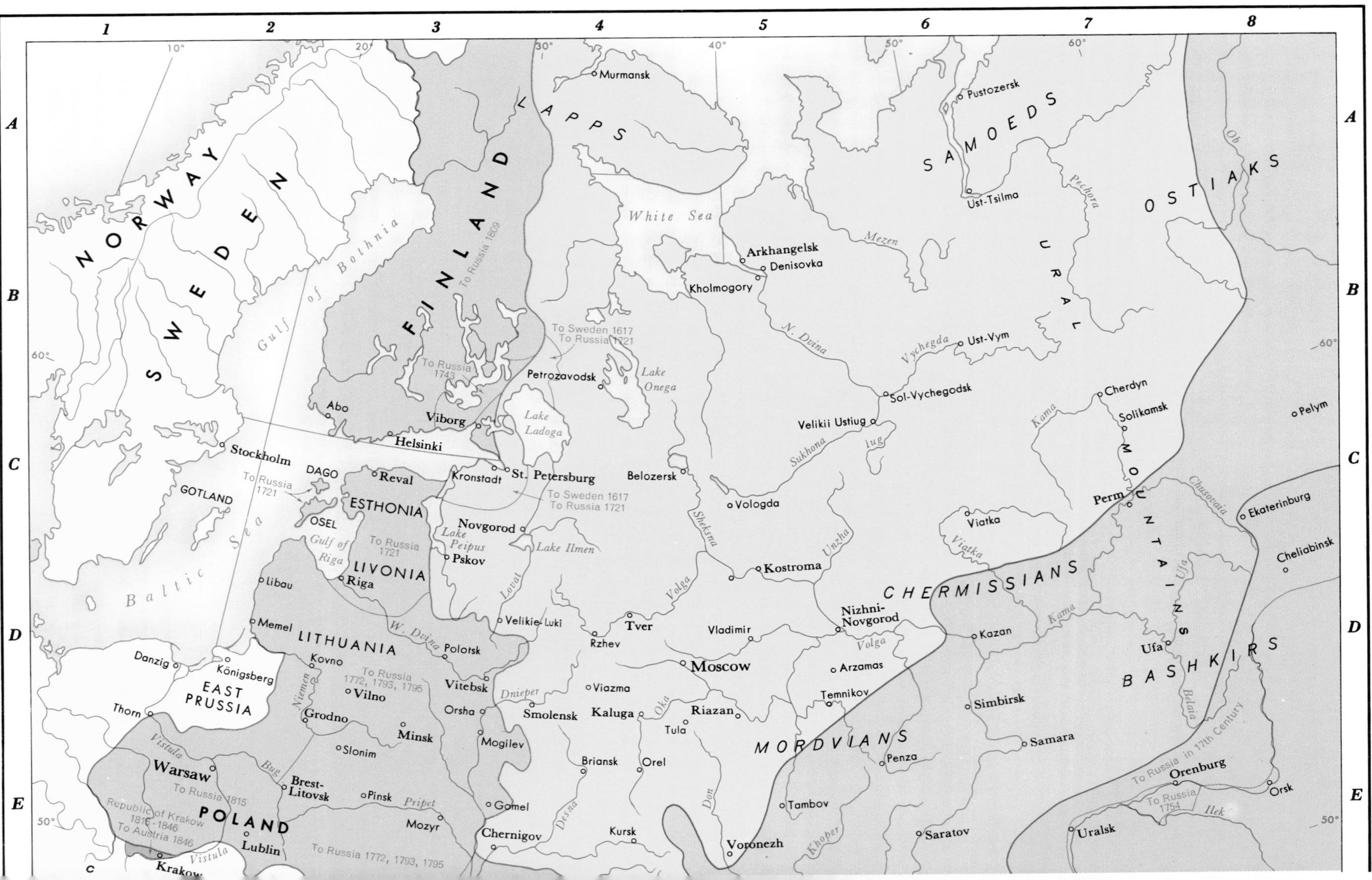
1
2
3
4
5
6
7
8
A
B
C
D
E
NORWAY
SWEDEN
FINLAND
LAPPS
SAMOEDS
OSTIAKS
URAL MOUNTAINS
CHERMISSIANS
BASHKIRS
MORDVIANS
ESTHONIA
LIVONIA
LITHUANIA
EAST PRUSSIA
POLAND
GOTLAND
DAGO
OSEL
Murmansk
Pustozersk
Ust-Tsilma
Arkhangelsk
Denisovka
Kholmogory
Ust-Vym
Sol-Vychegodsk
Cherdyn
Solikamsk
Pelym
Petrozavodsk
Velikii Ustiug
Abo
Viborg
Helsinki
Stockholm
Reval
Kronstadt
St. Petersburg
Belozersk
Vologda
Perm
Ekaterinburg
Viatka
Cheliabinsk
Novgorod
Pskov
Riga
Libau
Kostroma
Velikie Luki
Tver
Rzhev
Vladimir
Nizhni-Novgorod
Kazan
Ufa
Memel
Polotsk
Danzig
Königsberg
Kovno
Moscow
Arzamas
Vitebsk
Vilno
Viazma
Temnikov
Simbirsk
Thorn
Orsha
Smolensk
Kaluga
Riazan
Tula
Grodno
Minsk
Mogilev
Slonim
Samara
Penza
Briansk
Orel
Orenburg
Warsaw
Brest-Litovsk
Pinsk
Orsk
Gomel
Tambov
Mozyr
Chernigov
Kursk
Saratov
Uralsk
Lublin
Voronezh
Krakow
White Sea
Gulf of Bothnia
Lake Onega
Lake Ladoga
Lake Peipus
Lake Ilmen
Gulf of Riga
Baltic Sea
Ob
Pechora
Mezen
N. Dvina
Vychegda
Kama
Sukhona
Iug
Chusovaia
Ufa
Sheksna
Unzha
Viatka
Volga
Lovat
W. Dvina
Dnieper
Oka
Niemen
Belaia
Vistula
Bug
Pripet
Desna
Don
Khoper
Ilek
To Russia 1809
To Russia 1743
To Sweden 1617
To Russia 1721
To Russia 1721
To Sweden 1617
To Russia 1721
To Russia 1721
To Russia 1772, 1793, 1795
To Russia in 17th Century
To Russia 1815
Republic of Krakow 1815–1846
To Austria 1846
To Russia 1754
To Russia 1772, 1793, 1795

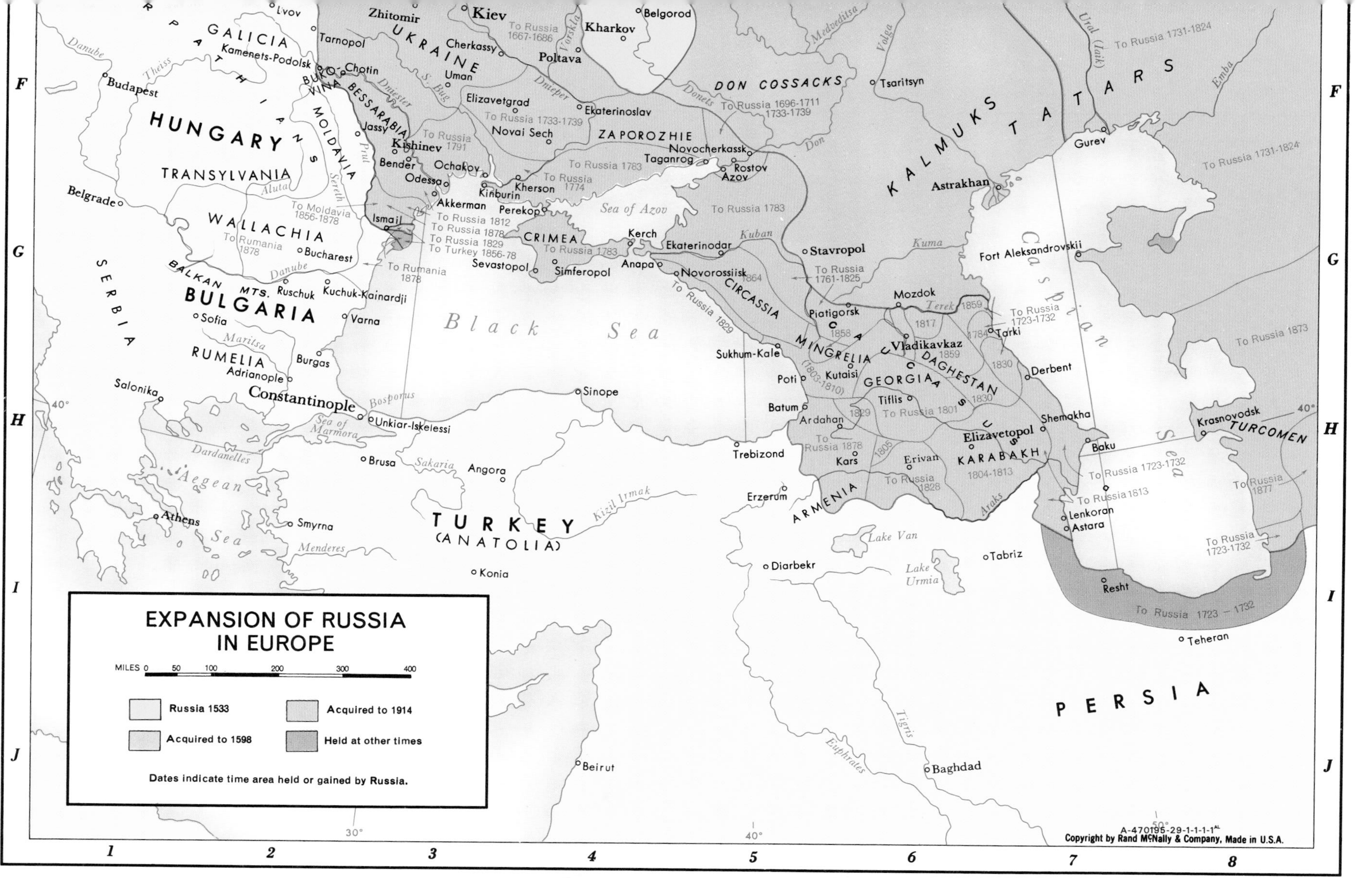
EXPANSION OF RUSSIA IN EUROPE
MILES 0 50 100 200 300 400
Russia 1533
Acquired to 1598
Acquired to 1914
Held at other times
Dates indicate time area held or gained by Russia.
GALICIA
Kamenets-Podolsk
Lvov
Tarnopol
Zhitomir
Kiev
To Russia 1667-1686
Kharkov
Belgorod
UKRAINE
Cherkassy
Uman
Poltava
BUKOVINA
Chotin
BESSARABIA
MOLDAVIA
HUNGARY
Budapest
TRANSYLVANIA
Belgrade
SERBIA
WALLACHIA
To Rumania 1878
Bucharest
BALKAN MTS.
BULGARIA
Sofia
Ruschuk
Kuchuk-Kainardji
Varna
RUMELIA
Adrianople
Burgas
Salonika
Constantinople
Unkiar-Iskelessi
Sea of Marmora
Bosporus
Dardanelles
Aegean Sea
Athens
Smyrna
Brusa
Angora
TURKEY (ANATOLIA)
Konia
Sinope
Black Sea
Elizavetgrad
To Russia 1733-1739
Novai Sech
Ekaterinoslav
ZAPOROZHIE
Jassy
Kishinev
To Russia 1791
Bender
Ochakov
Odessa
Kinburn
Kherson
To Russia 1774
Akkerman
To Moldavia 1856-1878
Ismail
To Russia 1812
To Russia 1878
To Russia 1829
To Turkey 1856-78
To Rumania 1878
Perekop
CRIMEA
To Russia 1783
Sevastopol
Simferopol
Sea of Azov
Kerch
Taganrog
Novocherkassk
Rostov
Azov
DON COSSACKS
To Russia 1696-1711 1733-1739
Tsaritsyn
KALMUKS
TATARS
To Russia 1731-1824
Gurev
Astrakhan
Ekaterinodar
Anapa
Novorossiisk
CIRCASSIA
To Russia 1829
Stavropol
To Russia 1761-1825
Mozdok
Piatigorsk
Sukhum-Kale
MINGRELIA
Kutaisi
Poti
Batum
Ardahan
To Russia 1878
Kars
Trebizond
Erzerum
ARMENIA
Vladikavkaz
DAGHESTAN
GEORGIA
Tiflis
To Russia 1801
Erivan
To Russia 1828
KARABAKH
1804-1813
Elizavetopol
Shemakha
Tarki
To Russia 1723-1732
Derbent
Baku
Lenkoran
Astara
To Russia 1813
Fort Aleksandrovskii
Caspian Sea
To Russia 1873
Krasnovodsk
TURCOMEN
To Russia 1877
Resht
To Russia 1723 – 1732
Teheran
PERSIA
Tabriz
Lake Van
Lake Urmia
Diarbekr
Baghdad
Beirut
A-470195-29-1-1-1

EUROPEAN INVASIONS OF RUSSIA
MILES 0 50 100 200 300 400
1815 Boundaries
1920 Boundaries
States colored as of 1920
INVASIONS OF RUSSIA
INVASION ROUTES
Swedish invasions by Charles XII 1700-1709
Napoleon's invasion and retreat from Moscow 1812
Crimean War—Allied invasion of Evpatoriia and battle of Sevastopol
WORLD WAR I
British, French, and U.S. intervention in Russia
Deepest penetrations: (1) German 1918; (2) Polish 1920; and (3) Allied
WORLD WAR II
German advance to Dec. 1941
German advance in 1942
Russian front Dec. 1943
Eastern front Dec. 1944
CRIMEAN WAR
Allied assaults on Russian Coastal areas
Barents Sea
Norwegian Sea
(British, French, American 1918-1919)
NORWAY
SWEDEN
FINLAND
Gulf of Bothnia
Petsamo
Murmansk
German advance to Dec. 1941
Eastern front Dec. 1944
White Sea
Arkhangelsk
Allies
Onega
Shenkursk
N. Dvina
Pechora
Ob
Lake Onega
Lake Ladoga
URAL MTS.
ALAND IS.
Helsinki
Vyborg
Kronstadt
Gulf of Finland
Leningrad was never captured by the Germans
(British) (1918-19)
DAGO
OSEL
Narva
Reval
St. Petersburg (Leningrad)
Tikhvin
Baltic Sea
GOTLAND
Parnau
ESTONIA
Novgorod
Lake Ilmen
Viatka (Kirov)
Perm (Molotov)
Kama
Pskov
1700-1702
LATVIA
Riga
Volga
Nizhni Novgorod (Gorki)
Kazan
Ufa
Dvinsk
German advance 1941
Velikie-Luki
Tver (Kalinin)
Moscow
Königsberg
LITHUANIA
Polotsk
Borodino
Kovno
Vitebsk
Viazma
Oka
EAST PRUSSIA
Vilno
Smolensk
Tula
GERMANY
Berlin
Thorn
Grodno
Niemen
Minsk
Mogilev
RUSSIA
Samara (Kuibyshev)
Penza
Orenburg (Chkalov)
Ural
Elbe
Kalisz
Warsaw
1705
Brest
Berezina
Desna
Orel
Tsna
POLAND
Oder
Warta
Vistula
1700-1702
Pripet
Chernigov
Kursk
Voronezh
Saratov
Uralsk
Prague
Polish 1920
Russian front Dec. 1943
Germans 1918
Baturin
Don
CZECHOSLOVAKIA
Krakow
Zhitomir
Lvov
1707-1709
Kiev
Kharkov
Danube
CARPATHIANS
Vienna
AUSTRIA
GALICIA
Tarnopol
UKRAINE
Poltava
Tsaritsyn (Stalingrad)
Theiss
Budapest
Dniester
Dnieper
Donets
Gurev
HUNGARY
BESSARABIA
S. Bug
Ekaterinoslav (Dnepropetrovsk)
German advance 1942
Drave
MOLDAVIA
Jassy
Allies
Taganrog
Rostov
Astrakhan
TRANSYLVANIA
Nikolaev
Kherson
Odessa
1855
Save
Eastern front Dec. 1944
Belgrade
RUMANIA
WALLACHIA
Galati
Prut
Kinburn
Sea of Azov
Ekaterinodar (Krasnodar)
Stavropol
Kuban
Kuma
Caspian Sea
YUGOSLAVIA
Morava
Bucharest
Evpatoriia
Kerch
Novorossiisk
Sevastopol
1854
BULGARIA
Varna
BALKAN MTS.
Sofia
Burgas
Maritsa
Black Sea
(French 1918-19)
(British 1918-1919)
Grozny
Allies
CAUCASUS
ALBANIA
Vardar
Salonika
Constantinople
Bosporus
Sinope
Batum
Tiflis
Kura
Baku
Krasnovodsk
GREECE
Sea of Marmora
Dardanelles
Sakaria
Angora
ARMENIA
Aras
Lenkoran
Aegean Sea
TURKEY
Kizil Irmak
Tabriz
Athens
Smyrna
Menderes
Konia
TAURUS MTS.
Euphrates
Tigris
PERSIA
Teheran
(British) (1918-19)
RHODES
Mosul
SYRIA
IRAQ
Aleppo
A-470196-29-1-1

Copyright by Rand McNally & Company, Made in U.S.A.

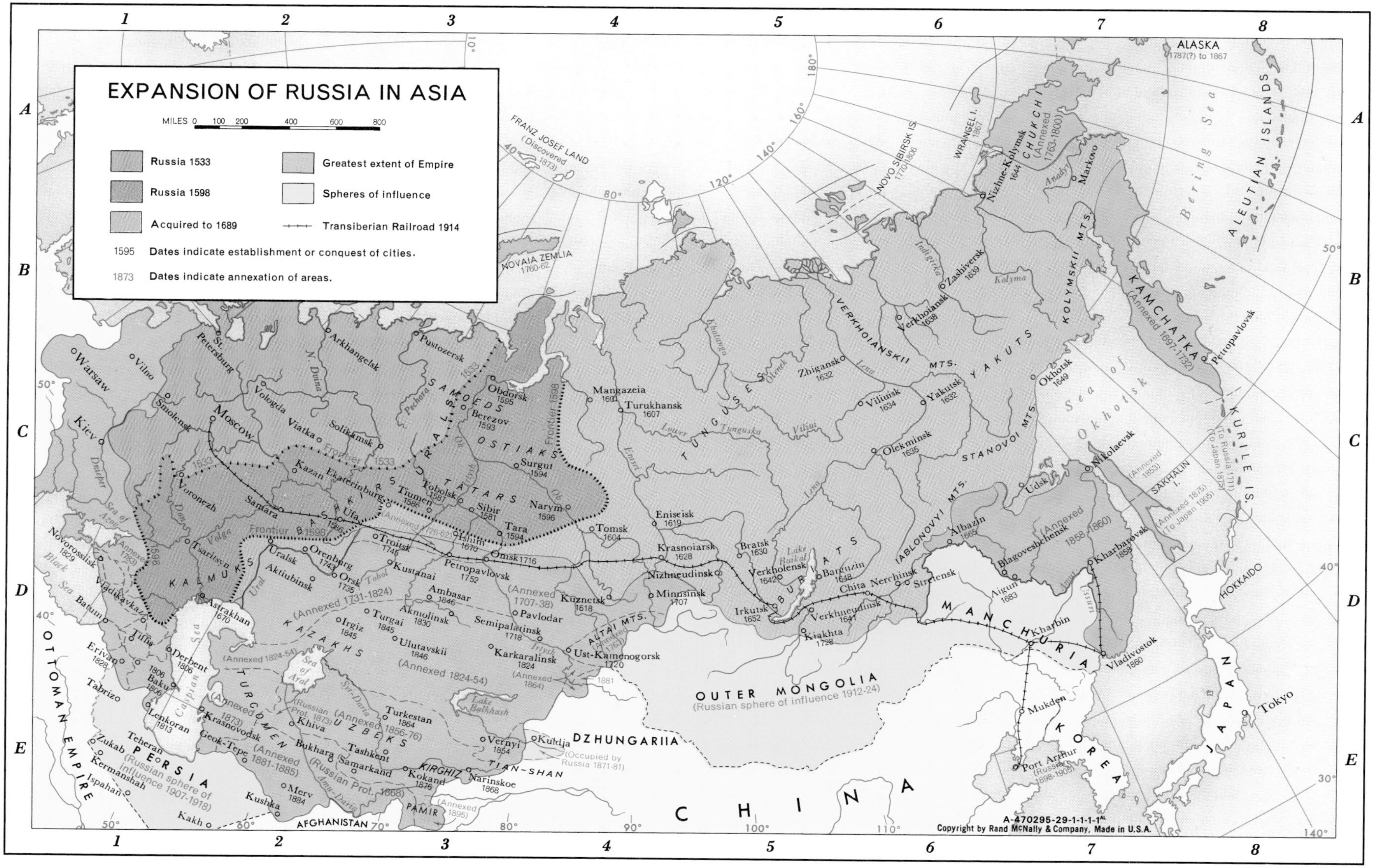

EXPANSION OF RUSSIA IN ASIA
MILES 0 100 200 400 600 800
Russia 1533
Russia 1598
Acquired to 1689
Greatest extent of Empire
Spheres of influence
Transiberian Railroad 1914
1595 Dates indicate establishment or conquest of cities.
1873 Dates indicate annexation of areas.
ALASKA 1787(?) to 1867
ALEUTIAN ISLANDS
Bering Sea
FRANZ JOSEF LAND (Discovered 1873)
NOVAIA ZEMLIA 1760-62
NOVO SIBIRSK IS. 1770-1806
WRANGEL I. 1867
CHUKCHI (Annexed 1763-1800)
Nizhne-Kolymsk 1644
Markovo
Anadyr
KAMCHATKA (Annexed 1697-1732)
Petropavlovsk
KURILE IS. (To Russia 1711) (To Japan 1875)
SAKHALIN I. (Annexed 1853) (Annexed 1875) (To Japan 1905)
Sea of Okhotsk
Okhotsk 1649
Nikolaevsk
Udsk
KOLYMSKII MTS.
STANOVOI MTS.
IABLONOVYI MTS.
VERKHOIANSKII MTS.
YAKUTS
Zashiversk 1639
Verkhoiansk 1638
Indigirka
Kolyma
Zhigansk 1632
Yakutsk 1632
Viliuisk 1634
Olekminsk 1635
Albazin 1665
Blagoveshchensk
(Annexed 1858-1860)
Kharbarovsk 1858
Aigun 1683
Amur
Ussuri
Vladivostok 1860
MANCHURIA
Kharbin
Mukden
Port Arthur (Russian 1898-1905)
KOREA
HOKKAIDO
JAPAN
Tokyo
Sretensk
Chita
Nerchinsk
Barguzin 1648
Verkholensk 1642
Lake Baikal
BURIATS
Bratsk 1630
Irkutsk 1652
Verkhneudinsk 1641
Kiakhta 1728
OUTER MONGOLIA (Russian sphere of influence 1912-24)
CHINA
DZHUNGARIIA
Kuldja (Occupied by Russia 1871-81)
TIAN-SHAN
Vernyi 1854
Narinskoe 1868
KIRGHIZ
Kokand 1876
PAMIR (Annexed 1895)
AFGHANISTAN
TUNGUSES
Khatanga
Olenek
Lower Tunguska
Viliui
Lena
Mangazeia 1601
Turukhansk 1607
Enisei
Eniseisk 1619
Krasnoiarsk 1628
Nizhneudinsk
Minusinsk 1707
Tomsk 1604
Kuznetsk 1618
ALTAI MTS.
(Annexed 1756)
Ust-Kamenogorsk 1720
1881
OSTIAKS
Frontier 1598
Obdorsk 1595
Berezov 1593
Surgut 1594
Narym 1596
Ob
Irtysh
TATARS
Tobolsk 1587
Tiumen 1586
Sibir 1581
Tara 1594
Omsk 1716
Ishim 1670
Petropavlovsk 1752
(Annexed 1707-38)
Pavlodar
Semipalatinsk 1718
Karkaralinsk 1824
(Annexed 1864)
Lake Balkhash
Ambasar 1846
Akmolinsk 1830
Ulutavskii 1846
(Annexed 1824-54)
KAZAKHS
(Annexed 1731-1824)
Turgai 1845
Irgiz 1845
Kustanai
Troitsk 1745
(Annexed 1726-62)
Orenburg 1743
Orsk 1735
Uralsk
Aktiubinsk
Ural
Tobol
Sea of Aral
Syr-Daria
Amu-Daria
Turkestan 1864
(Annexed 1856-76)
UZBEKS
(Russian Prot. 1873)
Khiva
Bukhara
Samarkand
Tashkent
(Russian Prot. 1868)
TURCOMEN
(Annexed 1881-1885)
Krasnovodsk
Geok-Tepe
Merv 1884
Kushka
(Annexed 1824-54)
(Annexed 1873)
URALS
SAMOEDS
Pustozersk
Pechora
Arkhangelsk
N. Dvina
Solikamsk
Frontier 1533
Viatka
Vologda
Kazan
Ekaterinburg
Ufa 1586
BASHKIRS
Frontier 1598
Samara
Moscow
St. Petersburg
Smolensk
Voronezh
Don
Volga
Tsaritsyn
KALMUKS
Astrakhan 1670
1533
1598
Vilno
Warsaw
Kiev
Dnieper
Sea of Azov
(Annexed 1783)
Novorossiisk 1829
Black Sea
Batum
Vladikavkaz
Tiflis
Erivan 1828
Tabrizo
Derbent 1806
Baku 1806
1806
Caspian Sea
Lenkoran 1813
Teheran
Zukab
Kermanshah
Ispahan
Kakh
PERSIA (Russian sphere of influence 1907-1918)
OTTOMAN EMPIRE
A-470295-29-1-1-1-1
Copyright by Rand McNally & Company, Made in U.S.A.

I. INDO-EUROPEAN
1. Germanic
English
German
Dutch
Flemish
Danish
Norwegian
Swedish
Faeroese
Frisian
2. Romanic
French
Italian
Rhaeto-Romanic
Ladinic
Friulian
Sardinian
Spanish
Catalan
Portuguese
Gallegan
Rumanian
Vlach
3. Slavonic
Great Russian
Ukrainian
White Russian
Polish
Serbo-Croatian
Slovenian
Czech
Slovakian
Bulgarian
Macedonian
Sorbian (Wendic)
4. Hellenic
Modern Greek
5. Baltic
Lettish
Lithuanian
6. Celtic
Irish
Gaelic
Welsh (Cymric)
Breton
7. Armenian
Armenian
8. Iranic
Ossetic
Kurdic
Yezidic
9. Thraco-Illyrian
Albanian
II. URAL-ALTAIC
1. Finno-Ugrian
Finnish (Suomi)
Estonian and Livonian
Lappish
Karelian
Cheremissian
Votiak
Mordvinian
Magyar
2. Turkish-Tataric
Turkish (Osmanli)
Kirghizic
Bashkirian
Tataric
Kumykian
Chuvashian
Karachaic
Nogaic
Karapapakian
Kizilbashian
Tahtajic
3. Mongolian
Kalmuckian
III. SEMITIC
Arabic
Maltese
Syrian
IV. HAMITIC
Berber
V. CAUCASIC
Caucasian
Northwest
Northeast
Southwest
VI. BASQUE
Basque
Atlantic Ocean
FAEROESE
SHETLAND IS.
ORKNEY IS.
HEBRIDES
GAELIC
SCOTS
North Chan.
Firth of Forth
Edinburgh
Belfast
IRISH
ENGLISH
Dublin
Irish Sea
St. Georges Chan.
WELSH
LANDS END
London
Thames
English Channel
Str. of Dover
North Sea
NORWEGIAN
Oslo
Glommen
Laagen
Skagerrak
Kattegat
SWEDISH
Lake Vänern
Stockholm
DANISH
Copenhagen
BORNHOLM
RÜGEN
FRISIAN
Amsterdam
The Hague
DUTCH
FLEMISH
Brussels
LOW GERMAN
Berlin
SORBIAN
MIDDLE GERMAN
Prague
CZECH
Danube
UPPER GERMAN
Vienna
Rhine
BRETON
Seine
Paris
Meuse
FRENCH
Saône
Geneva
Bern
Bay of Biscay
Gironde R.
BASQUE
Garonne
Rhone
PROVENÇAL
RHAETO-ROMANIC
LADINIC
FRIULIAN
SLOVENIAN
Trieste
Rijeka
Drave
Save
ITALIAN
Po
Gulf of Genoa
Gulf of Lions
GALLEGAN
PORTUGUESE
Lisbon
Duero
Ebro
Madrid
SPANISH
Guadiana
Guadalquivir
Barcelona
CATALAN
BALEARIC ISLANDS
IBIZA
MAJORCA
MINORCA
CORSICA
ELBA
SARDINIA
SARDINIAN
Rome
Tyrrhenian Sea
Adriatic Sea
G. of Taranto
SICILY
Str. of Gibraltar
Mediterranean
Algiers
Tunis
ARABIC
BERBER
MALTA
MALTESE

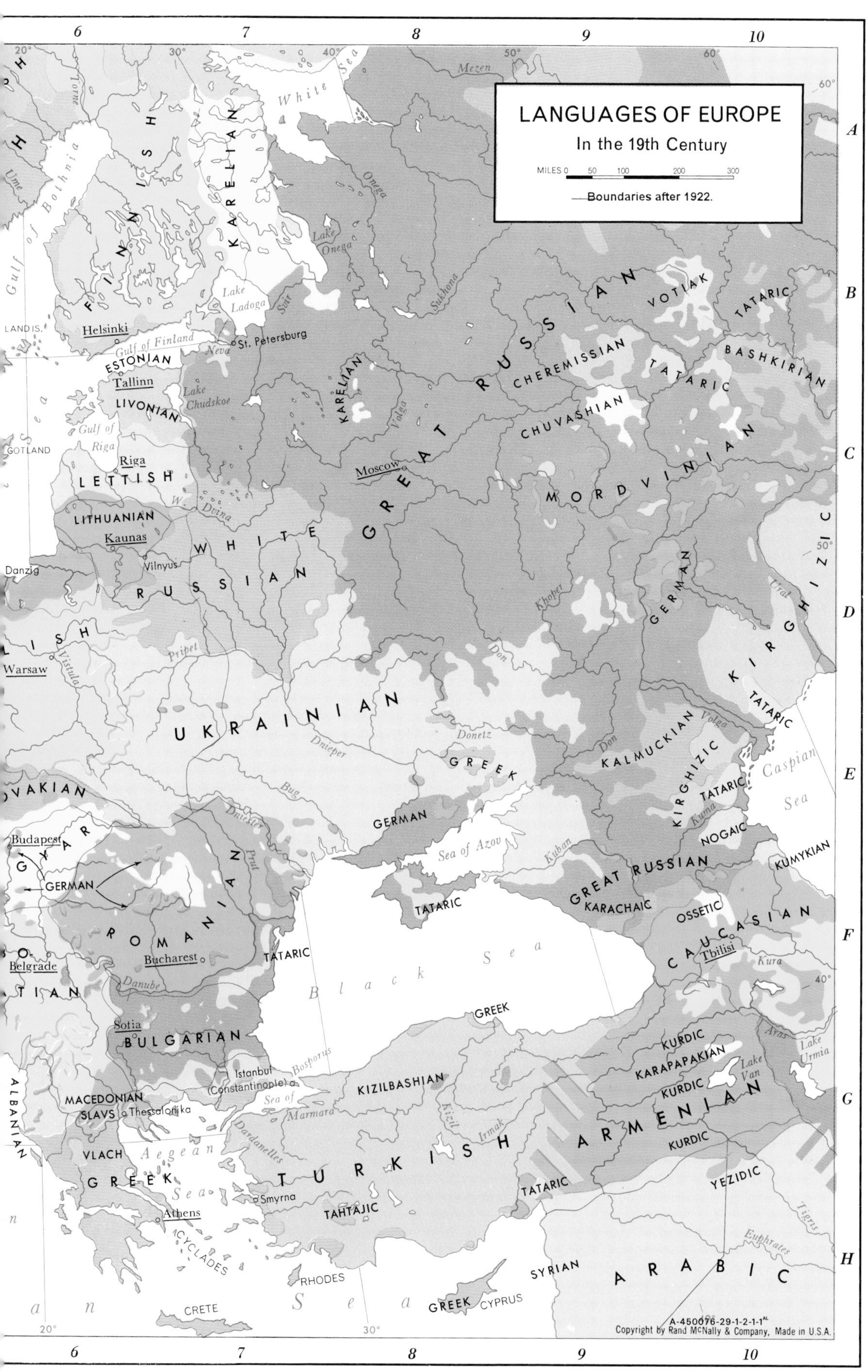
LANGUAGES OF EUROPE
In the 19th Century
MILES 0 50 100 200 300
Boundaries after 1922.
GREAT RUSSIAN
WHITE RUSSIAN
UKRAINIAN
FINNISH
KARELIAN
ESTONIAN
LIVONIAN
LETTISH
LITHUANIAN
VOTIAK
TATARIC
BASHKIRIAN
CHEREMISSIAN
CHUVASHIAN
MORDVINIAN
GERMAN
KIRGHIZIC
KALMUCKIAN
GREEK
NOGAIC
KUMYKIAN
KARACHAIC
OSSETIC
CAUCASIAN
ROMANIAN
MAGYAR
BULGARIAN
MACEDONIAN SLAVS
VLACH
ALBANIAN
KIZILBASHIAN
KURDIC
KARAPAPAKIAN
ARMENIAN
TURKISH
TAHTAJIC
YEZIDIC
SYRIAN
ARABIC
Helsinki
St. Petersburg
Tallinn
Riga
Kaunas
Vilnyus
Danzig
Warsaw
Moscow
Budapest
Bucharest
Belgrade
Sofia
Istanbul (Constantinople)
Thessaloníka
Athens
Smyrna
Tbilisi
White Sea
Lake Ladoga
Lake Onega
Gulf of Finland
Gulf of Riga
Gulf of Bothnia
Lake Chudskoe
Black Sea
Sea of Azov
Caspian Sea
Aegean Sea
Sea of Marmara
Lake Van
Lake Urmia
CYCLADES
RHODES
CRETE
CYPRUS
GOTLAND
LAND IS.
Volga
Don
Dnieper
Dniester
Danube
Bug
Prut
Pripet
Vistula
Donetz
Khoper
Ural
Kuban
Kuma
Kura
Aras
Tigris
Euphrates
Kizil Irmak
Onega
Sukhona
Mezen
Neva
Svir
W. Dvina
Tornio
Ume
Bosporus
Dardanelles
A-450076-29-1-2-1-1

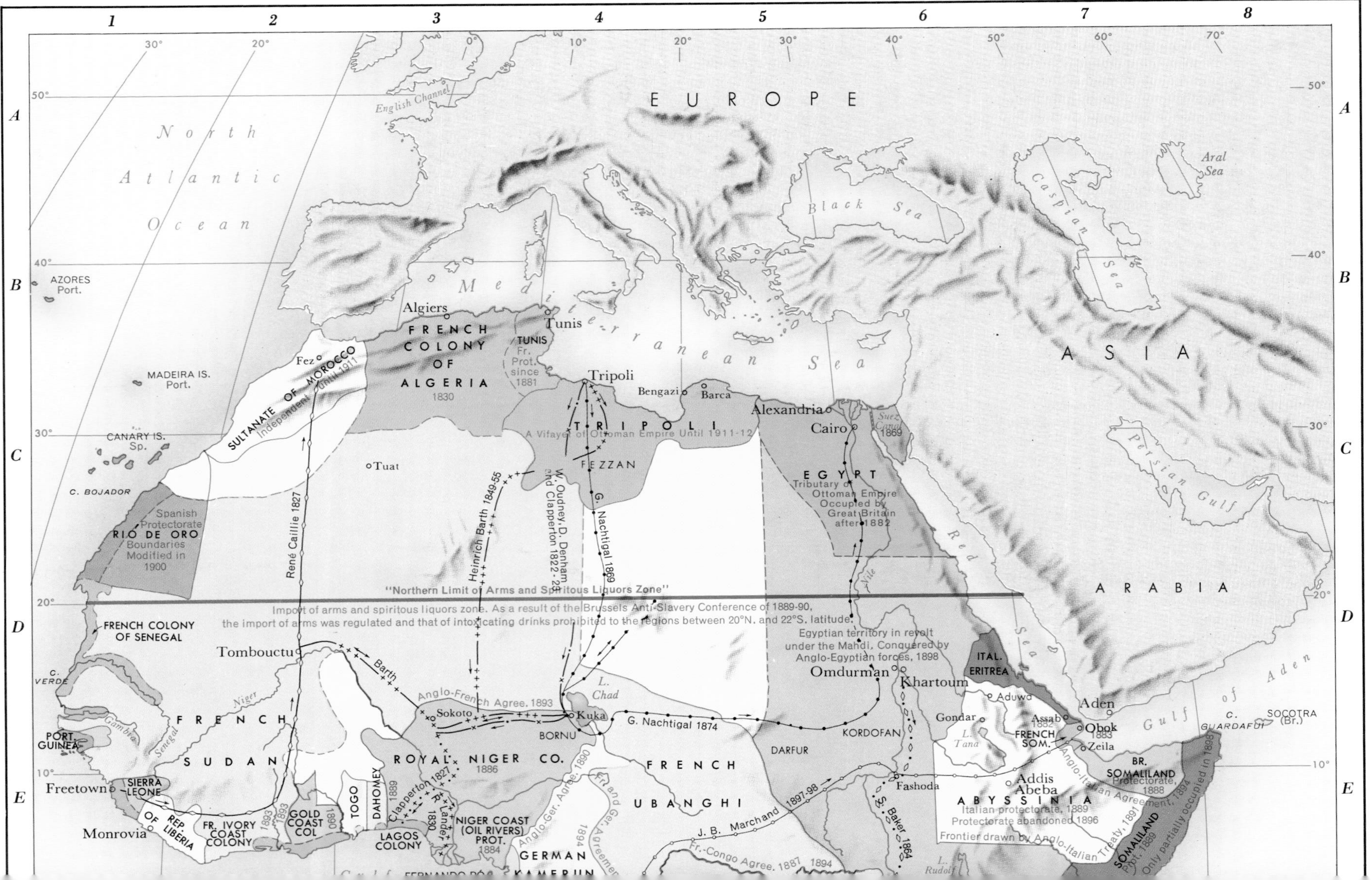

EUROPE
ASIA
ARABIA
North Atlantic Ocean
Mediterranean Sea
Black Sea
Caspian Sea
Aral Sea
Persian Gulf
Red Sea
Gulf of Aden
English Channel
AZORES Port.
MADEIRA IS. Port.
CANARY IS. Sp.
C. BOJADOR
C. VERDE
SOCOTRA (Br.)
C. GUARDAFUI
"Northern Limit of Arms and Spiritous Liquors Zone"
Import of arms and spiritous liquors zone. As a result of the Brussels Anti-Slavery Conference of 1889-90, the import of arms was regulated and that of intoxicating drinks prohibited to the regions between 20°N. and 22°S. latitude.
SULTANATE OF MOROCCO Independent Until 1911
Fez
FRENCH COLONY OF ALGERIA 1830
Algiers
TUNIS Fr. Prot. since 1881
Tunis
Tripoli
TRIPOLI A Vilayet of Ottoman Empire Until 1911-12
FEZZAN
Bengazi
Barca
Alexandria
Cairo
Suez Canal 1869
EGYPT Tributary of Ottoman Empire Occupied by Great Britain after 1882
Nile
Egyptian territory in revolt under the Mahdi, Conquered by Anglo-Egyptian forces, 1898
Omdurman
Khartoum
KORDOFAN
DARFUR
Fashoda
ITAL. ERITREA
Aduwa
Gondar
L. Tana
Assab 1882
FRENCH SOM.
Obok 1883
Zeila
Aden
BR. SOMALILAND Protectorate, 1888
ABYSSINIA
Addis Abeba
Italian protectorate, 1889 Protectorate abandoned 1896
Anglo-Italian Agreement, 1894
Frontier drawn by Anglo-Italian Treaty, 1891
SOMALILAND Prot. 1889 Only partially occupied in 1898
L. Rudolf
S. Baker 1864
J. B. Marchand 1897-98
Fr.-Congo Agree. 1887 1894
Tuat
Spanish Protectorate RIO DE ORO Boundaries Modified in 1900
René Caillie 1827
Heinrich Barth 1849-55
W. Oudney, D. Denham and Clapperton 1822-25
G. Nachtigal 1869
G. Nachtigal 1874
FRENCH COLONY OF SENEGAL
Tombouctu
Barth
Niger
Gambia
Senegal
FRENCH SUDAN
PORT. GUINEA
SIERRA LEONE
Freetown
REP. OF LIBERIA
Monrovia
FR. IVORY COAST COLONY
1893
GOLD COAST COL.
1890
TOGO
DAHOMEY 1889
LAGOS COLONY
Clapperton 1827
R. Lander 1830
NIGER COAST (OIL RIVERS) PROT. 1884
Anglo-French Agree. 1893
Sokoto
ROYAL NIGER CO. 1886
BORNU
Kuka
L. Chad
Anglo-Ger. Agree. 1890
Fr. and Ger. Agreement 1894
GERMAN KAMERUN
FERNANDO PÓO
FRENCH UBANGHI

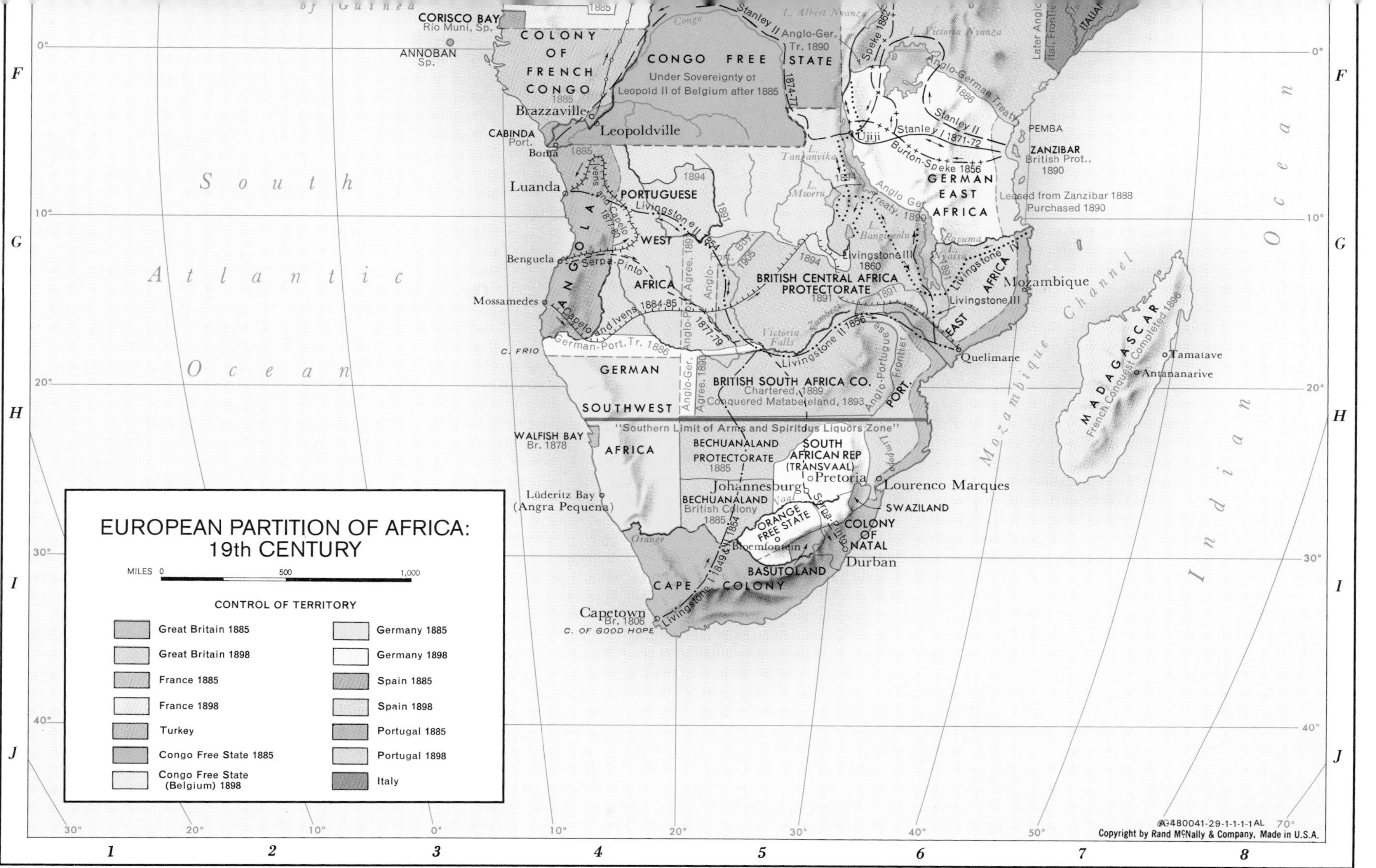

EUROPEAN PARTITION OF AFRICA:
19th CENTURY
MILES 0 500 1,000
CONTROL OF TERRITORY
Great Britain 1885
Great Britain 1898
France 1885
France 1898
Turkey
Congo Free State 1885
Congo Free State (Belgium) 1898
Germany 1885
Germany 1898
Spain 1885
Spain 1898
Portugal 1885
Portugal 1898
Italy
South Atlantic Ocean
Indian Ocean
Mozambique Channel
CORISCO BAY
Rio Muni, Sp.
ANNOBAN
Sp.
COLONY OF FRENCH CONGO
1885
CONGO FREE STATE
Under Sovereignty of Leopold II of Belgium after 1885
Brazzaville
Leopoldville
CABINDA
Port.
Boma
Luanda
Benguela
Mossamedes
C. FRIO
ANGOLA
PORTUGUESE WEST AFRICA
GERMAN SOUTHWEST AFRICA
WALFISH BAY
Br. 1878
Lüderitz Bay
(Angra Pequena)
Capetown
Br. 1806
C. OF GOOD HOPE
CAPE COLONY
BASUTOLAND
ORANGE FREE STATE
Bloemfontein
COLONY OF NATAL
Durban
SWAZILAND
Lourenco Marques
SOUTH AFRICAN REP (TRANSVAAL)
Pretoria
Johannesburg
BECHUANALAND PROTECTORATE
1885
BECHUANALAND
British Colony
1885
"Southern Limit of Arms and Spirituous Liquors Zone"
BRITISH SOUTH AFRICA CO.
Chartered, 1889
Conquered Matabeleland, 1893
BRITISH CENTRAL AFRICA PROTECTORATE
1891
PORT. EAST AFRICA
Mozambique
Quelimane
GERMAN EAST AFRICA
ZANZIBAR
British Prot.,
1890
PEMBA
Leased from Zanzibar 1888
Purchased 1890
MADAGASCAR
French Conquest Completed 1896
Tamatave
Antananarive
Ujiji
Stanley II
Stanley I 1871-72
Burton-Speke 1856
Speke 1862
Livingstone III
Livingstone I 1849 & 1854
Livingstone II 1856
Serpa-Pinto
Capelo and Ivens 1884-85
Capelo and Ivens 1877-80
German-Port. Tr. 1886
Anglo-German Treaty
Anglo-Ger. Tr. 1890
Anglo-Port. Agree. 1891
Anglo-Ger. Agree. 1890
Anglo-Portuguese Frontier
Victoria Falls
L. Tanganyika
L. Victoria Nyanza
L. Albert Nyanza
L. Mweru
L. Bangweolu
L. Nyasa
Congo
Zambezi
Limpopo
Orange
Vaal
Rovuma
Copyright by Rand McNally & Company, Made in U.S.A.

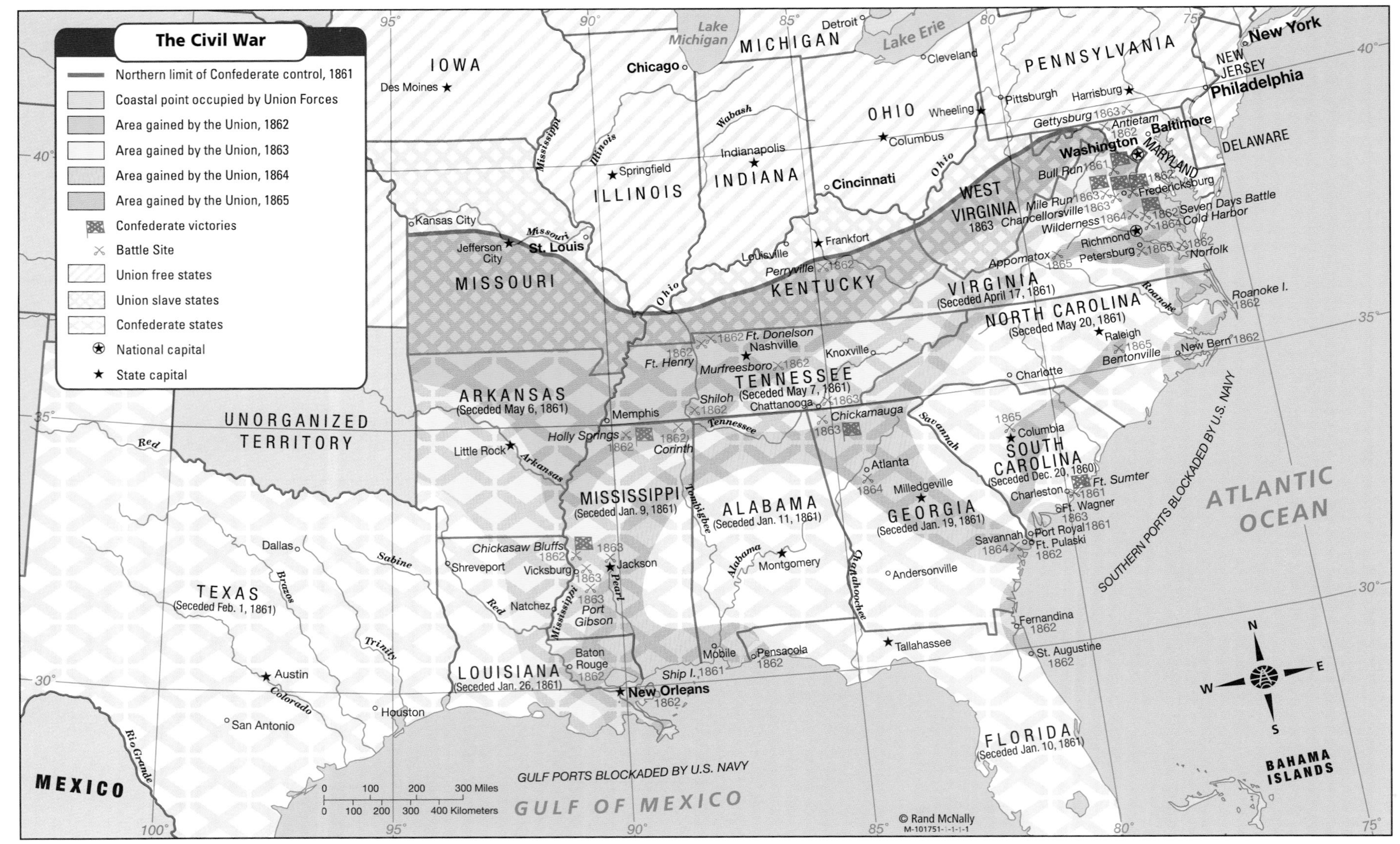
The Civil War
Northern limit of Confederate control, 1861
Coastal point occupied by Union Forces
Area gained by the Union, 1862
Area gained by the Union, 1863
Area gained by the Union, 1864
Area gained by the Union, 1865
Confederate victories
Battle Site
Union free states
Union slave states
Confederate states
National capital
State capital
IOWA
Des Moines
ILLINOIS
Chicago
Springfield
INDIANA
Indianapolis
MICHIGAN
Detroit
Lake Michigan
Lake Erie
OHIO
Cleveland
Columbus
Cincinnati
Wheeling
PENNSYLVANIA
Pittsburgh
Harrisburg
Philadelphia
Gettysburg 1863
NEW JERSEY
New York
DELAWARE
MARYLAND
Baltimore
Washington
Antietam 1862
Bull Run 1861
Mile Run 1863
Chancellorsville 1863
Wilderness 1864
Fredericksburg 1862
Seven Days Battle 1862
Cold Harbor 1864
Richmond
Petersburg 1865
Norfolk 1862
Appomatox 1865
WEST VIRGINIA 1863
VIRGINIA (Seceded April 17, 1861)
NORTH CAROLINA (Seceded May 20, 1861)
Raleigh
Bentonville 1865
New Bern 1862
Roanoke I. 1862
Roanoke
Charlotte
KENTUCKY
Frankfort
Louisville
Perryville 1862
MISSOURI
Kansas City
Jefferson City
St. Louis
Missouri
Mississippi
Illinois
Wabash
Ohio
Ft. Henry 1862
Ft. Donelson 1862
Nashville
Murfreesboro 1862
Knoxville
TENNESSEE (Seceded May 7, 1861)
Shiloh 1862
Chattanooga 1863
Chickamauga 1863
Tennessee
ARKANSAS (Seceded May 6, 1861)
Little Rock
Arkansas
Memphis
Holly Springs 1862
Corinth 1862
UNORGANIZED TERRITORY
Red
MISSISSIPPI (Seceded Jan. 9, 1861)
Jackson 1863
Vicksburg 1863
Chickasaw Bluffs 1862
Port Gibson 1863
Natchez
Pearl
Tombigbee
ALABAMA (Seceded Jan. 11, 1861)
Montgomery
Alabama
Mobile
Pensacola 1862
Ship I. 1861
GEORGIA (Seceded Jan. 19, 1861)
Atlanta 1864
Milledgeville
Andersonville
Savannah 1864
Ft. Pulaski 1862
Chattahoochee
Savannah
SOUTH CAROLINA (Seceded Dec. 20, 1860)
Columbia 1865
Charleston
Ft. Sumter 1861
Ft. Wagner 1863
Port Royal 1861
FLORIDA (Seceded Jan. 10, 1861)
Tallahassee
Fernandina 1862
St. Augustine 1862
LOUISIANA (Seceded Jan. 26, 1861)
Shreveport
Baton Rouge 1862
New Orleans 1862
TEXAS (Seceded Feb. 1, 1861)
Dallas
Austin
Houston
San Antonio
Sabine
Brazos
Trinity
Colorado
Rio Grande
MEXICO
GULF PORTS BLOCKADED BY U.S. NAVY
GULF OF MEXICO
SOUTHERN PORTS BLOCKADED BY U.S. NAVY
ATLANTIC OCEAN
BAHAMA ISLANDS
N
S
E
W
0 100 200 300 Miles
0 100 200 300 400 Kilometers
40°
35°
30°
100°
95°
90°
85°
80°
75°
© Rand McNally
M-101751-1-1-1-1

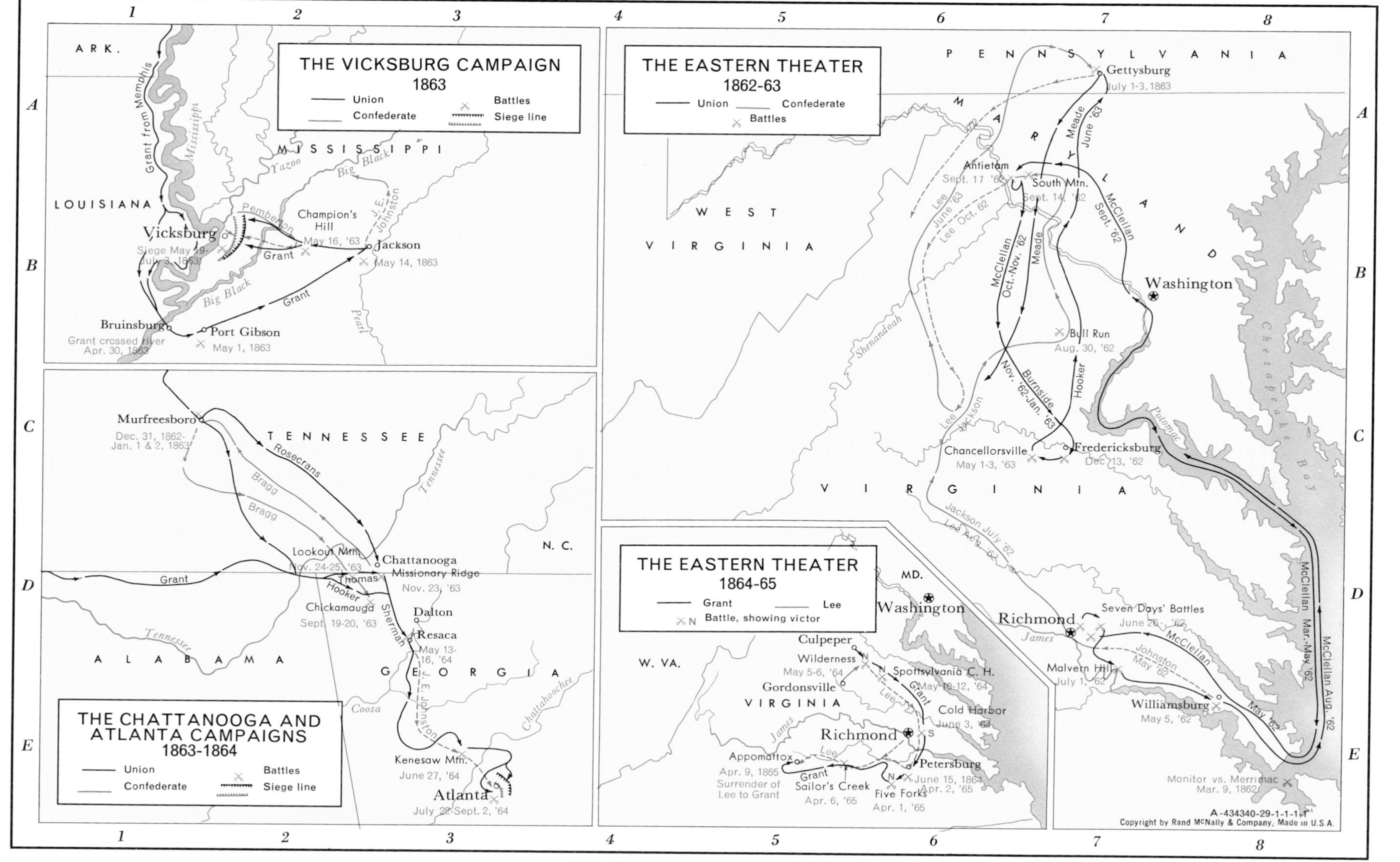

THE VICKSBURG CAMPAIGN
1863
Union
Confederate
Battles
Siege line
ARK.
LOUISIANA
MISSISSIPPI
Grant from Memphis
Mississippi
Yazoo
Big Black
Pemberton
Champion's Hill
May 16, '63
J. E. Johnston
Jackson
May 14, 1863
Vicksburg
Siege May 19-July 3, 1863
Grant
Big Black
Pearl
Bruinsburg
Grant crossed river
Apr. 30, 1863
Port Gibson
May 1, 1863
THE CHATTANOOGA AND ATLANTA CAMPAIGNS
1863-1864
Union
Confederate
Battles
Siege line
Murfreesboro
Dec. 31, 1862-Jan. 1 & 2, 1863
TENNESSEE
Rosecrans
Bragg
Bragg
Tennessee
N. C.
Lookout Mtn.
Nov. 24-25, '63
Chattanooga
Missionary Ridge
Nov. 23, '63
Grant
Thomas
Hooker
Chickamauga
Sept. 19-20, '63
Sherman
Dalton
Resaca
May 13-16, '64
Tennessee
ALABAMA
GEORGIA
J. E. Johnston
Coosa
Chattahoochee
Kenesaw Mtn.
June 27, '64
Atlanta
July 22-Sept. 2, '64
THE EASTERN THEATER
1862-63
Union
Confederate
Battles
PENNSYLVANIA
Gettysburg
July 1-3, 1863
MARYLAND
Meade
June '63
WEST VIRGINIA
Antietam
Sept. 17 '62
South Mtn.
Sept. 14, '62
Lee June '63
Lee Oct. '62
McClellan Sept. '62
McClellan Oct.-Nov. '62
Meade
Washington
Shenandoah
Bull Run
Aug. 30, '62
Burnside Nov. '62-Jan. '63
Hooker
Lee
Jackson
Potomac
Chancellorsville
May 1-3, '63
Fredericksburg
Dec. 13, '62
VIRGINIA
Chesapeake Bay
Jackson July '62
Lee Aug. '62
McClellan Mar.-May '62
McClellan Aug. '62
Richmond
James
Seven Days' Battles
June 26-July 1, '62
McClellan
Johnston May '62
Malvern Hill
July 1, '62
Williamsburg
May 5, '62
May '62
Monitor vs. Merrimac
Mar. 9, 1862
THE EASTERN THEATER
1864-65
Grant
Lee
Battle, showing victor
MD.
Washington
W. VA.
Culpeper
Wilderness
May 5-6, '64
Spottsylvania C. H.
May 10-12, '64
Gordonsville
VIRGINIA
Lee
Grant
Cold Harbor
June 3, '64
James
Richmond
Appomattox
Apr. 9, 1865
Surrender of Lee to Grant
Grant
Sailor's Creek
Apr. 6, '65
Five Forks
Apr. 1, '65
Petersburg
June 15, 1864-Apr. 2, '65
A-434340-29-1-1-1
Copyright by Rand McNally & Company, Made in U.S.A.

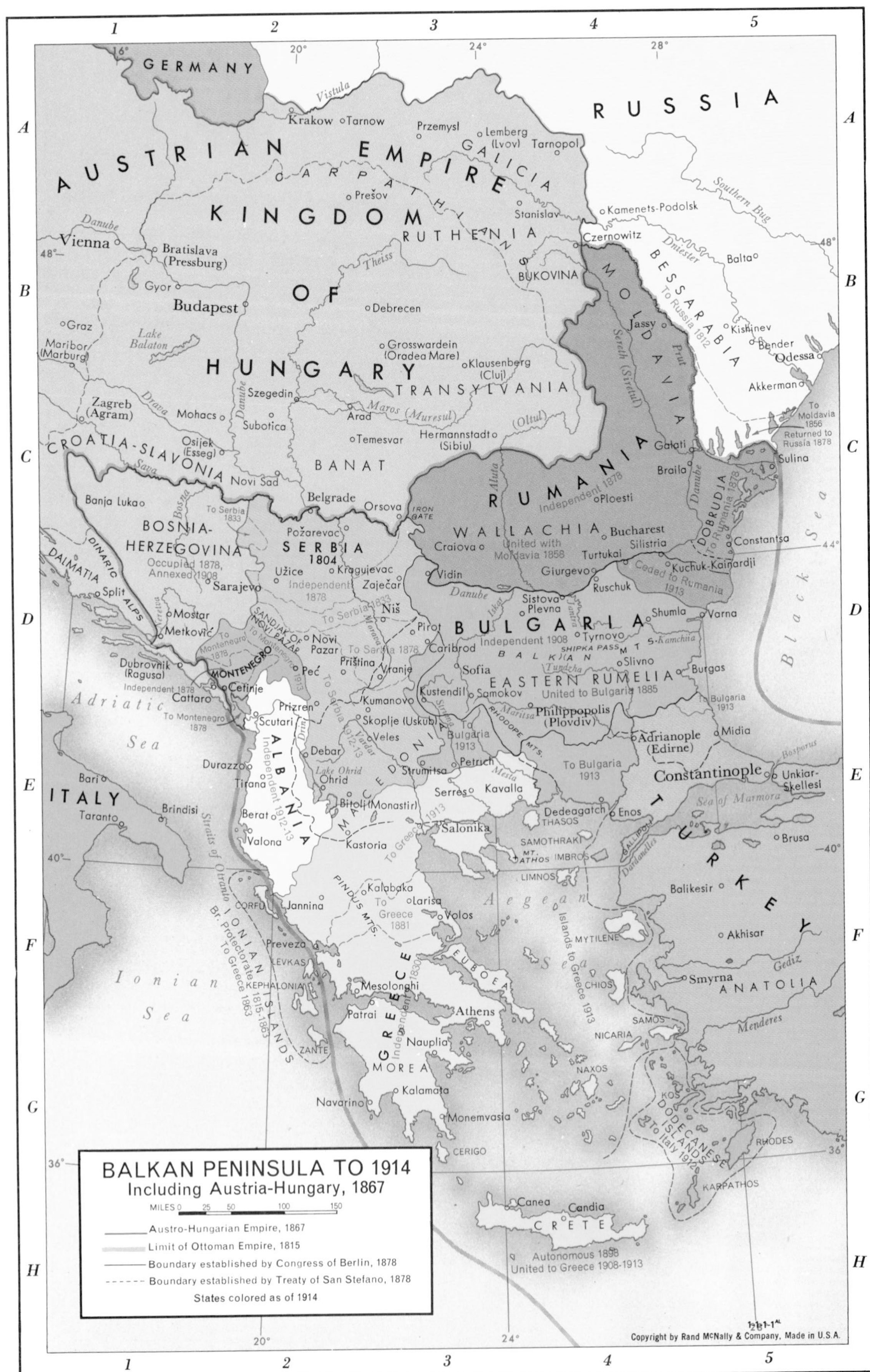
BALKAN PENINSULA TO 1914
Including Austria-Hungary, 1867
MILES 0 25 50 100 150
Austro-Hungarian Empire, 1867
Limit of Ottoman Empire, 1815
Boundary established by Congress of Berlin, 1878
Boundary established by Treaty of San Stefano, 1878
States colored as of 1914
Copyright by Rand McNally & Company, Made in U.S.A.
GERMANY
RUSSIA
AUSTRIAN EMPIRE
KINGDOM OF HUNGARY
GALICIA
CARPATHIANS
RUTHENIA
BUKOVINA
TRANSYLVANIA
BANAT
CROATIA-SLAVONIA
BOSNIA-HERZEGOVINA
Occupied 1878, Annexed 1908
DALMATIA
DINARIC ALPS
SERBIA
1804
Independent 1878
To Serbia 1833
To Serbia 1878
SANDJAK OF NOVI PAZAR
MONTENEGRO
Independent 1878
To Montenegro 1878
MOLDAVIA
BESSARABIA
To Russia 1812
To Moldavia 1856
Returned to Russia 1878
RUMANIA
Independent 1878
WALLACHIA
United with Moldavia 1858
DOBRUDJA
To Rumania 1878
Ceded to Rumania 1913
BULGARIA
Independent 1908
BALKAN MTS.
SHIPKA PASS
EASTERN RUMELIA
United to Bulgaria 1885
RHODOPE MTS.
To Bulgaria 1913
MACEDONIA
To Serbia 1912-13
To Greece 1913
ALBANIA
Independent 1912-13
PINDUS MTS.
To Greece 1881
GREECE
Independent 1830
MOREA
IONIAN ISLANDS
Br. Protectorate 1815-1863
To Greece 1863
EUBOEA
TURKEY
ANATOLIA
DODECANESE ISLANDS
To Italy 1912
CRETE
Autonomous 1898
United to Greece 1908-1913
Islands to Greece 1913
ITALY
Adriatic Sea
Ionian Sea
Aegean Sea
Black Sea
Sea of Marmora
Bosporus
Dardanelles
GALLIPOLI
Straits of Otranto
Lake Balaton
Lake Ohrid
IRON GATE
Danube
Vistula
Southern Bug
Dniester
Prut
Sereth (Siretul)
Theiss
Maros (Muresul)
Oltul
Aluta
Drava
Sava
Bosna
Morava
Drin
Vardar
Struma
Mesta
Maritsa
Tundzha
Isker
Jantra
Kamchia
Gediz
Menderes
Krakow
Tarnow
Przemysl
Lemberg (Lvov)
Tarnopol
Prešov
Stanislav
Kamenets-Podolsk
Czernowitz
Balta
Vienna
Bratislava (Pressburg)
Gyor
Budapest
Debrecen
Graz
Maribor (Marburg)
Grosswardein (Oradea Mare)
Klausenberg (Cluj)
Jassy
Kishinev
Bender
Odessa
Akkerman
Szegedin
Zagreb (Agram)
Mohacs
Subotica
Arad
Temesvar
Hermannstadt (Sibiu)
Osijek (Esseg)
Novi Sad
Galati
Braila
Sulina
Banja Luka
Belgrade
Orsova
Ploesti
Bucharest
Craiova
Silistria
Constantsa
Turtukai
Kuchuk-Kainardji
Požarevac
Užice
Kragujevac
Sarajevo
Zaječar
Vidin
Giurgevo
Ruschuk
Split
Niš
Sistova
Plevna
Shumla
Varna
Mostar
Metković
Pirot
Tyrnovo
Novi Pazar
Caribrod
Dubrovnik (Ragusa)
Priština
Slivno
Peć
Vranje
Sofia
Burgas
Cetinje
Cattaro
Kustendil
Samokov
Prizren
Kumanovo
Philippopolis (Plovdiv)
Scutari
Skoplje (Uskub)
Veles
Adrianople (Edirne)
Midia
Debar
Durazzo
Strumitsa
Petrich
Tirana
Ohrid
Serres
Kavalla
Constantinople
Unkiar-Skellesi
Bari
Brindisi
Taranto
Bitolj (Monastir)
Dedeagatch
Enos
Berat
Salonika
Valona
Kastoria
THASOS
SAMOTHRAKI
MT. ATHOS
IMBROS
LIMNOS
Brusa
Balikesir
Kalabaka
Larisa
CORFU
Jannina
Volos
Akhisar
MYTILENE
Preveza
LEVKAS
KEPHALONIA
Mesolonghi
CHIOS
Smyrna
Athens
Patrai
SAMOS
NICARIA
Nauplia
ZANTE
NAXOS
Kalamata
Navarino
KOS
Monemvasia
RHODES
CERIGO
KARPATHOS
Canea
Candia

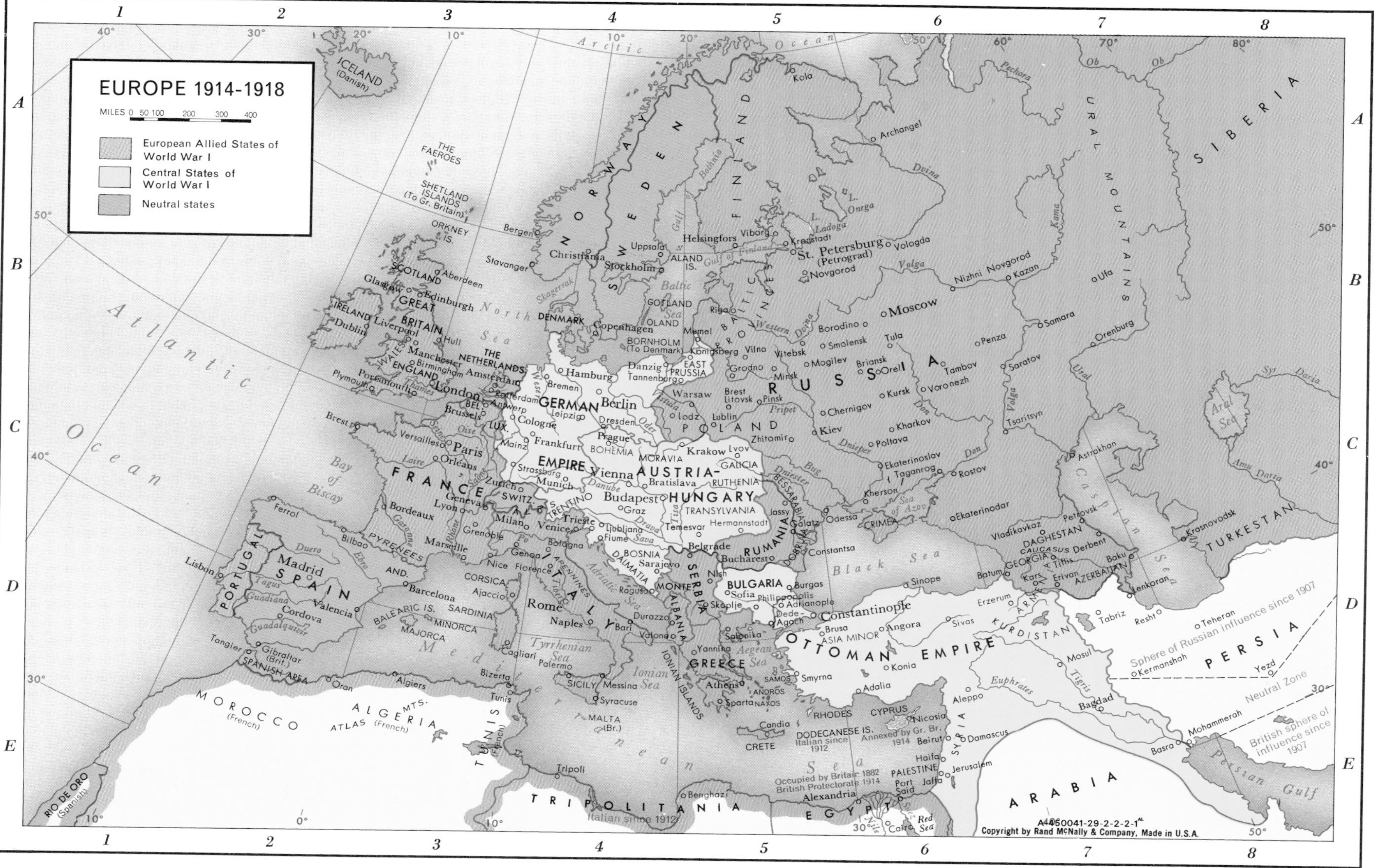
EUROPE 1914-1918
MILES 0 50 100 200 300 400
European Allied States of World War I
Central States of World War I
Neutral states
ICELAND (Danish)
THE FAEROES
SHETLAND ISLANDS (To Gr. Britain)
ORKNEY IS.
NORWAY
SWEDEN
FINLAND
SIBERIA
URAL MOUNTAINS
RUSSIA
POLAND
BALTIC PROVINCES
EAST PRUSSIA
GERMAN EMPIRE
AUSTRIA-HUNGARY
GREAT BRITAIN
SCOTLAND
IRELAND
WALES
ENGLAND
THE NETHERLANDS
BEL.
LUX.
DENMARK
FRANCE
SWITZ.
SPAIN
PORTUGAL
AND.
ITALY
SERBIA
MONTE.
ALBANIA
BULGARIA
RUMANIA
GREECE
OTTOMAN EMPIRE
PERSIA
TURKESTAN
ARABIA
EGYPT
TRIPOLITANIA
Italian since 1912
TUNIS (French)
ALGERIA (French)
MOROCCO (French)
RIO DE ORO (Spanish)
SPANISH AREA
Atlantic Ocean
Arctic Ocean
North Sea
Baltic Sea
Black Sea
Caspian Sea
Mediterranean Sea
Bay of Biscay
Adriatic Sea
Tyrrhenian Sea
Ionian Sea
Aegean Sea
Aral Sea
Persian Gulf
Red Sea
Sphere of Russian influence since 1907
Neutral Zone
British sphere of influence since 1907
Occupied by Britain 1882 British Protectorate 1914
CYPRUS Annexed by Gr. Br. 1914
DODECANESE IS. Italian since 1912
Moscow
St. Petersburg (Petrograd)
Berlin
Vienna
Budapest
Paris
London
Rome
Madrid
Constantinople
Copyright by Rand McNally & Company, Made in U.S.A.
A4450041-29-2-2-2-1

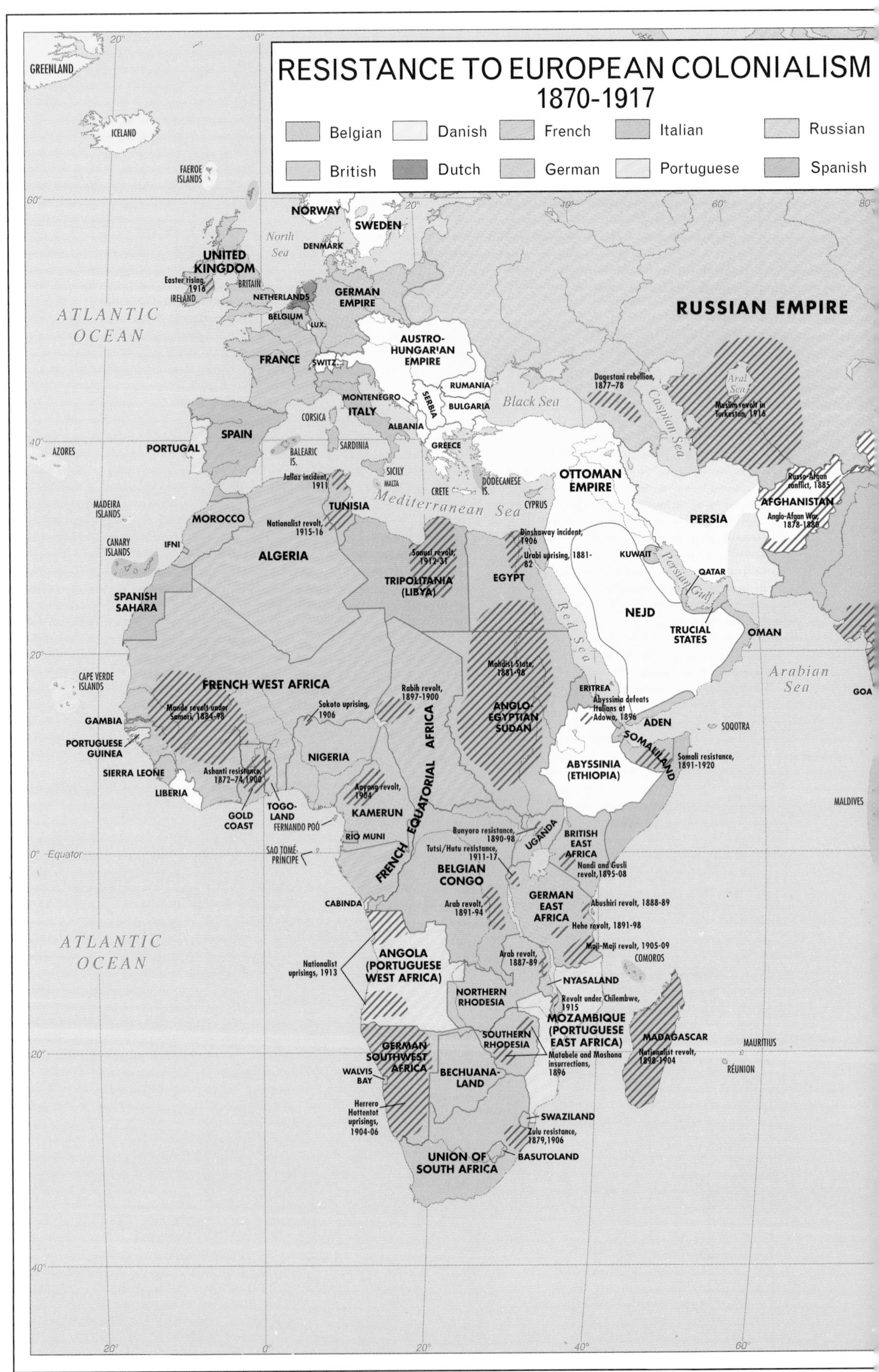
RESISTANCE TO EUROPEAN COLONIALISM
1870-1917
Belgian
Danish
French
Italian
Russian
British
Dutch
German
Portuguese
Spanish
GREENLAND
ICELAND
FAEROE ISLANDS
NORWAY
SWEDEN
North Sea
DENMARK
UNITED KINGDOM
Easter rising, 1916
IRELAND
BRITAIN
NETHERLANDS
GERMAN EMPIRE
BELGIUM
LUX.
ATLANTIC OCEAN
RUSSIAN EMPIRE
AUSTRO-HUNGARIAN EMPIRE
FRANCE
SWITZ.
RUMANIA
SERBIA
BULGARIA
MONTENEGRO
ITALY
CORSICA
Black Sea
Dagestani rebellion, 1877–78
Caspian Sea
Aral Sea
Muslim revolt in Turkestan, 1916
SPAIN
PORTUGAL
AZORES
ALBANIA
SARDINIA
GREECE
BALEARIC IS.
SICILY
MALTA
CRETE
DODECANESE IS.
Jallaz incident, 1911
TUNISIA
Mediterranean Sea
CYPRUS
OTTOMAN EMPIRE
PERSIA
Russo-Afgan conflict, 1885
AFGHANISTAN
Anglo-Afgan War, 1878-1880
MADEIRA ISLANDS
MOROCCO
Nationalist revolt, 1915-16
CANARY ISLANDS
IFNI
ALGERIA
Sanusi revolt, 1912-31
TRIPOLITANIA (LIBYA)
Dinshaway incident, 1906
Urabi uprising, 1881-82
EGYPT
KUWAIT
Persian Gulf
QATAR
SPANISH SAHARA
Red Sea
NEJD
TRUCIAL STATES
OMAN
Mahdist State, 1881-98
CAPE VERDE ISLANDS
FRENCH WEST AFRICA
Mande revolt under Samori, 1884-98
Rabih revolt, 1897-1900
Sokoto uprising, 1906
ANGLO-EGYPTIAN SUDAN
ERITREA
Abyssinia defeats Italians at Adowa, 1896
ADEN
SOQOTRA
Arabian Sea
GOA
GAMBIA
PORTUGUESE GUINEA
SIERRA LEONE
LIBERIA
Ashanti resistance, 1872–74,1900
NIGERIA
FRENCH EQUATORIAL AFRICA
ABYSSINIA (ETHIOPIA)
SOMALILAND
Somali resistance, 1891-1920
Anyang revolt, 1904
KAMERUN
GOLD COAST
TOGO-LAND
FERNANDO POÓ
RIO MUNI
Bunyoro resistance, 1890-98
UGANDA
BRITISH EAST AFRICA
MALDIVES
0° Equator
SAO TOMÉ-PRINCIPE
Tutsi/Hutu resistance, 1911-17
BELGIAN CONGO
Nandi and Gusli revolt, 1895-08
CABINDA
Arab revolt, 1891-94
GERMAN EAST AFRICA
Abushiri revolt, 1888-89
Hehe revolt, 1891-98
ATLANTIC OCEAN
Maji-Maji revolt, 1905-09
COMOROS
Nationalist uprisings, 1913
ANGOLA (PORTUGUESE WEST AFRICA)
Arab revolt, 1887-89
NYASALAND
NORTHERN RHODESIA
Revolt under Chilembwe, 1915
MOZAMBIQUE (PORTUGUESE EAST AFRICA)
SOUTHERN RHODESIA
MADAGASCAR
Nationalist revolt, 1898-1904
MAURITIUS
RÉUNION
GERMAN SOUTHWEST AFRICA
Matabele and Mashona insurrections, 1896
WALVIS BAY
BECHUANA-LAND
Herrero Hottentot uprisings, 1904-06
SWAZILAND
Zulu resistance, 1879,1906
UNION OF SOUTH AFRICA
BASUTOLAND

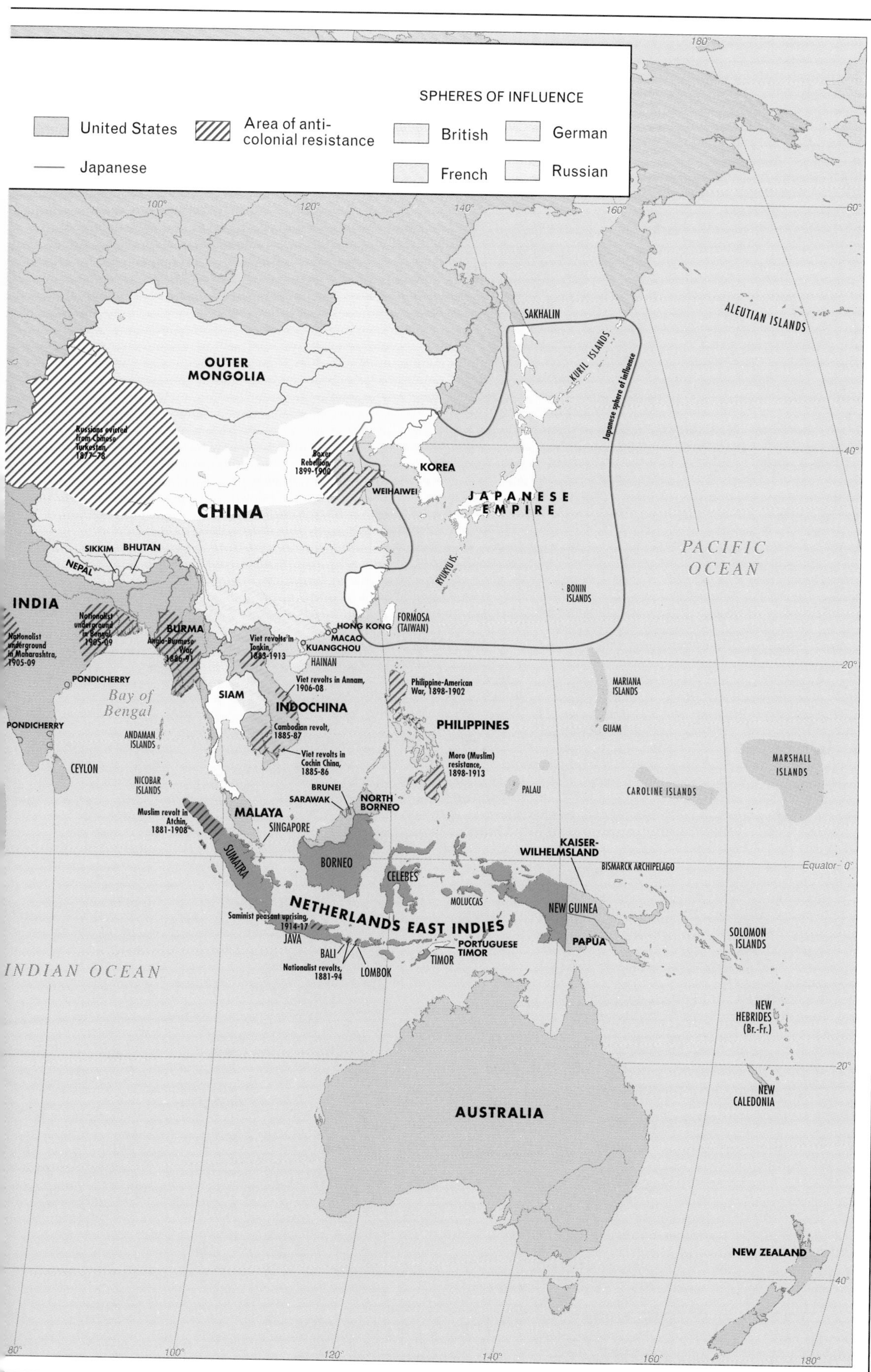

SPHERES OF INFLUENCE
United States
Area of anti-colonial resistance
British
German
Japanese
French
Russian
SAKHALIN
ALEUTIAN ISLANDS
KURIL ISLANDS
Japanese sphere of influence
OUTER MONGOLIA
Russians evicted from Chinese Turkestan, 1877-78
Boxer Rebellion, 1899-1900
KOREA
WEIHAIWEI
JAPANESE EMPIRE
CHINA
SIKKIM
BHUTAN
NEPAL
RYUKYU IS.
PACIFIC OCEAN
BONIN ISLANDS
INDIA
Nationalist underground in Bengal, 1905-09
BURMA
Anglo-Burmese War, 1886-91
Nationalist underground in Maharashtra, 1905-09
Viet revolts in Tonkin, 1883-1913
HONG KONG
MACAO
KUANGCHOU
FORMOSA (TAIWAN)
HAINAN
PONDICHERRY
Bay of Bengal
SIAM
Viet revolts in Annam, 1906-08
INDOCHINA
Philippine-American War, 1898-1902
MARIANA ISLANDS
PONDICHERRY
Cambodian revolt, 1885-87
PHILIPPINES
GUAM
ANDAMAN ISLANDS
Viet revolts in Cochin China, 1885-86
Moro (Muslim) resistance, 1898-1913
MARSHALL ISLANDS
CEYLON
NICOBAR ISLANDS
BRUNEI
SARAWAK
NORTH BORNEO
PALAU
CAROLINE ISLANDS
Muslim revolt in Atchin, 1881-1908
MALAYA
SINGAPORE
SUMATRA
BORNEO
CELEBES
KAISER-WILHELMSLAND
BISMARCK ARCHIPELAGO
Equator
MOLUCCAS
NEW GUINEA
NETHERLANDS EAST INDIES
Saminist peasant uprising, 1914-17
JAVA
BALI
PORTUGUESE TIMOR
TIMOR
PAPUA
SOLOMON ISLANDS
Nationalist revolts, 1881-94
LOMBOK
INDIAN OCEAN
NEW HEBRIDES (Br.-Fr.)
NEW CALEDONIA
AUSTRALIA
NEW ZEALAND

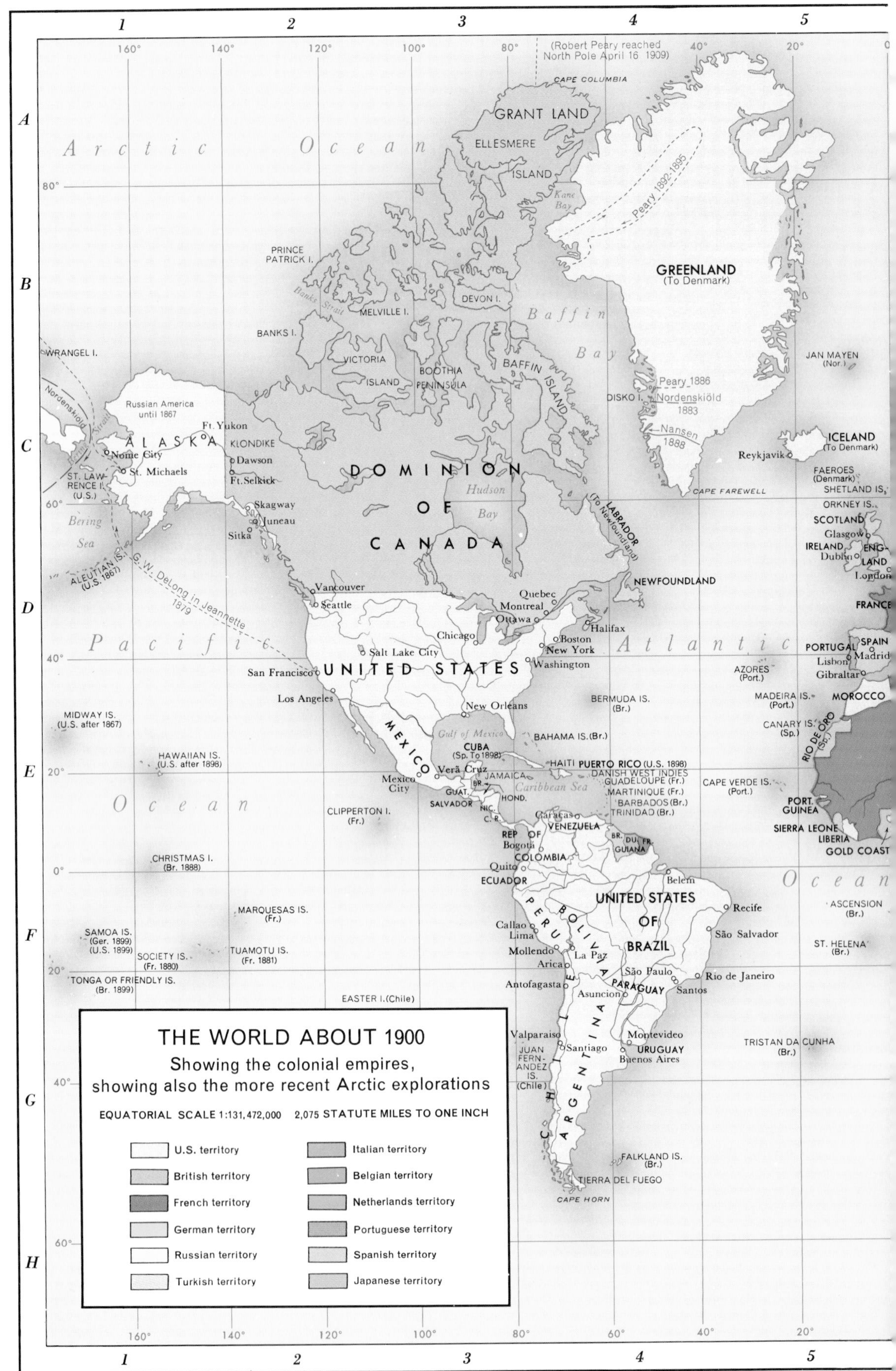

THE WORLD ABOUT 1900
Showing the colonial empires,
showing also the more recent Arctic explorations
EQUATORIAL SCALE 1:131,472,000 2,075 STATUTE MILES TO ONE INCH
U.S. territory
British territory
French territory
German territory
Russian territory
Turkish territory
Italian territory
Belgian territory
Netherlands territory
Portuguese territory
Spanish territory
Japanese territory
Arctic Ocean
Pacific Ocean
Atlantic Ocean
(Robert Peary reached North Pole April 16 1909)
CAPE COLUMBIA
GRANT LAND
ELLESMERE ISLAND
Kane Bay
Peary 1892-1895
GREENLAND (To Denmark)
PRINCE PATRICK I.
MELVILLE I.
DEVON I.
BANKS I.
Banks Strait
Baffin Bay
VICTORIA ISLAND
BOOTHIA PENINSULA
BAFFIN ISLAND
Peary 1886
DISKO I.
Nordenskiöld 1883
Nansen 1888
CAPE FAREWELL
JAN MAYEN (Nor.)
ICELAND (To Denmark)
Reykjavik
WRANGEL I.
Nordenskiöld
Russian America until 1867
ALASKA
Ft. Yukon
KLONDIKE
Dawson
Ft. Selkirk
Nome City
St. Michaels
ST. LAWRENCE I. (U.S.)
Skagway
Juneau
Sitka
Bering Sea
ALEUTIAN IS. (U.S. 1867)
G.W. DeLong in Jeannette 1879
DOMINION OF CANADA
Hudson Bay
LABRADOR (To Newfoundland)
NEWFOUNDLAND
Vancouver
Seattle
Quebec
Montreal
Ottawa
Halifax
Boston
New York
Washington
Chicago
Salt Lake City
San Francisco
UNITED STATES
Los Angeles
New Orleans
MIDWAY IS. (U.S. after 1867)
HAWAIIAN IS. (U.S. after 1898)
MEXICO
Gulf of Mexico
BAHAMA IS. (Br.)
BERMUDA IS. (Br.)
CUBA (Sp. To 1898)
HAITI
PUERTO RICO (U.S. 1898)
DANISH WEST INDIES
GUADELOUPE (Fr.)
MARTINIQUE (Fr.)
BARBADOS (Br.)
TRINIDAD (Br.)
Verã Cruz
Mexico City
JAMAICA
Caribbean Sea
GUAT.
SALVADOR
HOND.
NIC.
C.R.
Caracas
VENEZUELA
CLIPPERTON I. (Fr.)
REP OF COLOMBIA
Bogotá
BR.
DU.
FR.
GUIANA
Quito
ECUADOR
Belem
UNITED STATES OF BRAZIL
Recife
São Salvador
PERU
BOLIVIA
Callao
Lima
Mollendo
Arica
La Paz
Antofagasta
São Paulo
Rio de Janeiro
Santos
PARAGUAY
Asuncion
Valparaiso
Santiago
Montevideo
URUGUAY
Buenos Aires
JUAN FERNANDEZ IS. (Chile)
CHILE
ARGENTINA
FALKLAND IS. (Br.)
TIERRA DEL FUEGO
CAPE HORN
CHRISTMAS I. (Br. 1888)
MARQUESAS IS. (Fr.)
SAMOA IS. (Ger. 1899) (U.S. 1899)
SOCIETY IS. (Fr. 1880)
TUAMOTU IS. (Fr. 1881)
TONGA OR FRIENDLY IS. (Br. 1899)
EASTER I. (Chile)
FAEROES (Denmark)
SHETLAND IS.
ORKNEY IS.
SCOTLAND
Glasgow
IRELAND
Dublin
ENGLAND
London
FRANCE
PORTUGAL
SPAIN
Lisbon
Madrid
Gibraltar
AZORES (Port.)
MADEIRA IS. (Port.)
MOROCCO
CANARY IS. (Sp.)
RIO DE ORO (Sp.)
CAPE VERDE IS. (Port.)
PORT. GUINEA
SIERRA LEONE
LIBERIA
GOLD COAST
Ocean
ASCENSION (Br.)
ST. HELENA (Br.)
TRISTAN DA CUNHA (Br.)

6
7
8
9
10
A
B
C
D
E
F
G
H
Arctic Ocean
Fridtjof Nansen in Fram 1893-1896
FRANZ JOSEF LAND OR FRIDTJOF NANSEN LAND (Russia 1928)
NORTHERN LAND (NICHOLAS II)
SPITSBERGEN (Norway 1920)
Nansen 1893-1896
Abruzzi 1900
Duke of Abruzzi in Stella Polare 1900
Baron Adolf Erik
Nansen 1893 - 1896
NEW SIBERIAN ISLANDS
DE LONG IS.
DeLong 1879-1881
BEAR I. (Nor.)
Barents Sea
NOVAYA ZEMLYA
Kara Sea
TAIMYR PENINSULA
Nordenskiöld in 1878-1879 Vega
WRANGEL I.
De Long Strait
1879-1879
NORTH CAPE
Hammerfest
Vardö
Nordenskiöld
LOFOTEN IS.
KDM. OF SWEDEN AND NORWAY
NORWAY
SWEDEN
GR. DUCHY OF FINLAND
Russian Tsar Grand Duke since 1809
Archangel
RUSSIAN EMPIRE
Yakutsk
Christiania
St. Petersburg
Göteborg
Stockholm
North Sea
Baltic Sea
DEN.
NETH.
Hamburg
BEL.
GER. EMP.
Berlin
Warsaw
Paris
SWITZ.
AUS. HUNG.
Vienna
Budapest
Odessa
Marseille
SERB.
RUM.
BUL.
ITALY
Rome
Naples
Black Sea
Constantinople
TURKISH EMPIRE
GREECE
Mediterranean Sea
ALG.
TUNIS
MALTA (Br.)
CRETE (Gr. 1898)
CYPRUS (Br. 1878)
TRIPOLI (Turk.)
EGYPT
Alexandria
Moscow
Ufa
Kurgan
Omsk
Tomsk
Tobolsk
Krasnoyarsk
Trans-Siberian Railway
Samara
Volga
Don
Caspian Sea
Aral Sea
Lake Balkhash
Irtysh
Yenisei
Lena
Lake Baikal
Irkutsk
Chita
Sea of Okhotsk
Blagovyeshchensk
SAKHALIN (Russia 1875)
Petropavlovsk
MONGOLIA
Urga
MANCHURIA
Khabarovsk
KURILE IS.
Nordenskiöld 1879
Harbin
Vladivostok
Moukden
KULJA (Russia 1871-188)
EMPIRE OF CHINA
Merv (1885)
Teheran
Bagdad
PERSIA
AFG.
Kabul
SINKIANG
Kashgar
Peking
Huang Ho
Port Arthur (Russia 1898)
Weihaiwei (Br. 1898)
KOREA
EMPIRE OF JAPAN
Tokyo
Yokohama
Tsing Tao (Ger. 1897)
TIBET
Lhasa
China, Manchu Dynasty since 1644
CHINA PROPER
Shanghai
BALUCH. (Br. 1876)
Delhi
NEPAL
BHUTAN
Yangtze
BRITISH INDIAN EMPIRE
also many semiautonomous Indian states
INDIA
ARABIA
Persian Gulf
Red Sea
OMAN
Muscat
Mecca
Macao (Port.)
Hong Kong (Br.)
RYUKYU IS. (Jap. 1879)
OGASAWARA IS. (BONIN IS.) (Jap. 1878)
FORMOSA (Jap. since 1895)
MARCUS I. (Jap. 1899)
Pacific Ocean
SUDAN
ERIT.
KURIA MURIA IS. (Br.)
GOA (Port.)
Bombay
Calcutta
BURMA
Mandalay
Rangoon
Kwangchowwan (Fr. 1898)
FR. INDO-CHINA
SIAM
Bangkok
MARIANAS (Ger. 1899)
WAKE I. (U.S. 1898)
ADEN
SOCOTRA (Br. 1886)
Mahé (Fr.)
Madras
ANDAMAN IS. (Br.)
PHILIPPINE IS. (U.S. 1899)
GUAM (U.S. 1898)
CAROLINES (Ger. 1899)
MARSHALL IS. (Ger. 1899)
ABYSSINIA
LACCADIVE IS. (Br.)
Pondichéry
FR. SOM.
BR. SOM.
IT. SOM.
CEYLON
NICOBAR IS. (Br.)
STRAITS SETTLEMENTS
SARAWAK (Br. 1888)
N. BORNEO (1888)
PELEW IS. (Ger. 1899)
GILBERT IS. (Br. 1899)
MALDIVE IS. (Br.)
Singapore
SUMATRA
BORNEO
MOLUCCA
NEW GUINEA (Neth. 1901) (Ger. 1884) (Br. 1884)
NEW MECKLENBURG
BISMARCK IS. (Ger. 1884)
ELLICE IS. (Br. 1892)
NEW POMERANIA
SOLOMON IS. Div. between Br. and Ger. 1899
TOGO-LAND
Lake Chad
NIGERIA
KAMERUN
SP. GUINEA
CONGO FREE STATE Ruled by Leopold II of Belgium
E. AFR.
CABINDA (Port.)
Loanda
ANGOLA
GER. E. AFR.
ZANZIBAR (Br. 1890)
SEYCHELLES (Br.)
CELEBES
JAVA
(Port.) TIMOR (Neth.)
RHODESIA
PORT. E. AFR.
COMORO IS. (Fr.)
Mozambique
MADAGASCAR (Fr. 1896)
Indian Ocean
COCOS IS (Br. 1876)
Darwin
NORTHERN TERRITORY
NEW HEBRIDES
FIJI IS. (Br. 1874)
GER. S.W. AFR.
BECHUANA-LAND
TRANS-VAAL
MAURITIUS (Br.)
REUNION (Fr.)
COMMONWEALTH OF AUSTRALIA
WESTERN AUSTRALIA
QUEENSLAND
(including Tasmania formed in 1901)
NEW CALEDONIA (Fr.)
LOYALTY IS. (Fr. 1864)
ORANGE FREE STATE
Lourenço Marques
NATAL
CAPE COLONY
Capetown
Brisbane
SOUTH AUSTRALIA
Perth
NEW SOUTH WALES
Sydney
Adelaide
VICTORIA
Melbourne
TASMANIA
Wellington
NEW ZEALAND Organized as a Dominion in 1907
A-410041-29-1-1-1-1
Copyright by Rand McNally & Company, Made in U.S.A.

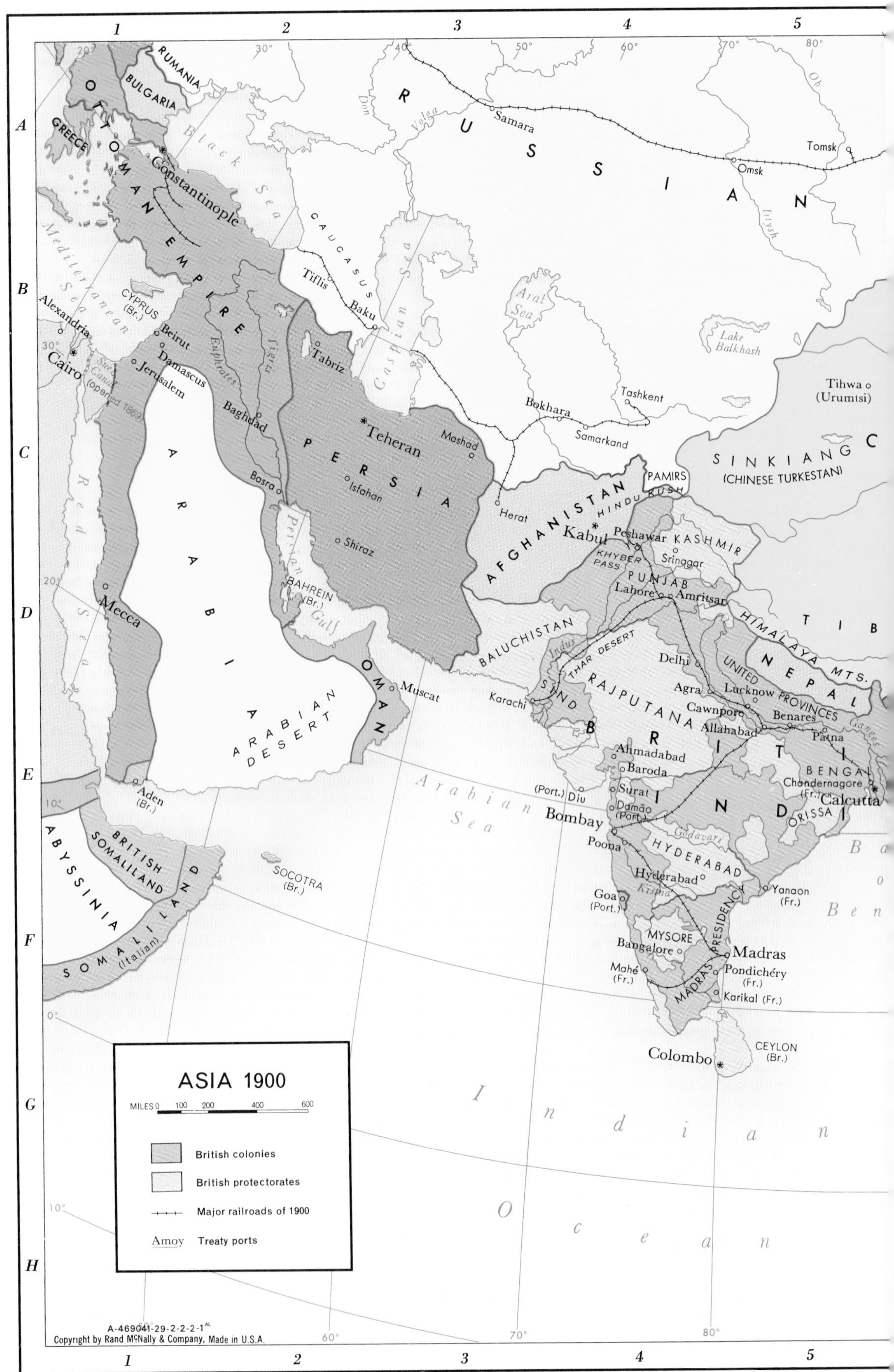
ASIA 1900
MILES 0 100 200 400 600
British colonies
British protectorates
Major railroads of 1900
Amoy Treaty ports
RUMANIA
BULGARIA
GREECE
OTTOMAN EMPIRE
Constantinople
Black Sea
Mediterranean Sea
CYPRUS (Br.)
Alexandria
Cairo
Suez Canal (opened 1869)
Beirut
Damascus
Jerusalem
Euphrates
Tigris
Baghdad
Basra
CAUCASUS
Tiflis
Baku
Caspian Sea
Tabriz
Teheran
PERSIA
Isfahan
Shiraz
Mashad
Persian Gulf
BAHREIN (Br.)
ARABIA
Mecca
Red Sea
OMAN
Muscat
ARABIAN DESERT
Aden (Br.)
RUSSIAN
Samara
Volga
Don
Tomsk
Omsk
Irtysh
Ob
Aral Sea
Lake Balkhash
Tashkent
Bokhara
Samarkand
Tihwa (Urumtsi)
SINKIANG (CHINESE TURKESTAN)
PAMIRS
AFGHANISTAN
HINDU KUSH
Herat
Kabul
Peshawar
KHYBER PASS
KASHMIR
Srinagar
PUNJAB
Lahore
Amritsar
BALUCHISTAN
Indus
THAR DESERT
SIND
Karachi
RAJPUTANA
Delhi
Agra
UNITED PROVINCES
Lucknow
Cawnpore
Allahabad
Benares
Patna
Ganges
NEPAL
HIMALAYA MTS.
TIB
BRITISH INDIA
BENGAL
Chandernagore (Fr.)
Calcutta
ORISSA
Ahmadabad
Baroda
Surat
(Port.) Diu
Damão (Port.)
Bombay
Poona
Arabian Sea
Godavari
HYDERABAD
Hyderabad
Kistna
Goa (Port.)
Yanaon (Fr.)
MADRAS PRESIDENCY
MYSORE
Bangalore
Madras
Mahé (Fr.)
Pondichéry (Fr.)
Karikal (Fr.)
CEYLON (Br.)
Colombo
Bay of Bengal
Indian Ocean
ABYSSINIA
BRITISH SOMALILAND
SOMALILAND (Italian)
SOCOTRA (Br.)
A-469041-29-2-2-2-1
Copyright by Rand McNally & Company, Made in U.S.A.

6
7
8
9
10
A
B
C
D
E
F
G
H
Yenisei
Lake Baikal
Irkutsk
Chita
E M P I R E
Heilung (Amur)
MANCHURIA
SAKHALIN (Russ.) (Southern half to Japan 1905)
CHISHIMA (KURILS) (Jap.)
HOKKAIDO
Hakodate
Vladivostok
Kirin
Urga
MONGOLIA
Sea of Japan
(Liaotung Peninsula Russ. lease 1898, transferred to Japan 1905)
Mukden
Newchwang
Yalu
Pyongyang
Wonsan
Seoul
KOREA
(Annexed by Japan 1910)
Chemulpo
Pusan
Niigata
Tokyo
Yokohama
Nagoya
Kyoto
Kobe
Osaka
(Treaty port status abolished in Japan 1899)
GOBI DESERT
Chinwangtao
Dalny (Dairen)
Port Arthur
Peking
Tientsin
Chefoo
Weihaiwei (Br. lease 1898)
Kiaochow Bay (Ger. lease 1898, Japan 1914)
Tsingtao
Tsinan
HONSHU
SHIKOKU
KYUSHU
Nagasaki
JAPAN
OGASAWARA (BONINS) (Jap.)
CHINESE EMPIRE
Huang
Lanchow
Kaifeng
Sian
Chinkiang
Soochow
Nanking
Wuhu
Shanghai
Hankow
Wuchang
Hangchow
Ningpo
Ichang
Shasi
Kiukiang
Yochow
Nanchang
Wenchow
Chengtu
CHINA
Chungking
Changsha
Santuao
Foochow
RYUKYU IS. (Japan)
Taihoku
TAIWAN (FORMOSA) (Japan) (from China 1895)
Pacific Ocean
Lhasa
Brahmaputra
Yangtze
BHUTAN
ASSAM
Amoy
Swatow
Yünnanfu
Hsi (West)
Canton
Mengtze
Wuchow
Samshui
Hong Kong (Br. 1842, Suppl. lease 1898)
Szemao
Lungchow
Macao (Port.)
Kwangchowwan (Fr. lease 1898)
Pakhoi
(Br. from 1885)
Mandalay
BURMA (Br. from 1852)
TONGKING (Fr. prot. from 1884)
Hanoi
Luang Prabang
(To Fr. 1907)
Kiungchow
HAINAN
LAOS (Fr. prot. 1893)
ANNAM (Fr. prot. from 1884)
FRENCH INDO-CHINA
Hué
Mekong
South China Sea
LUZON
PHILIPPINE ISLANDS
Manila
(U.S. from Spain 1898)
CAROLINE IS. (Ger.) (Purchased from Spain 1898)
Prome
Rangoon
SIAM
(To Fr. 1907)
Bangkok
Iloilo
Cebu
PALAU IS. (Ger.) (Purchased from Spain 1898)
ANDAMAN IS. (Br.)
Gulf of Siam
CAMBODIA (Fr. prot. from 1863)
Phnom Penh
Saigon
COCHIN CHINA (Fr. prot. 1862-67)
Zamboanga
MINDANAO
NICOBAR IS. (Br.)
NORTH BORNEO
BRUNEI
(To Br. prot. 1907-09)
NEW GUINEA
Penang
SARAWAK
(Finally subdued by the Dutch, 1899)
ACHEH
FEDERATED MALAY STATES (from 1895)
Malacca
JOHORE
Singapore
BORNEO
CELEBES
MOLUCCAS
Amboina
SUMATRA
BANKA
BILLITON
Palembang
DUTCH EAST INDIES
Semarang
Surabaya
JAVA
Batavia
Solo
Jokjakarta
BALI
TIMOR (Port.)
90°
100°
110°
120°
130°
140°
150°
160°
40°
30°
20°
10°
0°

1
2
3
4
5
A
B
C
D
E
F
G
H
30°
10°
0°
10°
20°
50°
40°
30°
Arctic
ICELAND
Reykjavik
Atlantic
Ocean
SHETLAND ISLANDS
HEBRIDES
ORKNEY IS.
Bergen
Stavanger
Oslo
NORWAY
Occupied by Germany 1940
SWEDEN
Tornio
Gulf of Bothnia
Vaasa (Vasa)
ALAND IS.
Helsingfors (Helsinki)
Uppsala
Stockholm
Gulf of Finland
Revel
ESTON
Annexed by USSR
Baltic
Sea
SCOTLAND
Aberdeen
North
Sea
Glasgow
Edinburgh
GREAT BRITAIN
IRISH FREE STATE
Dublin
Belfast
Cork
Liverpool
Manchester
Leeds
Hull
Sheffield
WALES
Birmingham
ENGLAND
Cardiff
Oxford
Bristol
Plymouth
Portsmouth
Thames
London
Dover
Göteborg
DENMARK
Occupied by Germany 1940
Aalborg
Hälsingborg
Copenhagen
ÖLAND
GOTLAND
LATV
Riga
Annexed by USSR
HELGOLAND
BORNHOLM
Kiel
Lübeck
Hamburg
Bremen
Elbe
Weser
MEMELAND
To Ger. 1939
Memel
Königsberg
LITHUANIA
Annexed by USSR 1940
Kovno (Kaunas)
Vilna
Danzig
EAST PRUSSIA
Tannenberg
Grodno
NETHERLANDS
Occ. by Ger. 1940
Rotterdam
Amsterdam
Hanover
Stettin
Berlin
Potsdam
Magdeburg
Essen
Cologne
Cassel
Leipzig
GERMANY
Dresden
Oder
Posen
Warsaw
Vistula
POLAND
Nazi-Soviet Pact Annexed by Germany 1939
Bialystok
Brest Litovsk
Lublin
Curzon Line 1919-1920
Annexed by USSR 1939
Nazi-Soviet Pact
English Channel
Dunkirk
Brussels
BEL
Occ. by Ger. 1940
Lille
Brest
CHANNEL IS.
Havre
Amiens
Caen
Seine
Rennes
Versailles
Paris
Reims
LORRAINE
Verdun
LUX.
Occ. 1940
SAAR
To Germany Plebiscite 1935
Mainz
Frankfurt
Weimar
Mannheim
Nürnberg
BAVARIA
Stuttgart
Strassburg
ALSACE
St. Nazaire
Nantes
Loire
Orléans
Occupied by Germany 1940
Fontainbleau
FRANCE
Bay of Biscay
La Rochelle
Dijon
Saône
Bordeaux
Limoges
Lyon
Basel
Zürich
Berne
SWITZERLAND
Geneva
LIECH.
Innsbruck
Munich
Danube
Vienna
AUSTRIA
To Germany Anschluss 1938
To Ger. at Munich 1938
SILESIA
Breslau
Pilsen
Prague
CZECHOSLOVAKIA
Cracow
To Pol. 1938
Tesin
Przemysl
Lemberg (Lwow)
Tarnopol
Bratislava (Pressburg)
Annexed by Hungary 1938
Kosice
RUTHENIA
Annexed by Hungary 1939
Budapest
HUNGARY
Oradea
Annexed by Hungary 1940
Cluj
TRANSYLVANIA
BUKOVINA
Corunna
Oporto
Coimbra
Lisbon
PORTUGAL
Burgos
Santander
Bayonne
Garonne
VICHY FRANCE 1940
Grenoble
TRENTINO
Drava
Graz
Duero
Valladolid
Salamanca
Madrid
Tagus
Toledo
SPAIN
Guadiana
Cordoba
Guadalquivir
Seville
Granada
Cadiz
Tangier
Gibralter (To Great Britain)
SPANISH AREA
Almeria
Cartagena
Valencia
Ebro
Saragossa
PYRENEES
ANDORRA
Toulouse
Montpellier
Rhone
Avignon
Marseille
Toulon
Nice
San Remo
Milan
Verona
Venice
Trieste
Ljubljana
Zagreb
Mohacs
Turin
Po
Parma
Genoa
Ravenna
Bologna
Fiume
Italy 1924
CROATIA
Sava
YUGOSLAVIA
Temisoara
Sibiu
RUMAN
WALLACHIA
Belgrade
Bucharest
Ruschuk
SAN MARINO
Florence
Ancona
Zara
BOSNIA
Sarajevo
DALMATIA
SERBIA
Morava
Nish
Sistova
Barcelona
BALERIC ISLANDS (To Spain)
MINORCA
MAJORCA
Ajaccio
CORSICA (To France)
ITALY
Tiber
Rome
Adriatic Sea
Split
LAGOSTA (To Italy)
Dubrovnik (Ragusa)
MONTENEGRO
Cattaro
Novi Pazar
BULGAR
Sofia
Antivari
Durazzo
ALBANIA
Tirana
Philippopolis
Skoplje
Adrianople
MACEDONIA
Dede-Agach
Kavala
Enos
Salonika
Vardar
SARDINIA (To Italy)
Naples
Bari
Taranto
Brindisi
Valona
CORFU
Yannina
Dardanelles
Cagliari
Tyrrhenian Sea
Palermo
Messina
SICILY
Syracuse
Ionian Sea
CEPHALLENIA
IONIAN ISLANDS
GREECE
Messolongi
Patras
Athens
Sparta
LESBOS
Aegean Sea
Mediterranean
MALTA (Br.)
Candi
CRETE
Rabat
MOROCCO
To France
ATLAS
MOUNTAINS
Oran
Algiers
Tunis
TUNIS
French Protectorate
ALGERIA
To France
AFRICA
Tripoli
TRIPOLITANIA
To Italy
LIBYA
Bengazi
Gulf of Sidra
CYRENAICA
To Italy

EUROPE 1922-40
MILES 0 50 100 200 300
Principal status quo powers
Principal Revisionist powers
1914 Boundaries
1922 Boundaries
UNION OF SOVIET SOCIALIST REPUBLICS
URAL MOUNTAINS
ASIA
UKRAINE
TURKEY
ASIA MINOR
SYRIA
IRAQ
Independent since 1932
PERSIA
TURKESTAN
ARABIA
KURDISTAN
PALESTINE
Br. Mandate
TRANSJORDAN
Br. Mandate
KUWAIT
REPUBLIC OF GEORGIA
REPUBLIC OF ARMENIA
REPUBLIC OF AZERBAIJAN
DAGHESTAN
KOLA PENINSULA
MURMAN COAST
Black Sea
Caspian Sea
Aral Sea
Sea of Azov
Persian Gulf
Red Sea
Dead Sea
White Sea
Lake Onega
Lake Ladoga
L. Urmia
Moscow
Leningrad (Petrograd)
Kronstadt
Archangel
Murmansk
Pechenga
Vologda
Yaroslavl
Novgorod
Pskov
Kalinin (Tver)
Gorkii (Nizhni Novgorod)
Kazañ
Kirov
Molotov
Sverdlovsk
Cheliabinsk
Magnitogorsk
Kustanai
Akmolinsk
Ufa
Kuibyshev
Chkalov
Orsk
Uralsk
Saratov
Penza
Tambov
Tula
Riazan
Orel
Briansk
Smolensk
Vitebsk
Minsk
Borisov
Mogilev
Kursk
Voronezh
Chernigov
Kiev
Zhitomir
Kharkov
Poltava
Kirovograd (Elizavetgrad)
Dnepropetrovsk (Ekaterinoslav)
Taganrog
Rostov
Stalingrad
Astrakhan
Voroshilovsk (Stavropol)
Krasnodar (Ekaterinodar)
Novorossiisk (Anapa)
Sevastopol
Cherson
Odessa
Kishinev
Czernowitz
BESSARABIA
Annexed by USSR 1940
Galatz
Constantsa
To Bulgaria 1940
Varna
Burgas
Grozni
Petrovsk
Ordzhonikidze (Vladikavkaz)
Derbent
Baku
Tiflis
Sukhumi
Poti
Batum
Kars
Erivan
Lenkoran
Krasnovodsk
Tabriz
Teheran
Trebizond
Samsun
Sinope
Tokat
Eregli
Skutari
Brusa
Ankara (Angora)
Smyrna
Aidin
Konia
Adana
Adalia
Makri
RHODES
ALEXANDRETTA
Annexed by Turkey 1939
Aleppo
Latakia
Homs
Beirut
Damascus
Nikosia
CYPRUS (Br.)
Limasol
Acre
Jaffa
Jerusalem
Amman
Alexandria
Port Said
Cairo
Mosul
Bagdad
Kuwait
Line of the treaty of Sevres
Bdry. between Syria and Turkey as Estab'd by Agree. Aug. 1921
Bdry. of Armenia by President Wilson arbitrated
Bdry. line between Fr. and Br. Mandate Terr's. as Estab'd. by Agree. Dec. 23, 1920
Independent Kingdom with British Protective Rights
EGYPT
Volga
Don
Dnieper
Oka
Kama
Belaia
Ural
Tobol
Ishim
Irtish
Ob
Pechora
Dvina
Vychegda
Kuban
Terek
Kura
Tigris
Euphrates
Kizil Irmak
Bosporus
Nile
Pripet
Bug
Dniester
Prut
30° 40° 50° 60° 70°
6 7 8 9 10
A B C D E F G H

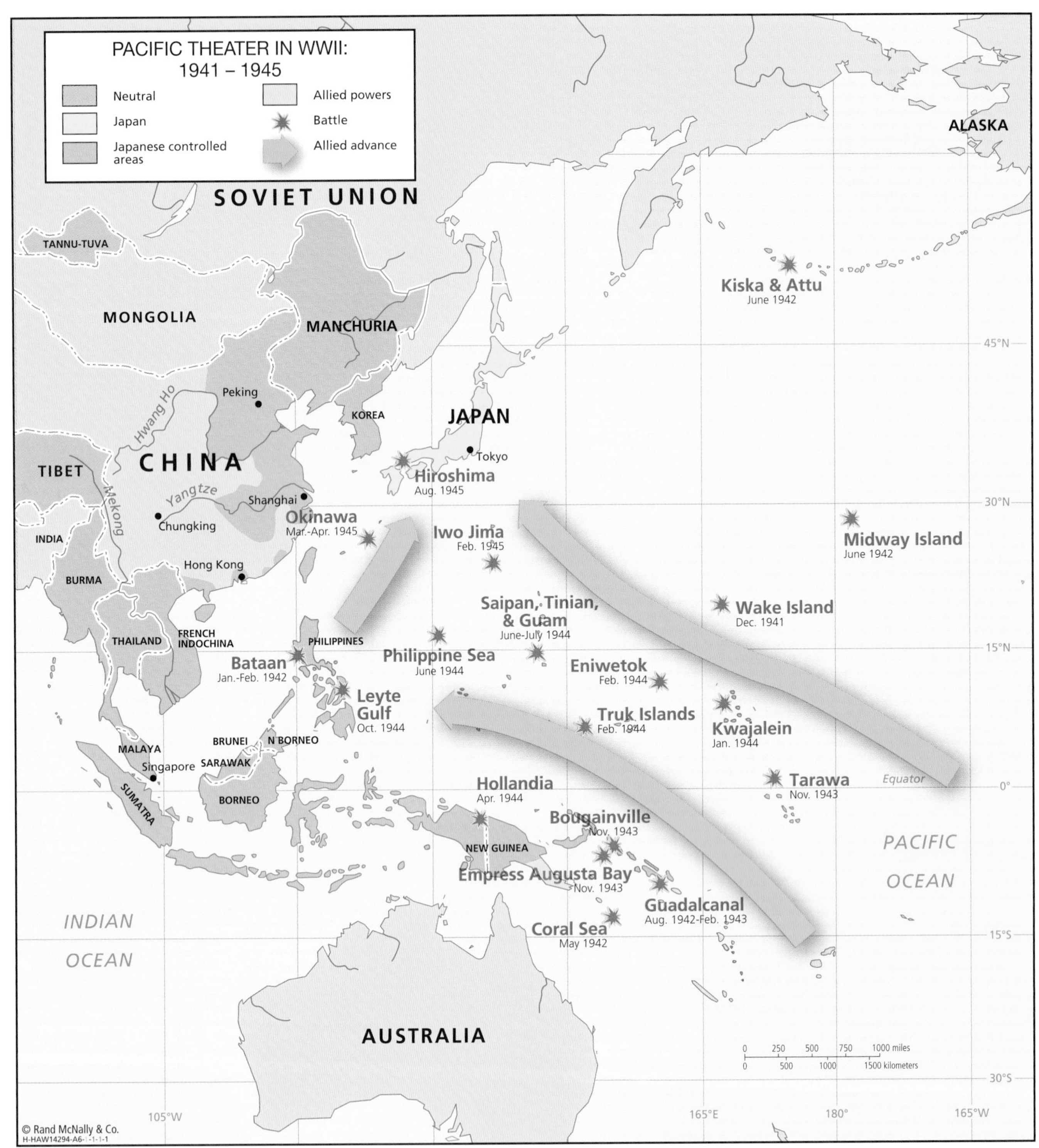

U.S. Casualties in World War II

BRANCH	NUMBERS ENGAGED	BATTLE DEATHS	OTHER DEATHS	TOTAL DEATHS	WOUNDS NOT MORTAL	TOTAL CASUALTIES
Army*	11,260,000	234,874	83,400	318,274	565,861	884,135
Navy	4,183,466	36,950	25,664	62,614	37,778	100,392
Marines	669,100	19,773	4,778	24,511	67,207	91,718
Total	**16,112,566**	**291,557**	**113,842**	**405,399**	**670,846**	**1,076,245**

*Includes Air Force

Source: *Information Please Almanac* (Boston: Houghton Mifflin Co., 1988)

World War II Casualties

COUNTRY	BATTLE DEATHS	WOUNDED
Australia	26,976	180,684
China	1,324,516	1,762,006
India	32,121	64,354
Japan	1,270,000	140,000
New Zealand	11,625	17,000
United Kingdom	357,116	369,267
United States	291,557	670,846

Source: *Information Please Almanac* (Boston: Houghton Mifflin Co., 1988)

World War II Casualties

COUNTRY	BATTLE DEATHS	WOUNDED
Austria	280,000	350,117
Canada	32,714	53,145
France	201,568	400,000
Germany	3,250,000	7,250,000
Hungary	147,435	89,313
Italy	149,496	66,716
Poland	320,000	530,000
Soviet Union	6,115,000	14,012,000

Source: *Information Please Almanac* (Boston: Houghton Mifflin Co., 1988)

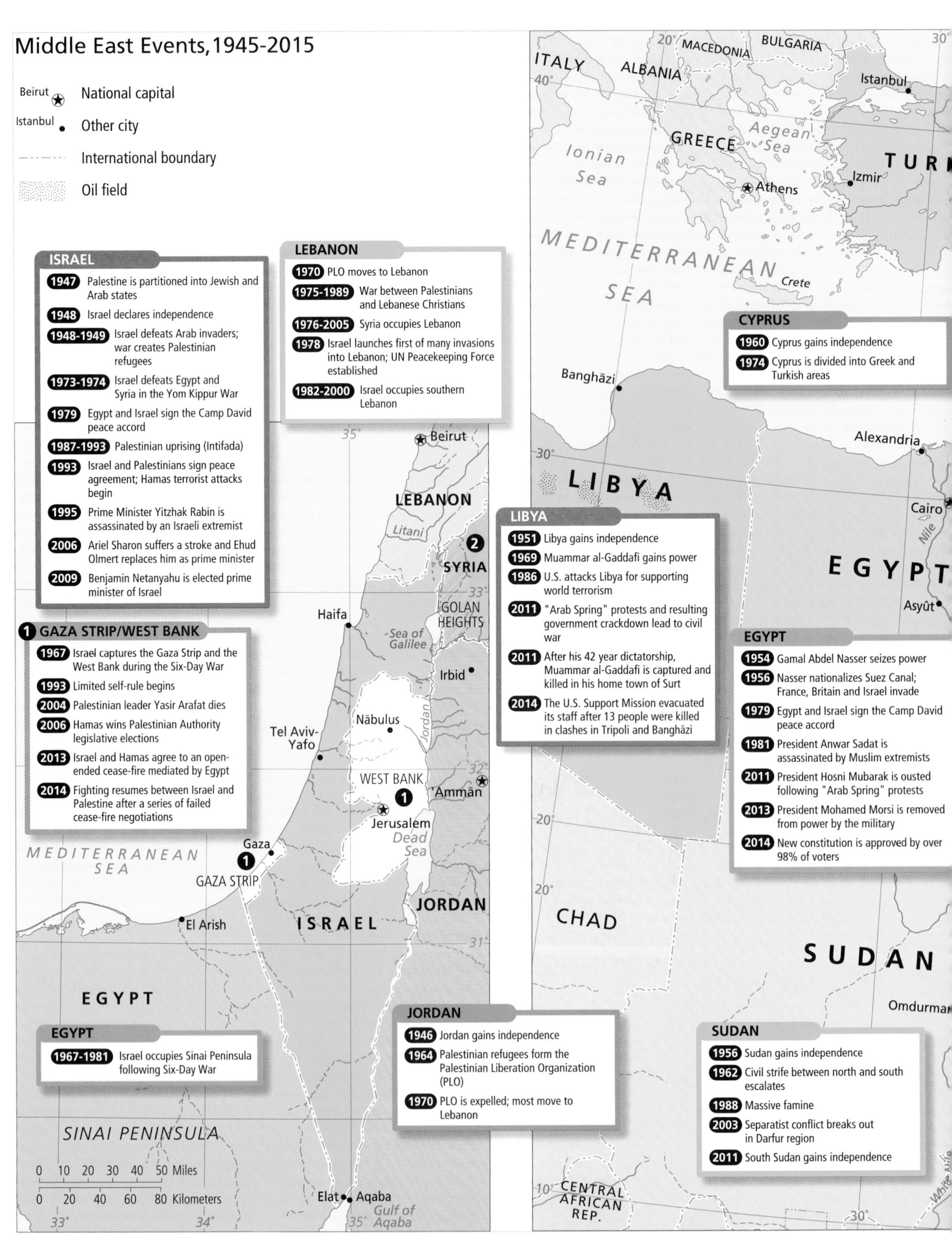
Middle East Events, 1945-2015
Beirut National capital
Istanbul Other city
International boundary
Oil field
ISRAEL
1947 Palestine is partitioned into Jewish and Arab states
1948 Israel declares independence
1948-1949 Israel defeats Arab invaders; war creates Palestinian refugees
1973-1974 Israel defeats Egypt and Syria in the Yom Kippur War
1979 Egypt and Israel sign the Camp David peace accord
1987-1993 Palestinian uprising (Intifada)
1993 Israel and Palestinians sign peace agreement; Hamas terrorist attacks begin
1995 Prime Minister Yitzhak Rabin is assassinated by an Israeli extremist
2006 Ariel Sharon suffers a stroke and Ehud Olmert replaces him as prime minister
2009 Benjamin Netanyahu is elected prime minister of Israel
LEBANON
1970 PLO moves to Lebanon
1975-1989 War between Palestinians and Lebanese Christians
1976-2005 Syria occupies Lebanon
1978 Israel launches first of many invasions into Lebanon; UN Peacekeeping Force established
1982-2000 Israel occupies southern Lebanon
1 GAZA STRIP/WEST BANK
1967 Israel captures the Gaza Strip and the West Bank during the Six-Day War
1993 Limited self-rule begins
2004 Palestinian leader Yasir Arafat dies
2006 Hamas wins Palestinian Authority legislative elections
2013 Israel and Hamas agree to an open-ended cease-fire mediated by Egypt
2014 Fighting resumes between Israel and Palestine after a series of failed cease-fire negotiations
EGYPT
1967-1981 Israel occupies Sinai Peninsula following Six-Day War
JORDAN
1946 Jordan gains independence
1964 Palestinian refugees form the Palestinian Liberation Organization (PLO)
1970 PLO is expelled; most move to Lebanon
LIBYA
1951 Libya gains independence
1969 Muammar al-Gaddafi gains power
1986 U.S. attacks Libya for supporting world terrorism
2011 "Arab Spring" protests and resulting government crackdown lead to civil war
2011 After his 42 year dictatorship, Muammar al-Gaddafi is captured and killed in his home town of Surt
2014 The U.S. Support Mission evacuated its staff after 13 people were killed in clashes in Tripoli and Banghāzi
CYPRUS
1960 Cyprus gains independence
1974 Cyprus is divided into Greek and Turkish areas
EGYPT
1954 Gamal Abdel Nasser seizes power
1956 Nasser nationalizes Suez Canal; France, Britain and Israel invade
1979 Egypt and Israel sign the Camp David peace accord
1981 President Anwar Sadat is assassinated by Muslim extremists
2011 President Hosni Mubarak is ousted following "Arab Spring" protests
2013 President Mohamed Morsi is removed from power by the military
2014 New constitution is approved by over 98% of voters
SUDAN
1956 Sudan gains independence
1962 Civil strife between north and south escalates
1988 Massive famine
2003 Separatist conflict breaks out in Darfur region
2011 South Sudan gains independence
ITALY
ALBANIA
MACEDONIA
BULGARIA
GREECE
Istanbul
Aegean Sea
Ionian Sea
Izmir
Athens
MEDITERRANEAN SEA
Crete
Banghāzi
Alexandria
LIBYA
Cairo
Nile
EGYPT
Asyût
CHAD
SUDAN
Omdurman
CENTRAL AFRICAN REP.
Beirut
LEBANON
Litani
SYRIA
GOLAN HEIGHTS
Haifa
Sea of Galilee
Irbid
Nābulus
Jordan
Tel Aviv-Yafo
WEST BANK
Ammān
Jerusalem
Dead Sea
Gaza
GAZA STRIP
MEDITERRANEAN SEA
El Arish
ISRAEL
JORDAN
EGYPT
SINAI PENINSULA
0 10 20 30 40 50 Miles
0 20 40 60 80 Kilometers
Elat
Aqaba
Gulf of Aqaba

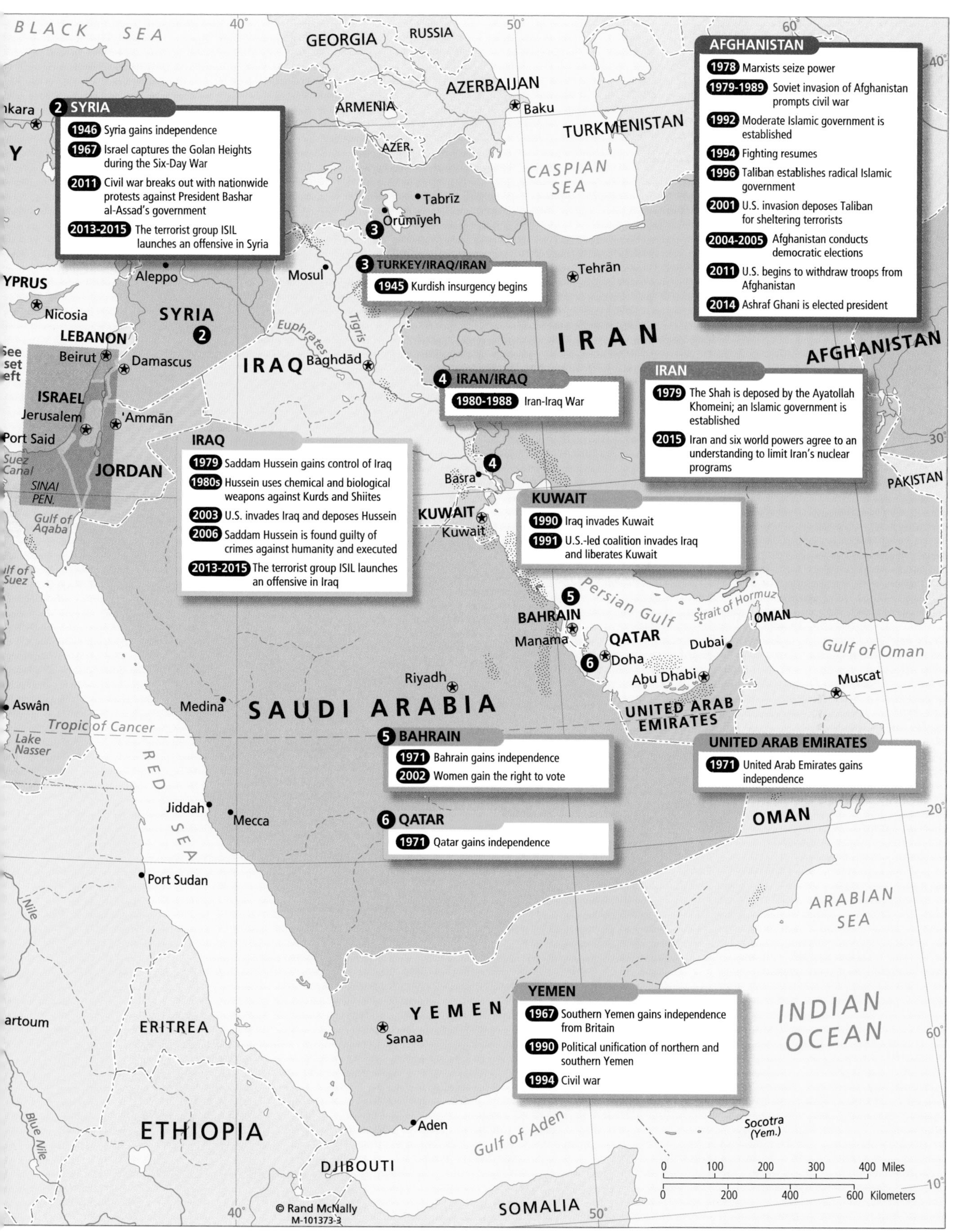
BLACK SEA
GEORGIA
RUSSIA
AZERBAIJAN
ARMENIA
AZER.
Baku
TURKMENISTAN
CASPIAN SEA
Tabrīz
Orūmīyeh
Tehrān
Ankara
CYPRUS
Nicosia
LEBANON
Beirut
Damascus
SYRIA
Aleppo
Mosul
IRAQ
Baghdād
Euphrates
Tigris
ISRAEL
Jerusalem
'Ammān
JORDAN
Port Said
Suez Canal
SINAI PEN.
Gulf of Aqaba
Gulf of Suez
IRAN
AFGHANISTAN
PAKISTAN
Basra
KUWAIT
Kuwait
Persian Gulf
Strait of Hormuz
BAHRAIN
Manama
QATAR
Doha
Dubai
Abu Dhabi
UNITED ARAB EMIRATES
OMAN
Muscat
Gulf of Oman
Riyadh
SAUDI ARABIA
Medina
Mecca
Jiddah
Aswân
Tropic of Cancer
Lake Nasser
RED SEA
Port Sudan
Nile
ARABIAN SEA
YEMEN
Sanaa
Aden
Gulf of Aden
Socotra (Yem.)
INDIAN OCEAN
Khartoum
ERITREA
ETHIOPIA
Blue Nile
DJIBOUTI
SOMALIA
40°
50°
60°
30°
20°
10°
0 100 200 300 400 Miles
0 200 400 600 Kilometers
© Rand McNally
M-101373-3
2 SYRIA
1946 Syria gains independence
1967 Israel captures the Golan Heights during the Six-Day War
2011 Civil war breaks out with nationwide protests against President Bashar al-Assad's government
2013-2015 The terrorist group ISIL launches an offensive in Syria
3 TURKEY/IRAQ/IRAN
1945 Kurdish insurgency begins
AFGHANISTAN
1978 Marxists seize power
1979-1989 Soviet invasion of Afghanistan prompts civil war
1992 Moderate Islamic government is established
1994 Fighting resumes
1996 Taliban establishes radical Islamic government
2001 U.S. invasion deposes Taliban for sheltering terrorists
2004-2005 Afghanistan conducts democratic elections
2011 U.S. begins to withdraw troops from Afghanistan
2014 Ashraf Ghani is elected president
4 IRAN/IRAQ
1980-1988 Iran-Iraq War
IRAN
1979 The Shah is deposed by the Ayatollah Khomeini; an Islamic government is established
2015 Iran and six world powers agree to an understanding to limit Iran's nuclear programs
IRAQ
1979 Saddam Hussein gains control of Iraq
1980s Hussein uses chemical and biological weapons against Kurds and Shiites
2003 U.S. invades Iraq and deposes Hussein
2006 Saddam Hussein is found guilty of crimes against humanity and executed
2013-2015 The terrorist group ISIL launches an offensive in Iraq
KUWAIT
1990 Iraq invades Kuwait
1991 U.S.-led coalition invades Iraq and liberates Kuwait
5 BAHRAIN
1971 Bahrain gains independence
2002 Women gain the right to vote
6 QATAR
1971 Qatar gains independence
UNITED ARAB EMIRATES
1971 United Arab Emirates gains independence
YEMEN
1967 Southern Yemen gains independence from Britain
1990 Political unification of northern and southern Yemen
1994 Civil war

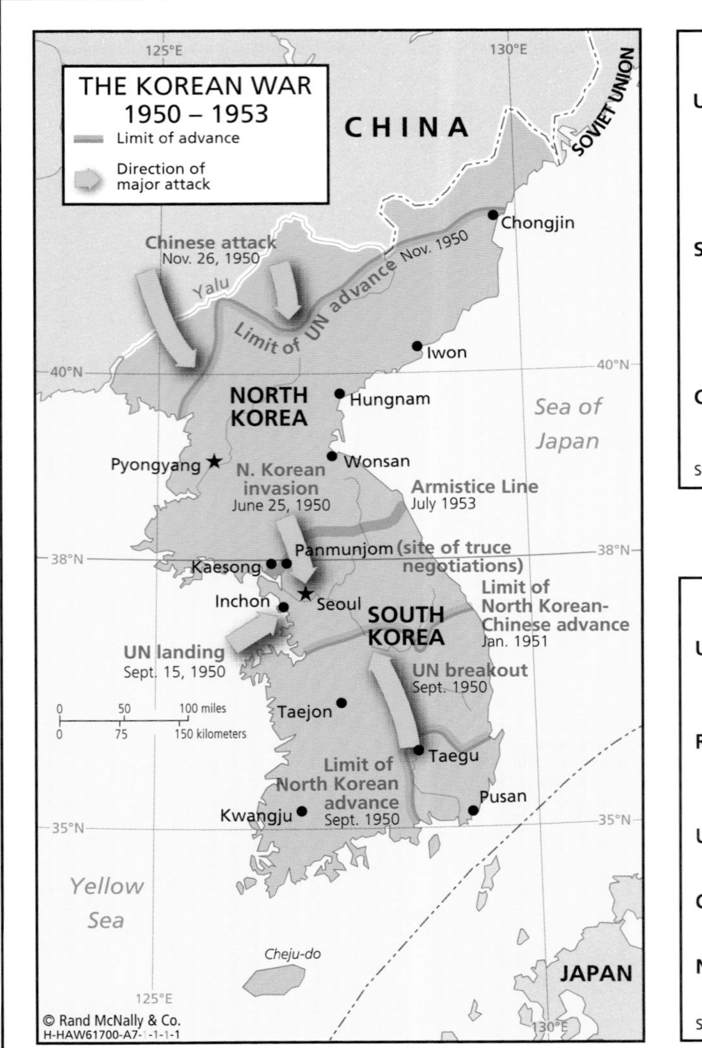

VIETNAM WAR CASUALTIES

United States	
Battle deaths	47,382
Wounded	153,303
Died, non-combat	1,811
Missing, captured	10,753
South Vietnam	
Military killed in action	110,357
Military wounded	499,026
Civilian killed	415,000
Civilian wounded	913,000
Communist Regulars and Guerillas	
Killed in action	666,000

Source: U.S. Department of Defense

KOREAN WAR CASUALTIES

United States	
Killed	36,913
Wounded	103,284
Republic of Korea	
Killed	415,004
Wounded	482,568
United Nations	
Killed and wounded	15,465
China	
Killed and wounded	900,000
North Korea	
Killed and wounded	520,000

Source: U.S. Department of Defense

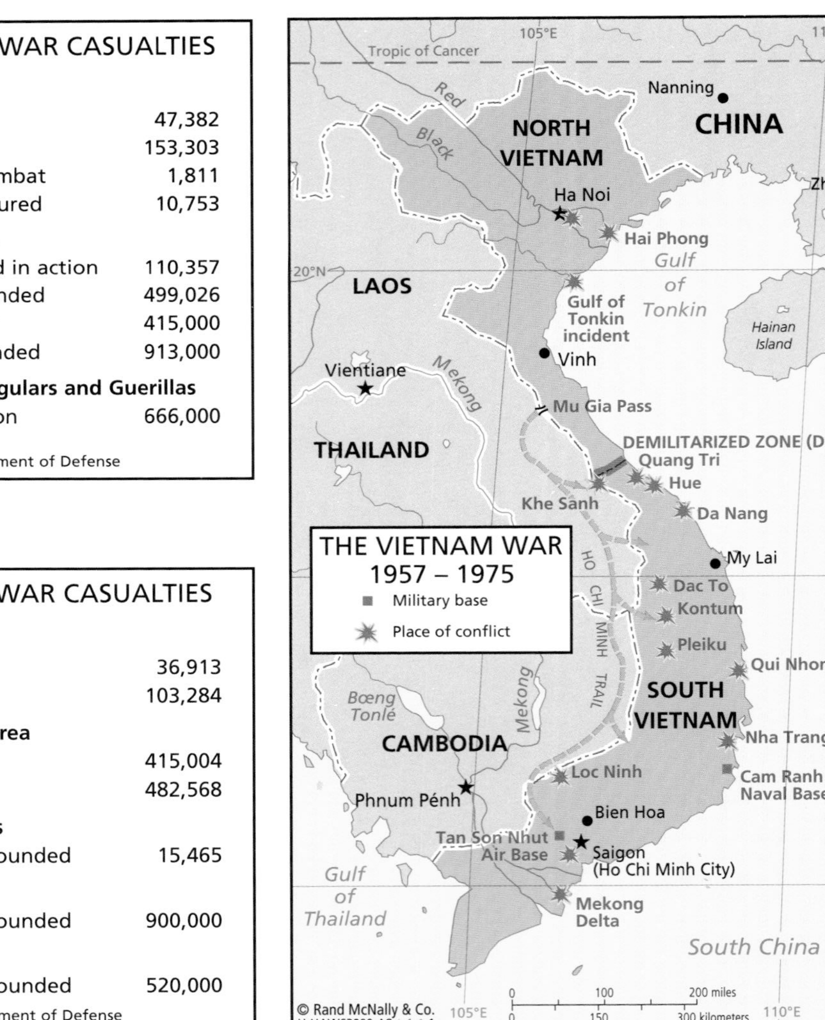

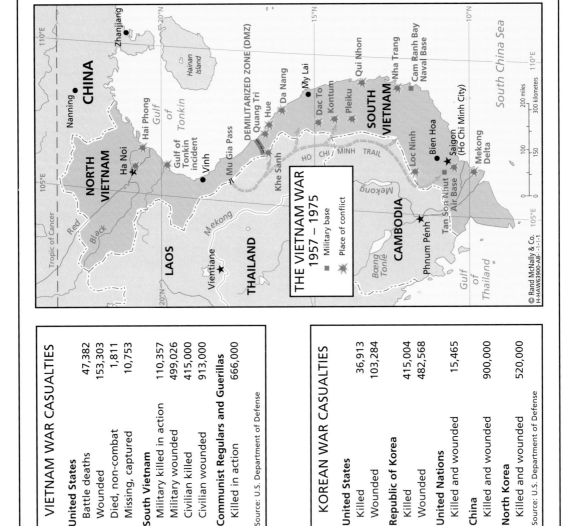

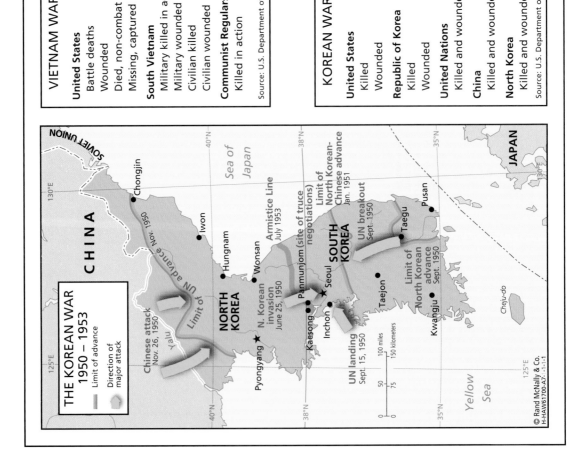

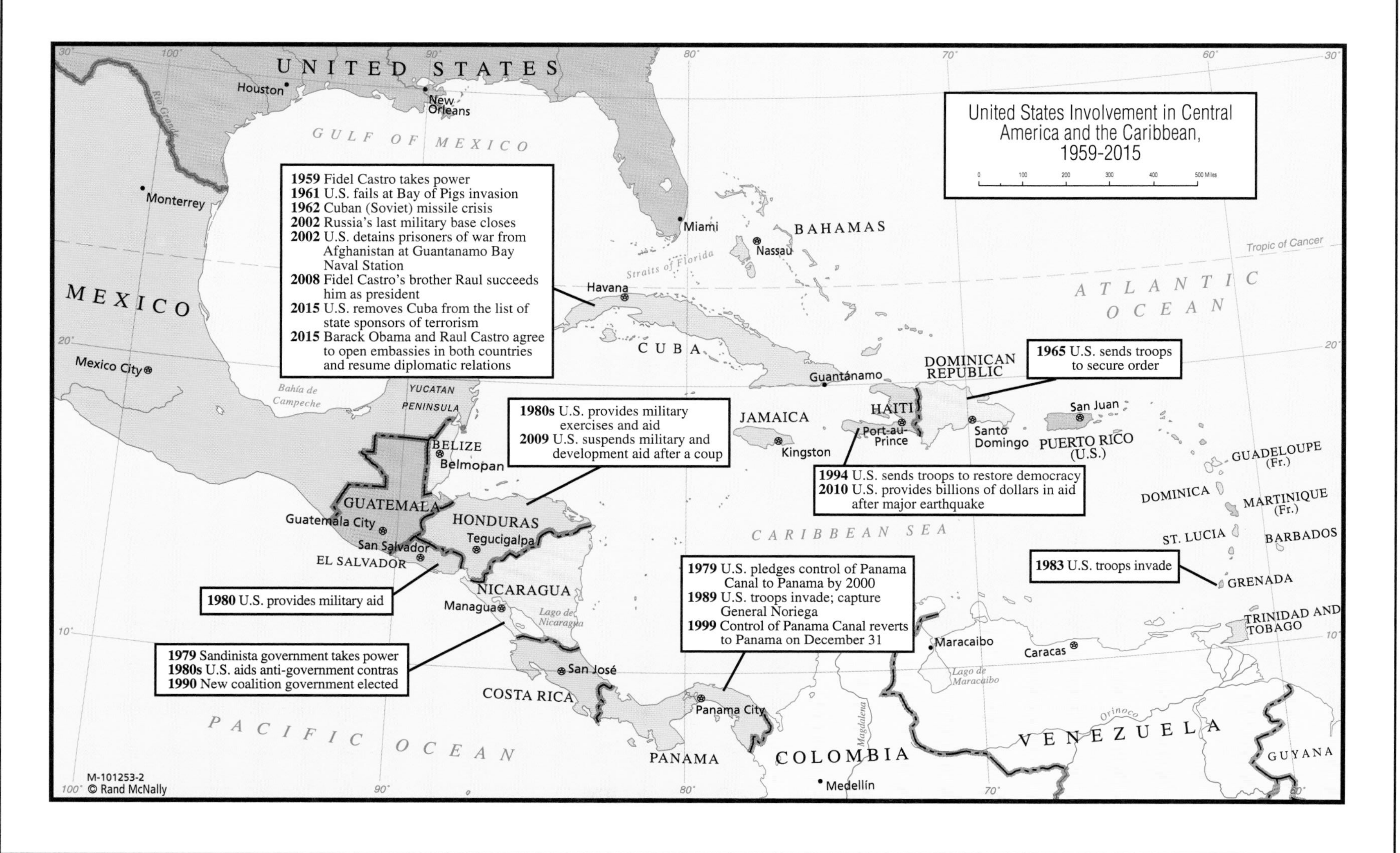
United States Involvement in Central America and the Caribbean, 1959-2015
0 100 200 300 400 500 Miles
UNITED STATES
Houston
New Orleans
Miami
GULF OF MEXICO
MEXICO
Monterrey
Mexico City
Rio Grande
Bahía de Campeche
YUCATAN PENINSULA
1959 Fidel Castro takes power
1961 U.S. fails at Bay of Pigs invasion
1962 Cuban (Soviet) missile crisis
2002 Russia's last military base closes
2002 U.S. detains prisoners of war from Afghanistan at Guantanamo Bay Naval Station
2008 Fidel Castro's brother Raul succeeds him as president
2015 U.S. removes Cuba from the list of state sponsors of terrorism
2015 Barack Obama and Raul Castro agree to open embassies in both countries and resume diplomatic relations
Havana
Straits of Florida
CUBA
Guantánamo
BAHAMAS
Nassau
Tropic of Cancer
ATLANTIC OCEAN
DOMINICAN REPUBLIC
1965 U.S. sends troops to secure order
HAITI
Port-au-Prince
Santo Domingo
San Juan
PUERTO RICO (U.S.)
JAMAICA
Kingston
1994 U.S. sends troops to restore democracy
2010 U.S. provides billions of dollars in aid after major earthquake
GUADELOUPE (Fr.)
DOMINICA
MARTINIQUE (Fr.)
ST. LUCIA
BARBADOS
1983 U.S. troops invade
GRENADA
TRINIDAD AND TOBAGO
CARIBBEAN SEA
BELIZE
Belmopan
1980s U.S. provides military exercises and aid
2009 U.S. suspends military and development aid after a coup
GUATEMALA
Guatemala City
HONDURAS
Tegucigalpa
San Salvador
EL SALVADOR
1980 U.S. provides military aid
NICARAGUA
Managua
Lago de Nicaragua
1979 Sandinista government takes power
1980s U.S. aids anti-government contras
1990 New coalition government elected
San José
COSTA RICA
1979 U.S. pledges control of Panama Canal to Panama by 2000
1989 U.S. troops invade; capture General Noriega
1999 Control of Panama Canal reverts to Panama on December 31
Panama City
PANAMA
COLOMBIA
Medellín
Magdalena
Maracaibo
Lago de Maracaibo
Caracas
Orinoco
VENEZUELA
GUYANA
PACIFIC OCEAN
M-101253-2
© Rand McNally

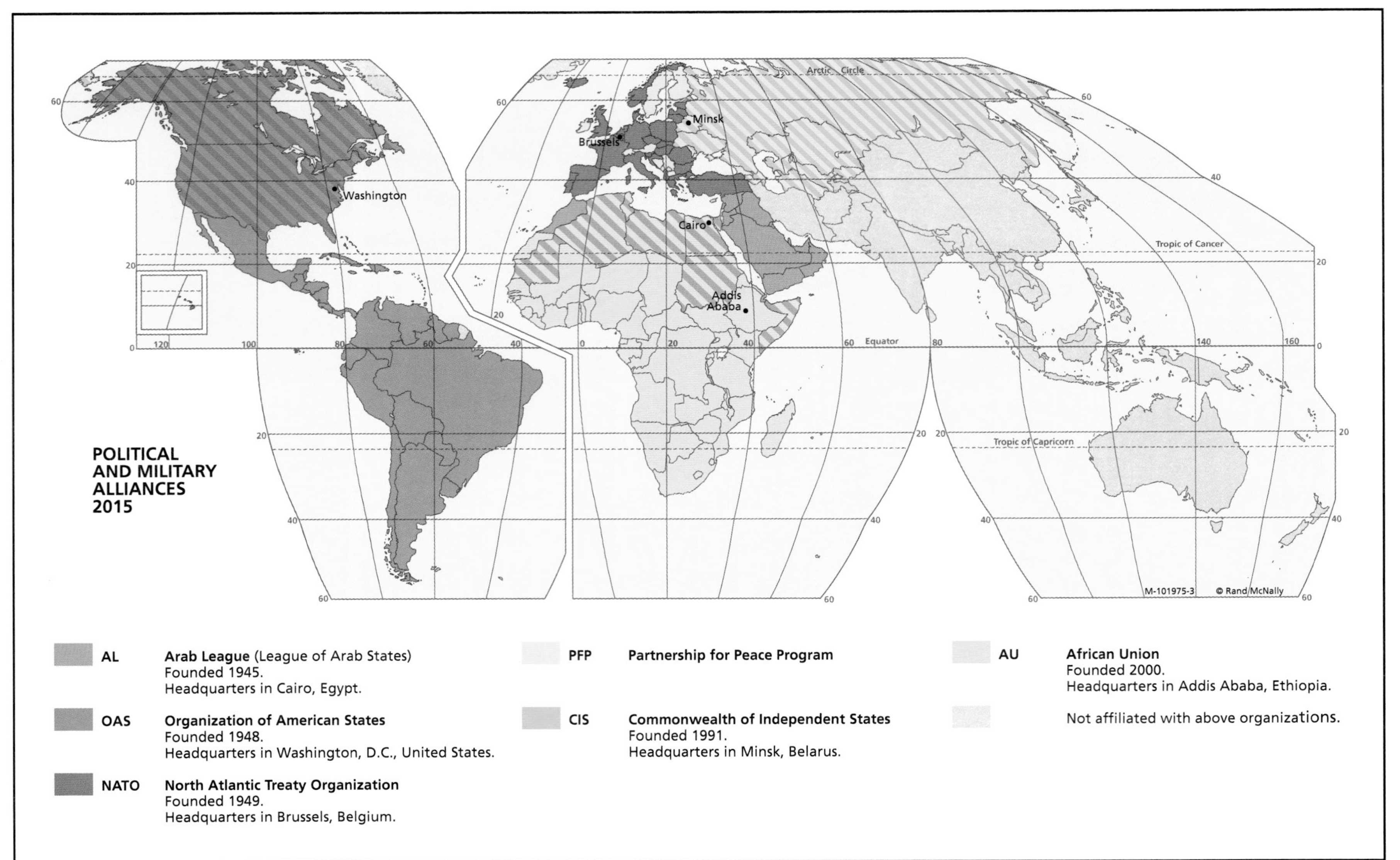
POLITICAL
AND MILITARY
ALLIANCES
2015
Washington
Brussels
Minsk
Cairo
Addis
Ababa
Arctic Circle
Tropic of Cancer
Equator
Tropic of Capricorn
M-101975-3
© Rand McNally
AL
Arab League (League of Arab States)
Founded 1945.
Headquarters in Cairo, Egypt.
OAS
Organization of American States
Founded 1948.
Headquarters in Washington, D.C., United States.
NATO
North Atlantic Treaty Organization
Founded 1949.
Headquarters in Brussels, Belgium.
PFP
Partnership for Peace Program
CIS
Commonwealth of Independent States
Founded 1991.
Headquarters in Minsk, Belarus.
AU
African Union
Founded 2000.
Headquarters in Addis Ababa, Ethiopia.
Not affiliated with above organizations.

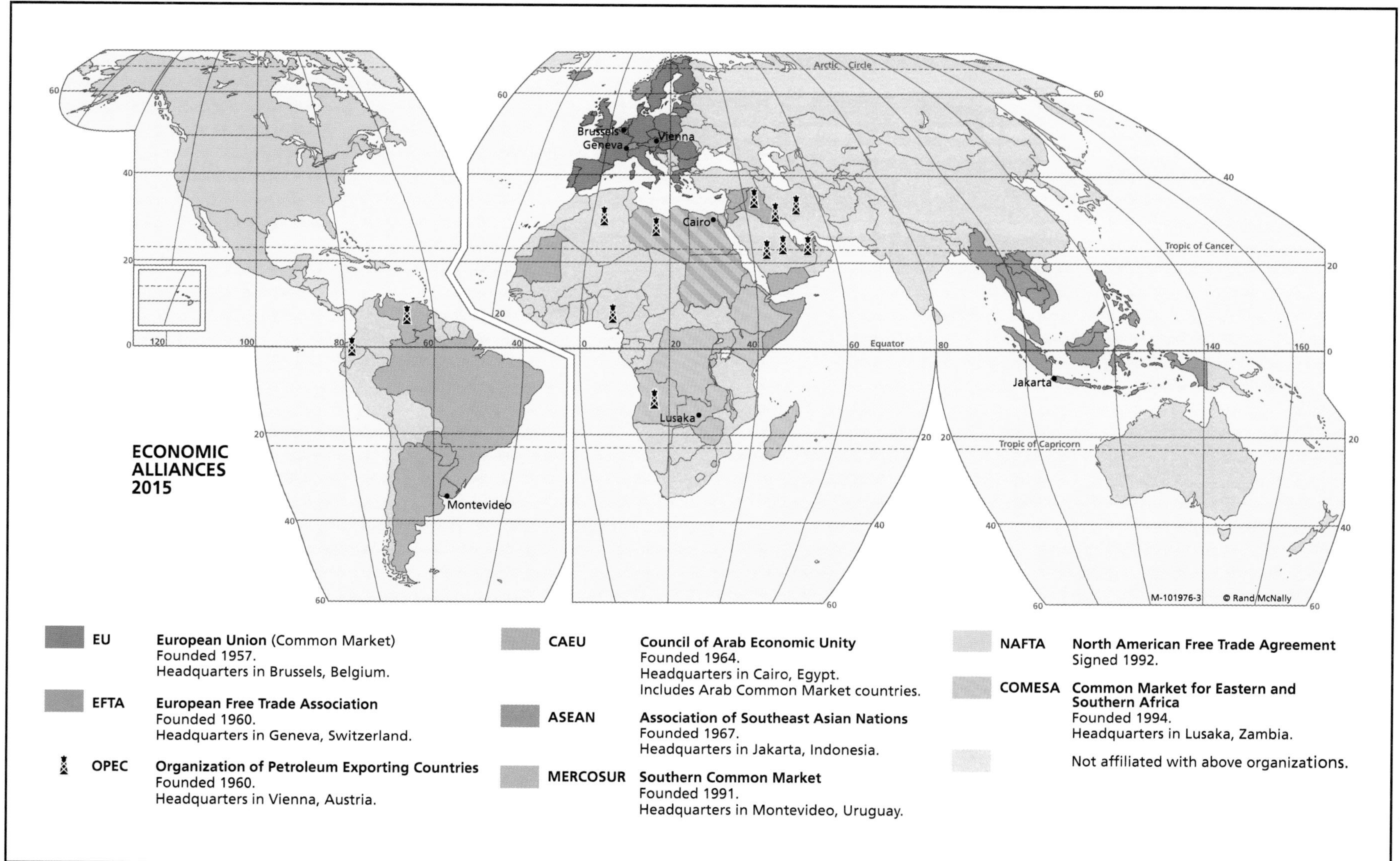
ECONOMIC ALLIANCES 2015
Arctic Circle
Tropic of Cancer
Equator
Tropic of Capricorn
Brussels
Geneva
Vienna
Cairo
Lusaka
Jakarta
Montevideo
M-101976-3
© Rand McNally
EU European Union (Common Market)
Founded 1957.
Headquarters in Brussels, Belgium.
EFTA European Free Trade Association
Founded 1960.
Headquarters in Geneva, Switzerland.
OPEC Organization of Petroleum Exporting Countries
Founded 1960.
Headquarters in Vienna, Austria.
CAEU Council of Arab Economic Unity
Founded 1964.
Headquarters in Cairo, Egypt.
Includes Arab Common Market countries.
ASEAN Association of Southeast Asian Nations
Founded 1967.
Headquarters in Jakarta, Indonesia.
MERCOSUR Southern Common Market
Founded 1991.
Headquarters in Montevideo, Uruguay.
NAFTA North American Free Trade Agreement
Signed 1992.
COMESA Common Market for Eastern and Southern Africa
Founded 1994.
Headquarters in Lusaka, Zambia.
Not affiliated with above organizations.

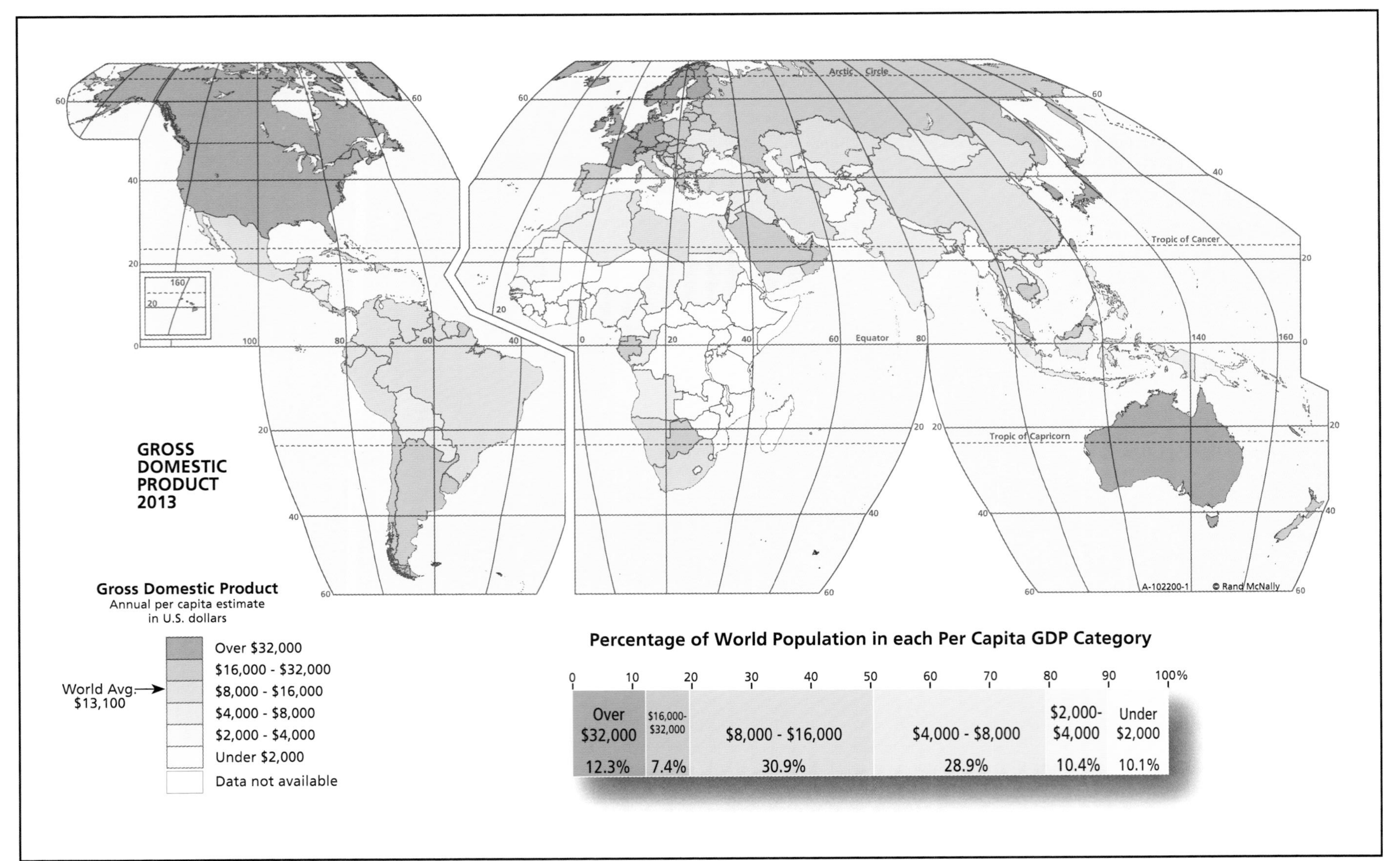

GROSS DOMESTIC PRODUCT 2013
Gross Domestic Product
Annual per capita estimate in U.S. dollars
World Avg. $13,100
Over $32,000
$16,000 - $32,000
$8,000 - $16,000
$4,000 - $8,000
$2,000 - $4,000
Under $2,000
Data not available
Arctic Circle
Tropic of Cancer
Equator
Tropic of Capricorn
A-102200-1
© Rand McNally
Percentage of World Population in each Per Capita GDP Category
0 10 20 30 40 50 60 70 80 90 100%
Over $32,000 12.3%
$16,000-$32,000 7.4%
$8,000 - $16,000 30.9%
$4,000 - $8,000 28.9%
$2,000-$4,000 10.4%
Under $2,000 10.1%

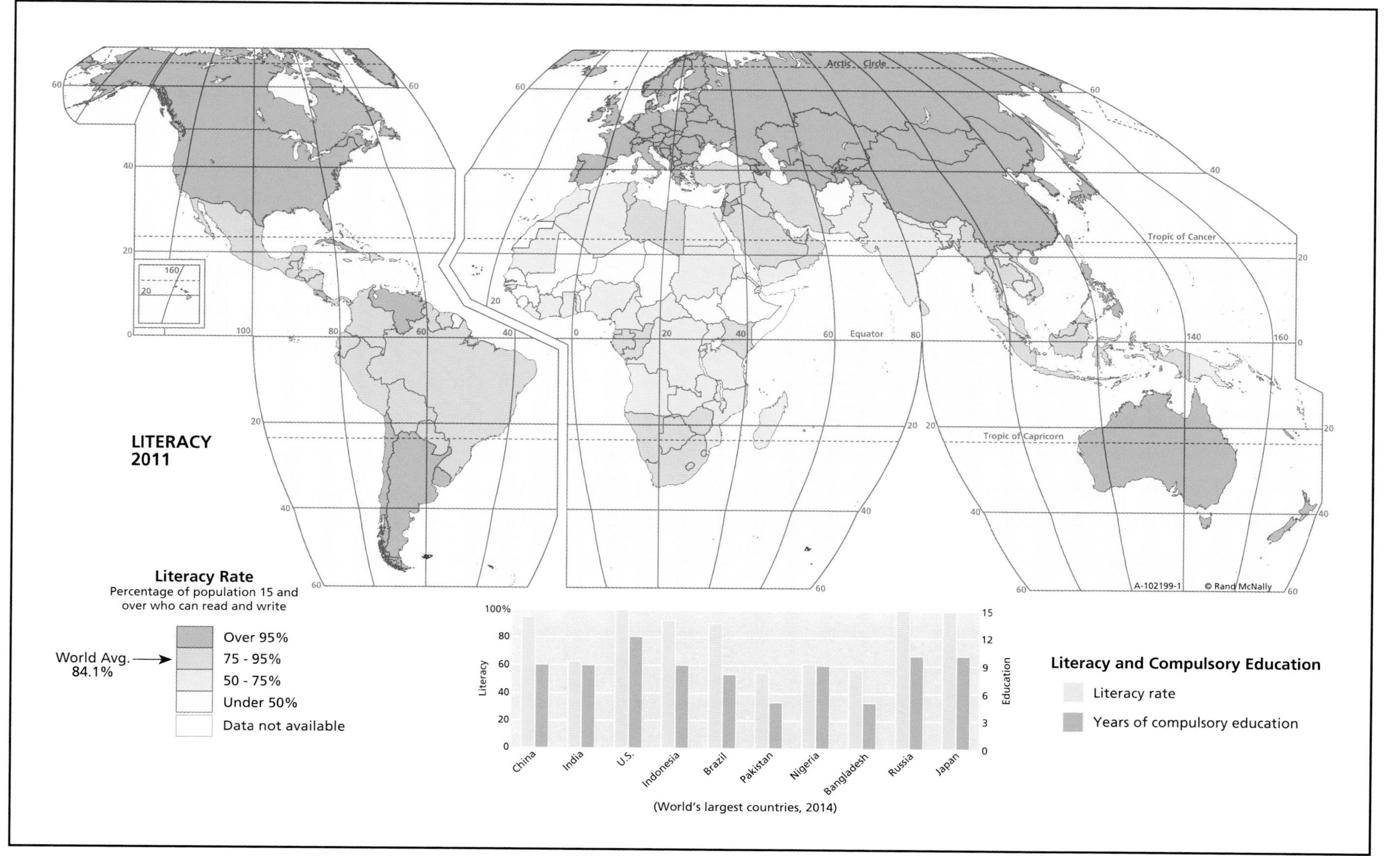

LITERACY
2011
Literacy Rate
Percentage of population 15 and over who can read and write
World Avg. 84.1%
Over 95%
75 - 95%
50 - 75%
Under 50%
Data not available
Arctic Circle
Tropic of Cancer
Equator
Tropic of Capricorn
A-102199-1
© Rand McNally
Literacy and Compulsory Education
Literacy rate
Years of compulsory education
Literacy
Education
100%
80
60
40
20
0
15
12
9
6
3
0
China
India
U.S.
Indonesia
Brazil
Pakistan
Nigeria
Bangladesh
Russia
Japan
(World's largest countries, 2014)

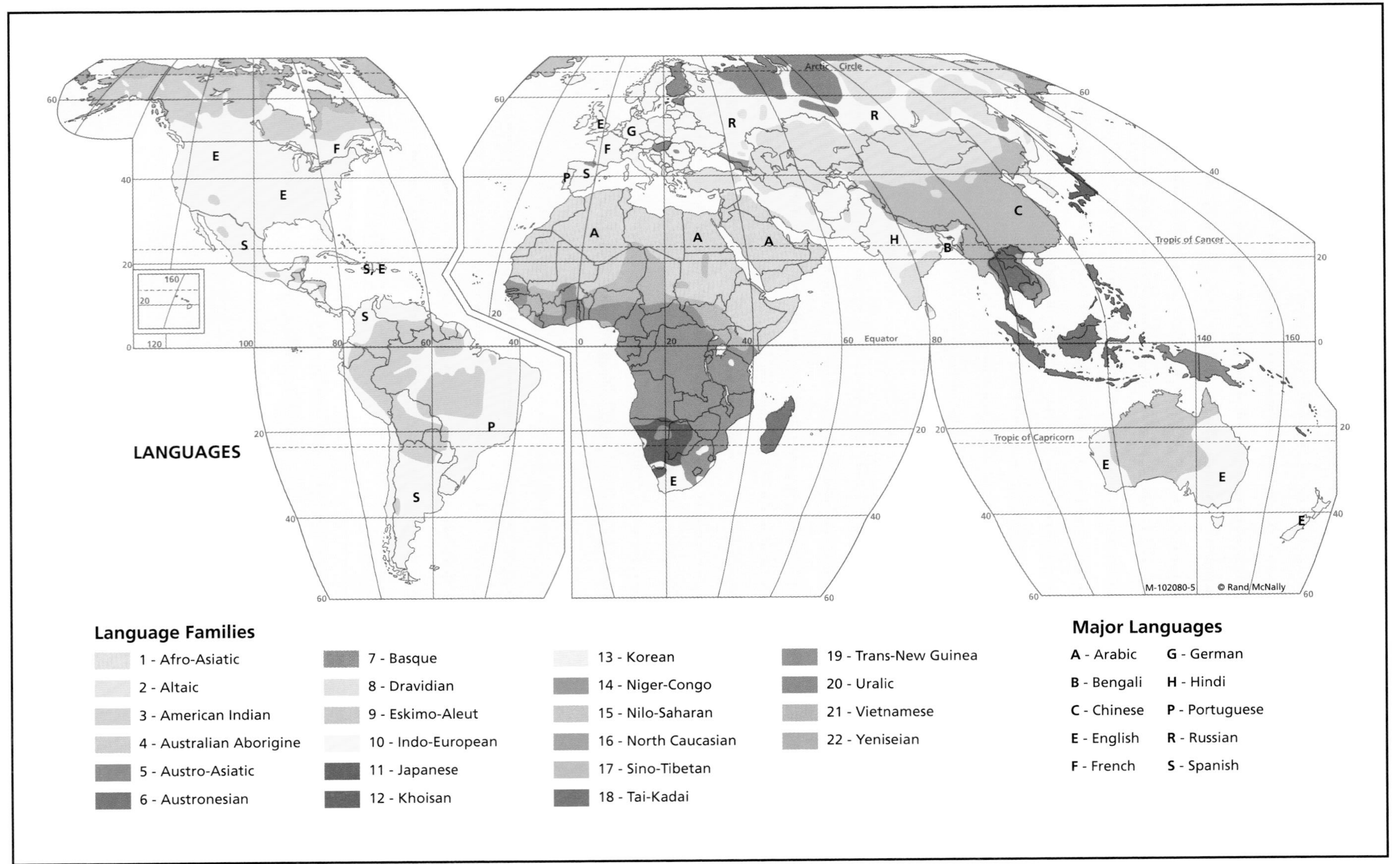
LANGUAGES
Language Families
1 - Afro-Asiatic
2 - Altaic
3 - American Indian
4 - Australian Aborigine
5 - Austro-Asiatic
6 - Austronesian
7 - Basque
8 - Dravidian
9 - Eskimo-Aleut
10 - Indo-European
11 - Japanese
12 - Khoisan
13 - Korean
14 - Niger-Congo
15 - Nilo-Saharan
16 - North Caucasian
17 - Sino-Tibetan
18 - Tai-Kadai
19 - Trans-New Guinea
20 - Uralic
21 - Vietnamese
22 - Yeniseian
Major Languages
A - Arabic
B - Bengali
C - Chinese
E - English
F - French
G - German
H - Hindi
P - Portuguese
R - Russian
S - Spanish
Arctic Circle
Tropic of Cancer
Equator
Tropic of Capricorn
M-102080-5
© Rand McNally

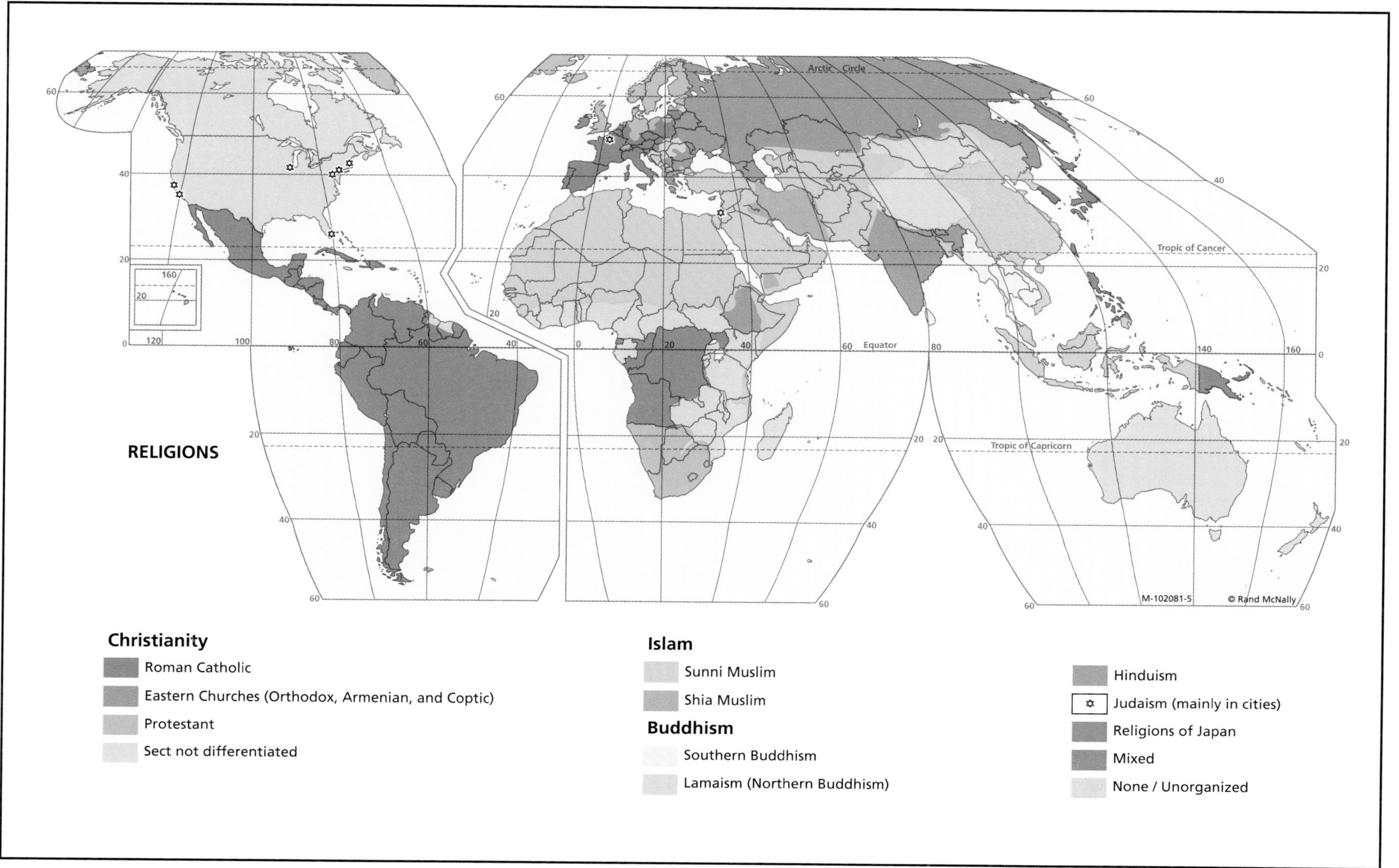
RELIGIONS
Arctic Circle
Tropic of Cancer
Equator
Tropic of Capricorn
M-102081-5
© Rand McNally
Christianity
Roman Catholic
Eastern Churches (Orthodox, Armenian, and Coptic)
Protestant
Sect not differentiated
Islam
Sunni Muslim
Shia Muslim
Buddhism
Southern Buddhism
Lamaism (Northern Buddhism)
Hinduism
Judaism (mainly in cities)
Religions of Japan
Mixed
None / Unorganized

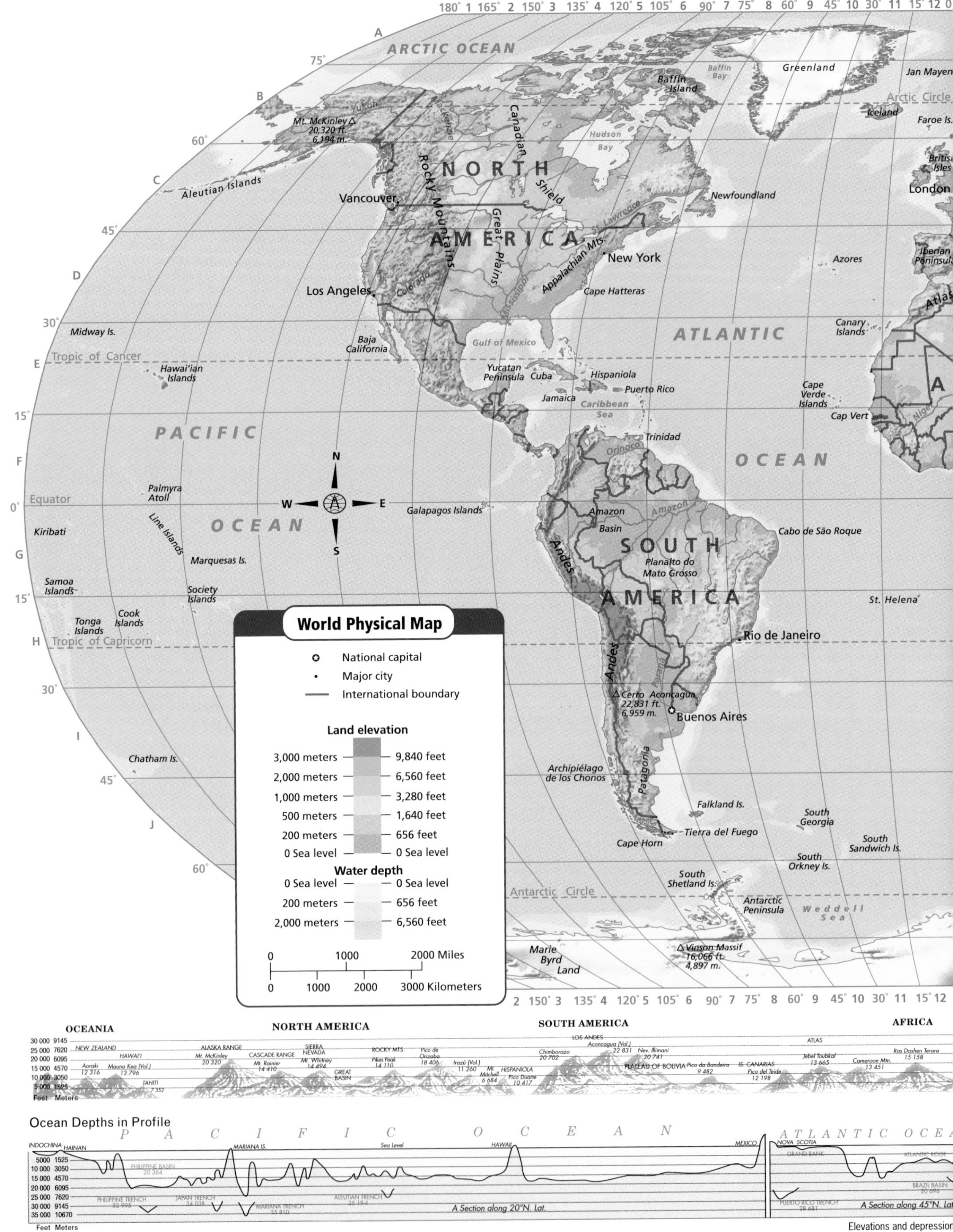
World Physical Map
ARCTIC OCEAN
PACIFIC OCEAN
ATLANTIC OCEAN
NORTH AMERICA
SOUTH AMERICA
Greenland
Baffin Island
Baffin Bay
Hudson Bay
Jan Mayen
Arctic Circle
Iceland
Faroe Is.
British Isles
London
Mt. McKinley
20,320 ft.
6,194 m.
Yukon
Mackenzie
Canadian Shield
Rocky Mountains
Aleutian Islands
Vancouver
Great Plains
St. Lawrence
Newfoundland
Appalachian Mts.
New York
Iberian Peninsula
Azores
Los Angeles
Colorado
Mississippi
Cape Hatteras
Canary Islands
Atlas
Midway Is.
Baja California
Gulf of Mexico
Tropic of Cancer
Hawai'ian Islands
Yucatan Peninsula
Cuba
Hispaniola
Puerto Rico
Jamaica
Caribbean Sea
Cape Verde Islands
Cap Vert
Niger
Trinidad
Orinoco
Equator
Palmyra Atoll
Galapagos Islands
Kiribati
Line Islands
Amazon
Amazon Basin
Andes
Cabo de São Roque
Marquesas Is.
Planalto do Mato Grosso
Samoa Islands
Society Islands
St. Helena
Tonga Islands
Cook Islands
Tropic of Capricorn
Rio de Janeiro
Paraná
Cerro Aconcagua
22,831 ft.
6,959 m.
Buenos Aires
Chatham Is.
Archipiélago de los Chonos
Patagonia
Falkland Is.
South Georgia
South Sandwich Is.
Tierra del Fuego
Cape Horn
South Orkney Is.
South Shetland Is.
Antarctic Circle
Antarctic Peninsula
Weddell Sea
Marie Byrd Land
Vinson Massif
16,066 ft.
4,897 m.
National capital
Major city
International boundary
Land elevation
3,000 meters — 9,840 feet
2,000 meters — 6,560 feet
1,000 meters — 3,280 feet
500 meters — 1,640 feet
200 meters — 656 feet
0 Sea level — 0 Sea level
Water depth
0 Sea level — 0 Sea level
200 meters — 656 feet
2,000 meters — 6,560 feet
0 1000 2000 Miles
0 1000 2000 3000 Kilometers
OCEANIA
NORTH AMERICA
SOUTH AMERICA
AFRICA
NEW ZEALAND
Aoraki 12 316
HAWAI'I
Mauna Kea (Vol.) 13 796
TAHITI 7 352
ALASKA RANGE
Mt. McKinley 20 320
CASCADE RANGE
Mt. Rainier 14 410
SIERRA NEVADA
Mt. Whitney 14 494
GREAT BASIN
ROCKY MTS.
Pikes Peak 14 110
Pico de Orizaba 18 406
Irazú (Vol.) 11 260
Mt. Mitchell 6 684
HISPANIOLA
Pico Duarte 10 417
Chimborazo 20 702
LOS ANDES
Aconcagua (Vol.) 22 831
Nev. Illimani 20 741
PLATEAU OF BOLIVIA
Pico da Bandeira 9 482
IS. CANARIAS
Pico del Teide 12 198
ATLAS
Jebel Toubkal 13 665
Cameroon Mtn. 13 451
Ras Dashen Terara 15 158
Feet Meters
Ocean Depths in Profile
PACIFIC OCEAN
ATLANTIC OCEAN
INDOCHINA
HAINAN
PHILIPPINE BASIN 20 364
MARIANA IS.
Sea Level
HAWAII
MEXICO
NOVA SCOTIA
GRAND BANK
ATLANTIC RIDGE
BRAZIL BASIN
PHILIPPINE TRENCH 32 995
JAPAN TRENCH 34 038
MARIANA TRENCH 35 810
ALEUTIAN TRENCH 25 194
PUERTO RICO TRENCH 28 681
A Section along 20°N. Lat.
A Section along 45°N. Lat.
Elevations and depressions

ARCTIC OCEAN
Spitsbergen
Franz Josef Land
Novaya Zemlya
Nordkapp
Scandinavia
Siberia
EUROPE
Moscow
Ural Mts.
Alps
Balkan Peninsula
Black Sea
Caucasus
Gora El'brus 18,510 ft. 5,642 m.
Sardinia
Sicily
Crete
Cyprus
Cairo
ASIA
Altai Mts.
Gobi Desert
Beijing
Sea of Okhotsk
Sakhalin
Kamchatka Peninsula
Bering Sea
Hokkaidō
Honshū
Sea of Japan (East Sea)
Pamir
Plateau of Tibet
Himalayas
Mt. Everest 29,028 ft. 8,848 m.
Zagros Mts.
East China Sea
Kyūshū
PACIFIC
Tropic of Cancer
Sahara
Arabian Peninsula
Mumbai (Bombay)
Deccan
Taiwan
Hainan Dao
South China Sea
Luzon
Mariana Islands
Wake Island
Guam
AFRICA
Sahel
Arabian Sea
Bay of Bengal
Socotra
Lakshadweep
Sri Lanka
Ethiopian Plateau
Mindanao
Palau Islands
OCEAN
Caroline Islands
Marshall Islands
Malay Peninsula
Congo Basin
Maldive Islands
Borneo
Celebes
Equator
Kilimanjaro 19,340 ft. 5,895 m.
Seychelles
Sumatra
New Guinea
Solomon Islands
Java
INDIAN
Cocos Islands
New Hebrides
Coral Sea
Madagascar
Mauritius
Reunion
Great Sandy Desert
New Caledonia
Fiji Is.
Kalahari Desert
Johannesburg
OCEAN
AUSTRALIA
Tropic of Capricorn
Great Dividing Range
Darling
Sydney
Cape of Good Hope
Cape Leeuwin
North Island
Aoraki (Mt. Cook) 12,316 ft. 3,754 m.
Tasmania
South Island
Îles Kerguélen
SOUTHERN OCEAN
Antarctic Circle
Enderby Land
Wilkes Land
Queen Maud Land
Victoria Land
ANTARCTICA
© Rand McNally
Made in U.S.A.
M-101117-4
EUROPE
ASIA
OCEANIA
MEDITERRANEAN SEA
INDIAN OCEAN
A Section along 10°S. Lat.
ARCTIC OCEAN
PACIFIC OCEAN
Meters Feet
e given in feet

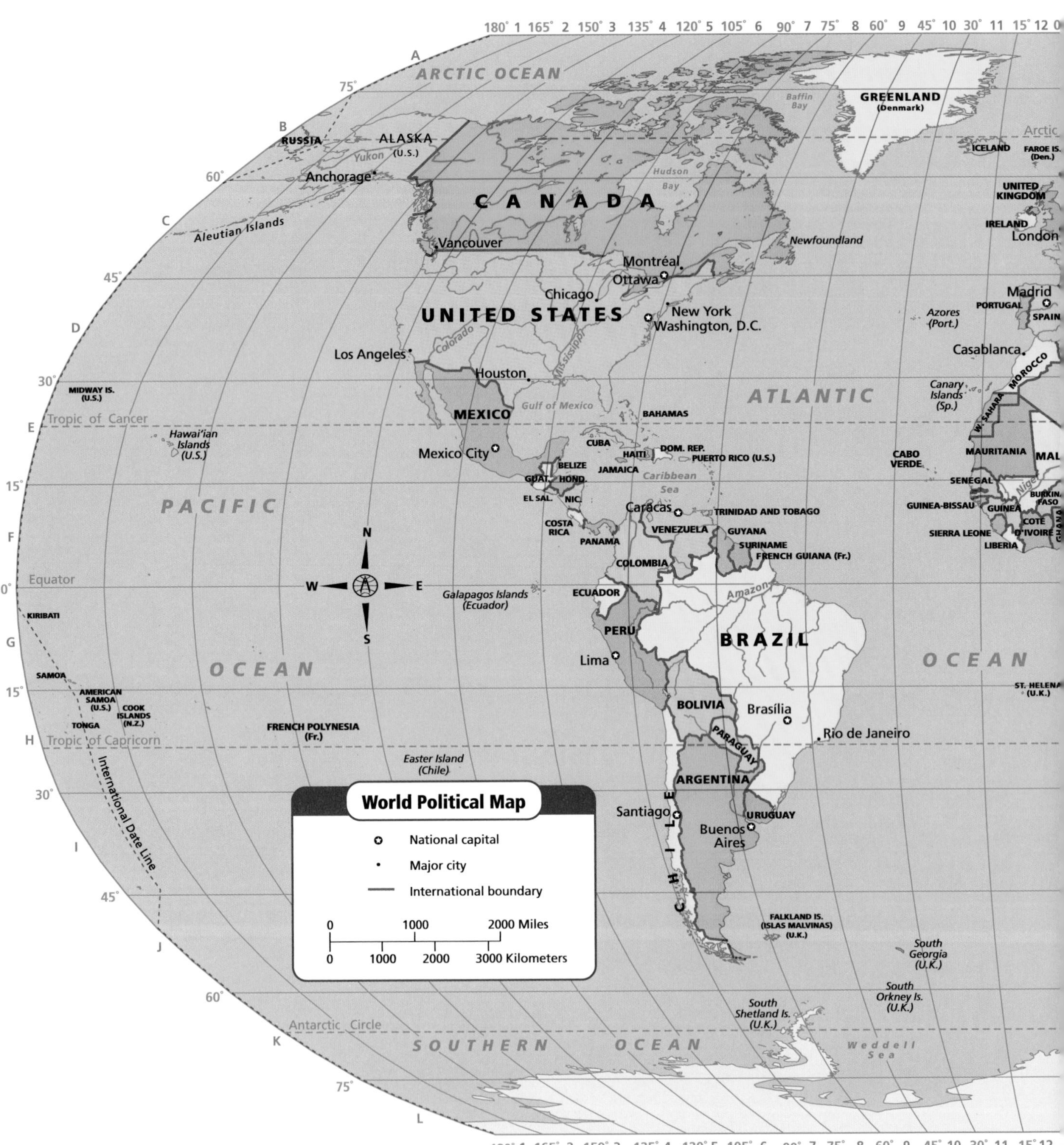

World Political Map
National capital
Major city
International boundary
0
1000
2000 Miles
0
1000
2000
3000 Kilometers
ARCTIC OCEAN
PACIFIC
OCEAN
ATLANTIC
OCEAN
SOUTHERN
OCEAN
Weddell Sea
Baffin Bay
Hudson Bay
Gulf of Mexico
Caribbean Sea
GREENLAND (Denmark)
ICELAND
FAROE IS. (Den.)
UNITED KINGDOM
IRELAND
London
RUSSIA
ALASKA (U.S.)
Yukon
Anchorage
Aleutian Islands
CANADA
Vancouver
Newfoundland
Montréal
Ottawa
Chicago
UNITED STATES
New York
Washington, D.C.
Los Angeles
Colorado
Mississippi
Houston
MIDWAY IS. (U.S.)
Tropic of Cancer
Hawai'ian Islands (U.S.)
MEXICO
Mexico City
BAHAMAS
CUBA
HAITI
DOM. REP.
PUERTO RICO (U.S.)
JAMAICA
BELIZE
GUAT.
HOND.
EL SAL.
NIC.
COSTA RICA
PANAMA
Caracas
TRINIDAD AND TOBAGO
VENEZUELA
GUYANA
SURINAME
FRENCH GUIANA (Fr.)
COLOMBIA
Equator
Galapagos Islands (Ecuador)
ECUADOR
Amazon
PERU
BRAZIL
Lima
KIRIBATI
SAMOA
AMERICAN SAMOA (U.S.)
COOK ISLANDS (N.Z.)
TONGA
FRENCH POLYNESIA (Fr.)
Tropic of Capricorn
Easter Island (Chile)
International Date Line
BOLIVIA
Brasília
PARAGUAY
Rio de Janeiro
ARGENTINA
Santiago
URUGUAY
Buenos Aires
CHILE
FALKLAND IS. (ISLAS MALVINAS) (U.K.)
South Georgia (U.K.)
South Orkney Is. (U.K.)
South Shetland Is. (U.K.)
Antarctic Circle
Arctic
Madrid
PORTUGAL
SPAIN
Azores (Port.)
Casablanca
MOROCCO
Canary Islands (Sp.)
W. SAHARA
MAURITANIA
CABO VERDE
SENEGAL
GUINEA-BISSAU
GUINEA
SIERRA LEONE
LIBERIA
COTE D'IVOIRE
ST. HELENA (U.K.)
N
S
E
W
A
B
C
D
E
F
G
H
I
J
K
L
180° 1 165° 2 150° 3 135° 4 120° 5 105° 6 90° 7 75° 8 60° 9 45° 10 30° 11 15° 12
75°
60°
45°
30°
15°
0°
15°
30°
45°
60°
75°

ARCTIC OCEAN
Franz Josef Land
Novaya Zemlya
RUSSIA
FINLAND
NORWAY
SWEDEN
EST.
LAT.
LITH.
DEN.
POLAND
BELARUS
GERMANY
UKRAINE
MOLD.
ROM.
BUL.
GREECE
TURKEY
ITALY
Rome
Moscow
Novosibirsk
KAZAKHSTAN
MONGOLIA
UZBEKISTAN
TURKMENISTAN
KYRG.
TAJIK.
GEO.
ARM.
AZER.
Black Sea
Mediterranean Sea
Crete
CYPRUS
LEB.
SYRIA
ISRAEL
IRAQ
JORDAN
Tehrān
IRAN
AFGHANISTAN
PAKISTAN
KUWAIT
QATAR
U.A.E.
SAUDI ARABIA
OMAN
YEMEN
Karāchi
Cairo
TUNISIA
LIBYA
EGYPT
NIGER
CHAD
SUDAN
NIGERIA
Lagos
CAMEROON
ERITREA
DJIBOUTI
Addis Ababa
ETHIOPIA
SOMALIA
SOUTH SUDAN
CENTRAL AFRICAN REPUBLIC
KENYA
UGANDA
RWANDA
BURUNDI
DEM. REP. OF THE CONGO
CONGO
GABON
TANZANIA
ANGOLA
ZAMBIA
MALAWI
MOZAMBIQUE
ZIMBABWE
NAMIBIA
BOTSWANA
Johannesburg
SWAZILAND
LESOTHO
SOUTH AFRICA
MADAGASCAR
COMOROS
SEYCHELLES
MAURITIUS
REUNION (Fr.)
MALDIVES
SRI LANKA
CHINA
Beijing
Shanghai
NORTH KOREA
SOUTH KOREA
Seoul
Sea of Japan (East Sea)
JAPAN
Tōkyō
Sea of Okhotsk
Bering Sea
NEPAL
BHU.
BNGL.
INDIA
Kolkata (Calcutta)
Mumbai (Bombay)
Arabian Sea
Bay of Bengal
MYANMAR
LAOS
THAILAND
Bangkok
CAMBODIA
VIETNAM
South China Sea
Hong Kong
TAIWAN
PHILIPPINES
Manila
BRUNEI
MALAYSIA
SINGAPORE
Borneo
Sumatra
Jakarta
Java
INDONESIA
TIMOR-LESTE
New Guinea
PAPUA NEW GUINEA
PALAU
NORTHERN MARIANA ISLANDS (U.S.)
GUAM (U.S.)
WAKE ISLAND (U.S.)
FED. STATES OF MICRONESIA
MARSHALL ISLANDS
SOLOMON ISLANDS
PACIFIC OCEAN
INDIAN OCEAN
Coral Sea
VANUATU
NEW CALEDONIA (Fr.)
FIJI
AUSTRALIA
Brisbane
Perth
Sydney
Melbourne
Tasmania
Auckland
NEW ZEALAND
Îles Kerguélen (Fr.)
SOUTHERN OCEAN
ANTARCTICA
Arctic Circle
Tropic of Cancer
Equator
Tropic of Capricorn
Antarctic Circle
International Date Line
Yenisey
Lena
Ob
Volga
Yangtze
Ganges
Nile
Congo
Darling
Red Sea
© Rand McNally
Made in U.S.A.
M-101116-4

Index

The following index lists important place names appearing on the maps in the *Historical Atlas of the World*. Countries and regions are indexed to the several maps which portray their areal and political development at successive periods. In general, each index entry includes a map reference key and the page number of the map. Alternate names and spellings are added in parentheses.

L

M

N

O

P